D1477126

# IAN MIKARDO

## BACK-BENCHER

*for*
*Mary*


*without words,*
*since none would be*
*adequate*

# IAN MIKARDO

## BACK-BENCHER

Weidenfeld and Nicolson
London

# *Preface*

THIS book is a mémoir, not an autobiography, a telerecording of high-lights of a long innings rather than a ball-by-ball commentary.

Highlights naturally present a more interesting picture than a full report does: you see the poetry of the magnificent hooks, sweeps and cover-drives and the excitement of the near-misses, dropped catches and rejected appeals without the dreary longueurs of slow field-changing or the boring stonewalling of the nervous nineties and of the last few overs of the day.

But that's not the reason why I haven't tried to write a work of record, with a bushel of references at the end of every chapter – the type of day-to-day revelations that some of my former colleagues, notably some ex-Ministers, have produced. The fact is that even if I wanted to do it that way, and I don't, I haven't the raw material for it. I've never kept a diary or papers or notes or press-cuttings or the usual great album of photographs and cartoon originals. Truth to tell, I was always puzzled by the willingness of some of my friends to enslave themselves to the incubus, the treadmill, of keeping a diary. Some of those diaries – Dick Crossman's and Hugh Gaitskell's in particular – contain periodic groans of protest at the daily and weekend tyranny of the relentless tape-recorder. I reckoned there were better things – or at least a better choice of things – to do with my time.

Barbara Castle used to write furiously right through every committee meeting she attended, simultaneously recording the proceedings and taking an active part in them. We all greatly admired her capacity to be in two places at once: writing down what one of her colleagues

1

was saying, and at the same time working out what she was going to say in reply. It must have been pretty wearing.

In February 1973 I went, as chairman of the Labour Party's International Committee, on a study tour of Hong Kong, North and South Vietnam, Laos and Thailand with Jim Callaghan, the Shadow Foreign Secretary, and Tom McNally, who was then the International Secretary of the Party (but later became Callaghan's political adviser and then an MP and finally a defector to the SDP, where he duly vanished into obscurity). It was a densely packed trip, teeming with arresting discussions and exciting new perceptions. After every one of our many formal meetings with all sorts of distinguished persons (some genuinely distinguished and some phoney distinguished), Tom and I would go off to look round the joint, to absorb the atmosphere, and to chit-chat (from which we learned a great deal) with some of the local citizenry in a café or two over a drink or two; but Jim wasn't free to come with us because he had to go off to his room, like a monk to his cell, in order to intone the responses to his ever-demanding deity, his tape-recorder. I hope, and I'm sure, that he's now enjoying those cassettes, but he missed a lot of life in order to get them.

I suppose I ought to confess that I was too lazy (or maybe too pleasure-loving) and too unambitious (indeed, totally without personal ambition) to follow the example of these colleagues of mine and match their nose-to-the-grindstone dedication. Dick Crossman once told me, as we were sharing a meal after a meeting, that he spent the first hour and a half of every day going through the newspapers. 'I just couldn't do that,' I said; 'I get only one newspaper at home: I read the sports pages in the morning and do the crossword in bed at night, and get all the rest I want from the radio.' Dick looked at me with a mixture of incomprehension, pity and scorn: I felt that he was instantly writing me off as a political dilettante whom he needn't bother with any further.

With this sort of attitude I was never likely to make a great push forward from the back benches to the front. I remember clearly the precise moment when I decided that I never wanted to be a Minister. It was not long after I became an MP. One of my constituents in Reading came to my 'surgery' (I believe I may have been the first, certainly I was among the first, to hold regular surgeries on advertised dates). She was a young Englishwoman who had married a foreigner, and her husband had been recommended for deportation. She knew he had committed some commercial offence, but she asked me to appeal to the Home Secretary, on her behalf and on behalf of her baby daughter, to let him stay.

The Home Secretary at the time was Chuter Ede, a highly respected man who had got the office as a just reward for a very sound job he had done in the wartime coalition government. I went to see him and asked him if he would re-examine the case himself. 'If you do that,' I said to him, 'and then tell me the man ought to be deported I'll of course accept that: I just don't want his wife and child to suffer on the automatic say-so of some desiccated civil servant.'

That day the House was on the Committee Stage of the Finance Bill, and we were expecting to sit all through the night. (In those years it was considered de rigueur to have two or three all-night sittings on the Finance Bill, rather like the set rituals of medieval jousting or the exaggerated punctilio of duelling.) Chuter Ede said he would get my constituent's file and go through it during the course of the evening, and if I would come to see him in his room at midnight he would tell me about it.

Punctually at midnight I presented myself to his room on the ministerial corridor. Chuter Ede had the file on the desk in front of him. 'I've been through it,' he said, 'carefully and sympathetically, but the man really is a bad egg and I couldn't justify overturning the recommendation to deport.'

I thanked him for his trouble, and we went on chatting for a bit about other things, and then, to the great and pleasant surprise of both of us, the bells rang and we heard the cry 'Who Goes Home?' With somewhat corny humour I said 'I for one Goes Home.'

Ede looked up at me and asked, somewhat wistfully, 'Where's home for you, and how long will it take you to get there?'

The question surprised me more than somewhat. Ede was a man well past middle age, white-haired and stiff-walking – a rather formal unbending withdrawn character who didn't easily enter into personal relationships outside his own circle.

'Home for me,' I said, 'is three miles north of here, and at this time of night I'll get there in fifteen minutes.'

'And what will you do when you get there?'

'Depends,' I said, 'on whether my Mary is still up. If she is we'll play a ten-minute game of *klabjascz*, loser to get up first in the morning and make the tea. But if she's gone to bed I'll swallow a quick nightcap and crawl in beside her. What about you?' I asked.

'My home,' he said, and there was no mistaking the envy in his voice, 'is in Epsom. I'll get there in forty minutes now, but in the morning it will take more than an hour to get back. I've got to be in Downing Street by 9.30, and some time between now and then I've got to wade through those two "boxes": the red one's the papers for tomorrow morning's Cabinet, and the black one's got the papers for a Cabinet committee before that.'

'My dear friend,' I said, 'you're a better man than I' – but tactfully refrained from adding that I was a happier man than he. And that was the moment I decided I never wanted to be a Minister.

[*Digression*. Did I but know it, I wasn't in the least danger of becoming a Minister at that time, or at any time as long as Clem Attlee was Prime Minister. I didn't discover that until nearly forty years later, when I read (and reviewed) Ben Pimlott's superb biography of Hugh Dalton. He records a meeting of Attlee's Inner Cabinet to consider a reshuffle of some senior Ministers, and then 'at a second meeting, the Prime Minister turned to junior posts. Dalton praised Jim Callaghan, John Freeman, Geoffrey de Freitas, Arthur Bottomley and Fred Peart. They agreed that Ian Mikardo and Austen Albu were unsuitable, Attlee apparently on racial grounds ('they both belonged to the Chosen People, and he didn't think he wanted any more of *them*').

It would be interesting to know where this antisemitism of Attlee's came from. It may have derived from his contacts with Jews during the many years he spent in the East End; it may have been a fall-out from his long-running bad-tempered disagreements with Harold Laski, who would be in Attlee's black book not merely as a Jew but also as an intellectual and a doctrinal socialist; and it may have been a transference from Ernest Bevin, by whom he was always greatly influenced and who as Foreign Secretary developed a bitter hatred of the Jews because a few thousand of them successfully defied him, and hurt his pride, by running the gauntlet of his warships, in unsafe cockleshell boats, to get out of concentration camps in Germany and join their own, and welcoming, people in Palestine, and because in the end he had to admit defeat at the hands of the Palestinian Jews and leave others to solve a problem which he couldn't solve because he never understood it. This was one of several examples in British colonial history – Ireland preceded it and Kenya was to follow – where the Imperial Power ended its occupation by yielding to force what it had refused to moderation. Will Ulster, some years ahead, prove to be the last chapter in that unhappy story?]

So I was explaining before that digression how I wasn't assiduous enough to preserve all the material which would have enabled me now to write a book of record like those of Barbara Castle and Dick Crossman and Hugh Gaitskell and Harold Wilson and Jim Callaghan and Tony Benn and others of my former colleagues. Running through many of those diaries and autobiographies are two features which I find unlovable: first, the authors' repeated claim 'I got it right, all the others got it wrong'; and second, their tendency to write bitchily about colleagues for whom they had, over many years, professed brotherly love. Many of them lowered, rather than enhanced, their reputations by what they wrote. It's perhaps not surprising that an acerbic and unloving character like Tom Driberg, riddled right through with all sorts of torturing complexes, should produce a posthumous book which leaves a sour taste in the reader's mouth, but even former Speaker George Thomas, the most gentle and kindly of men, managed to offend many of his friends by what he wrote about them.

So this book consists only of those flashbacks which have stuck in my memory. I'm well aware that memory is an impressionist painting, not a photograph: it is inescapably selective, and it's often impossible to know to what extent any particular story has grown in the telling or any particular recollection is coloured by hindsight or wishful thinking or vanity – or just colouring. I've tried hard to tell it as it was.

I've been greatly helped to do that by some of my friends who have filled lacunae in my memory with their recollections and with papers, pictures and cartoons that they've lent me: they include Andy and Judy Becker, Tony Benn, the Cheadle Labour Club, Bill and Pauline Davidson, Michael Foot, Joyce Gould, John Hall, Judith Hart, Eric Heffer, Clive Jenkins, Greta Karpin, Jenny Little, John Mackie, Tom McNally, Roy Mason, Sidney Mikardo, Stan Orme, Chaim Raphael, Jo Richardson, David Stoddart and Aubrey Weinberg. I'm greatly indebted, too, to the library staffs of the Labour Party, the Borough of Tower Hamlets and the University of Warwick; to Howard Fidderman and Jeannette Gould for some patient research; and to Jeannette again for magically translating my scrawl into hi-tech reproduction. But if there's anything wrong in what I've written it is of course *mea culpa* and nobody else's.

# *Chapter 1*

BOTH my parents came to Britain in the massive Jewish exodus from the tsarist empire in the last decades of the nineteenth century and the first of the twentieth.

My mother, Bluma, came from a village (which has now grown into a town) called Yampol (Yiddish speakers pronounced it Yompella) in the province of Podolia in the Western Ukraine. One of her brothers, Louis (anglicised from Leib), had settled here some years before: he had started a family, and his wife was chronically sick, so in 1902 or 1903 he sent for his young sister to help in the house.

Like most other immigrants she had no birth certificate or identity document or other papers, and so she was subsequently able to claim that she was still a teenager when she arrived, though I always suspected that that was, in the Yiddish phrase, missing out a few Sabbaths and High Holydays. She was a handsome statuesque woman, and very vain, and she went on being comically economical with the truth about her age until the day of her death, when, by my calculation, she was about eighty.

Of the rest of my mother's family there was another brother in London and two more and a sister in New York. They all had large families, and in later years I met many of them and their descendants on their trips to England and mine to the United States. Only one of my mother's siblings, her elder sister Bassia, stayed in Yampol: we had some intermittent correspondence with her up to 1939, but there was no trace of her or her family when I checked after the end of the War.

My father, Morris (anglicised from Moshe), arrived just before the turn of the century, during the Boer War. Almost the first English he learned was the current top-of-the-pops jingo song 'We're soldiers of the Queen, my lads', which he was still singing, with the words almost unrecognisably mispronounced, more than ten years later when everyone else had forgotten it, and when it was soon to be replaced by the jingo songs of another and a bloodier war.

Like most of the immigrants (some smaller numbers entered through Leith, Harwich and the Humber), he landed at London Dock, which is now part of the new yuppie colony on East London's riverside. He came from Kutno, a textile manufacturing town, a satellite of the great textile centre of Łódź, both of them to the west of Warsaw.

His three sisters all emigrated at about the same time, two to New York and the other to London, and after his marriage he brought over his widowed mother to live with us. He left behind in Kutno a family of cousins: during the nineteen-twenties I exchanged letters with one of them of my own age, but after that we lost touch. During the war Kutno was fought through twice: I went there a year or so after the end of the War to look for any trace of my cousins and found only rubble and silence. Doubtless they met their end either in battle or in air-raids or at Auschwitz.

When Morris disembarked at London Dock his total possessions were the clothes he stood up in, plus a little bag containing a change of shirt and underclothes and his accessories for prayer – a *talis* (prayer-shawl) and a *sidur* (prayer book) and *tefilin* (phylacteries) – plus one rouble.

In common with all other immigrants, except those who were lucky enough to have a relative or a friend meeting them off the ship, his first port of call was the Poor Jews' Temporary Shelter in Leman Street, close by the dock. The Shelter, founded in 1885, was a bit of first-aid for Jewish newcomers. It had its ups and downs: in good times, when the flow of immigrants was relatively slow, it could provide up to two weeks' accommodation for those who had nowhere to go, and some good counselling services as well. My father must have arrived at a very bad time, when the immigrants were flooding in and the Shelter's resources were overstretched, so the help they could offer was minimal. He had a bath, to get rid of the odour of the ship, which was very dirty and verminous; his rouble was changed into two shillings; and he was handed a little book of do's and don'ts in English, which of course was incomprehensible to him. (There were times when the Shelter did much better: they produced a Yiddish-English manual which was not only helpful to the immigrants on their arrival, but also came to be used in the Russian-Jewish Committee's Free Evening Classes and some others at which the more literate of the immigrants began to learn English.)

Thus inadequately accoutred with his booklet and his florin, Morris sallied forth along Leman Street towards the Aldgate tram terminus to face the perils of an unknown new world. He didn't know a word of English, or indeed of any language other than Yiddish. The only schooling he had had was in synagogue classes, where he was taught to read the Hebrew prayers and recite them by rote without at all understanding what he was saying to his deity. He couldn't read or write a word of even his own language, nor sign his name. The only skill he had was operating a sewing-machine.

Doubtless he walked that first half-mile of alien streets with a little knot of his fellow-immigrants; and doubtless they discussed how to go about achieving their immediate and urgent objectives, which were to find somewhere to eat, and somewhere to live, and somewhere to pray, and somewhere to work and earn a living.

These immigrants were not altogether without recourse. Many of them had one or more relatives or friends who had come over earlier and were settled and were available for guidance and help. Even if there wasn't a relative or friend there would always be a *lantzman* (a native of the same town or village) to turn to. The solidarity of *lantzleit* was a strong and practical bond, and each of the larger East European cities had a *lantzmanshaft*, which was a sort of mutual aid society: for example, the *Vilner lantzmanshaft* was the association of immigrants from Vilna. These primitive community centres were a comforting port in a storm: the newcomers would go along there to talk nostalgically about their growing up and about the old folks at home. (It may sound incongruous, but I always think I'm in a sort of exiles' *lantzmanshaft* whenever, in an upper room in some pub in Waterloo or Maida Vale, I attend a get-together of the London Section of the Portsmouth Football Supporters' Club.) If one of the newcomers (they were called *greeners*, the green, unripe ones: the term is obviously cognate with 'greenhorn') walked into a synagogue on a Friday evening for Sabbath-eve prayers and looked a bit lost, there would always be a member of the congregation who would invite him home to break bread by the Sabbath candles, recite a blessing over it, and then dig into the salt herring and fried fish and *gefilte* fish. And as a last resort, any door with a *mezuza* on the doorpost had a Jewish family behind it, and nobody was ever turned away: nearly all of them were poor, some very poor, but they were all ready to share what they had. (The *mezuza* is a small metal tube, a few centimetres long and about a centimetre in diameter, containing a tiny scroll with a Hebrew prayer written on it; and a religious Jew nails one to his doorpost. It's believed by some to be a hangover from the biblical story of the Lord smiting the firstborn of Egypt, and being able to miss the firstborn of the Jews because they had an identification symbol on their doorposts.)

There was also some help for the immigrants provided by philanthropic institutions, mostly set up and supported by a few of the wealthy Jewish families who had been settled in England for a long time – some from as far back as the 1650s, when Oliver Cromwell revoked Edward I's edict of 1290 banning Jews from Britain.

In addition to the Shelter (and at times in conflict with it), there was the Jewish Board of Guardians, which combined the functions of a charity with those of a social services department (it still exists as the Jewish Welfare Board), and a number of smaller organisations, including the Soup Kitchens for the Jewish Poor, the Bread and Coals Society, the Sabbath Meals Society, and the Children's Country Holiday Fund, which gave East End children their first sight of the countryside. My wife, Mary, remembers to this day the summer week she spent in a cottage in Loudwater, near High Wycombe, when she was nine years old: it was the first time she had seen farms and fields and hedgerows and wild flowers and heard bird-song in the morning. (Some thirty years later, when we were driving along the A40 towards one of our Cotswold weekends, we stopped in Loudwater and knocked on the door of that cottage. The woman who opened it looked at my wife and said, 'Goodness me, you're Mary, the little Jew-girl.')

Virtually all the immigrants were semi-skilled and unskilled workers in a limited number of trades: the main *dramatis personae* of many Yiddish folk-tales are the tailor, the cobbler, the carpenter and the wagoner. That situation derived from the conditions of life of the Jews in the tsarist empire, where they were subject to severe restrictions on movement and on access to educational and vocational opportunities. They were required to live in a defined area called the Pale of Settlement, and it was only in exceptional cases that a Jew could move out of the Pale. ('Pale' means, literally, a fenced area: the term was also used, over a period, to denote the area of Ireland owned and controlled, and sometimes partially occupied, by the English.)

The East European Pale was a bantustan without the least semblance of autonomy: within it the Jews were the victims of a system of apartheid as brutal as that of present-day South Africa. They had very little access to education, especially higher education; they were denied any opportunity of entering the professions or skilled vocations; and they were subjected to many other forms of discriminatory oppression.

In spite of that, there were two small groups of Russian Jews who broke out of these chains. There were a few who made their way upwards from petty trading into an area of middle-class prosperity – but these entrepreneurial types didn't take part in the emigration. There were a few others who managed somehow to give themselves a wider-than-Jewish education, and read extensively in Hebrew and Russian and German and in Yiddish translations, and out of that reading escaped from religious fundamentalism into political theory and activity: these were an important element in the immigrant community, as you will discover later in my story. But the great majority of the immigrants were, like my parents, illiterate and unskilled. The only intellectual baggage they carried with them was the sharp consciousness, derived from the synagogue and the synagogue-class and from Yiddish folk-lore, of being a separate people with a religion of their own, a history of their own, a culture of their own and two languages of their own.

The poverty and bleakness of life within the Pale was one of the potent incentives to emigration. But there were many others, including periodic famines and epidemics of cholera. Every few years the anti-semites of the tsarist peoples (notably the Ukrainians, who to this day are more antisemitic than the other nationalities of the Soviet Union) erupted into pogroms of murder, rape, pillage and arson, and every such wave, such as the massive Kishinev pogrom of 1903, added a sharp stimulus to the urge to emigrate. Another factor inducing Jewish young men to escape from the Pale was that Jewish conscripts into the tsarist army, almost always the sons of the poor, were put through the tortures of hell. In the worst periods a Jewish conscript would get out of the army, if indeed he got out alive, only after twenty-five years or more, and then almost always after a forced conversion. The family of a conscript would pronounce over him the *kadish* (the ritual prayer for the dead), and if he were married he would offer his wife a divorce.

By the end of the nineteenth century this horrendous situation had improved, but not all that much, so whenever there was an increase in the rate of conscription, as at the time of the Russo-Japanese war, there was a parallel increase in the number of young Jews ducking under the wire and getting out.

Refugees are by definition vulnerable, dependent, defensive and overwhelmed by their circumstances. That generation of Jewish immigrants into England over the forty years or so before 1914 overcame that handicap, and many others, and created a stable and honourable place in society for themselves and their children. How they did it, how they succeeded against all the odds, is a story of no mean achievement. It is one that was to have a profound effect in shaping my thinking and my life, and one which provided me with guidance and help when, in 1964, I found myself representing the heart of that same East End area in Parliament and coping with the very similar problems of a later and different and even more vulnerable immigrant community. So I now recount a little of that struggle before I come back to where I left my father, a few pages back, walking towards Aldgate on his first morning in London.

Apart from the obstacles presented to the newcomers by living in a strange new environment surrounded by a strange new people speaking a strange new tongue, their ills were compounded by being crowded into awful dwellings and working in awful sweatshops, and facing the active hostility of some racists without much support from the long-settled Anglo-Jewish community from whom they might reasonably have expected much more sympathy and help than they got.

The state of the slum dwellings of East London – dark, damp, decrepit, dirty and dangerous – has been so well documented that it is now an all-too-familiar story. One doesn't need to read about it: one can go and see it, because in some streets, notably in Spitalfields, the same buildings are still there, and in a condition not very different from that of a century ago. The pressure for space created by the immigrants led to rack-renting and overcrowding: the average number of residents per house in Whitechapel rose from nine in 1871 to fourteen in 1901. Toilet facilities were sparse, primitive and intermittent, and there were frequent water famines until an Act of Parliament in 1903 set up a public water authority – a process which the third Thatcher government is to reverse, doubtless as a sharp, specific, practical manifestation of a return to the Victorian values which are the Prime Minister's highest aspiration.

In spite of that, contemporary statistics show that the immigrants had, except for one disease, a significantly better health record than their indigenous neighbours. One can only guess at why this was so: perhaps it's because they were very moderate drinkers; or because their separate and distinct diet, derived from the Hebrew dietary laws and from consequent tradition and taste, was healthier; or because they were intensely family-oriented, with always an extended family to fall back on when the resources of the immediate family were insufficient.

The exceptional disease to which they were more prone than the host community was tuberculosis, and that was a direct product of the conditions in their sweatshops, most of them in the needle trades. Those conditions, like the state of the slum housing, have been well documented by many researchers, including Sidney and Beatrice Webb. As with the housing, one doesn't need to read about the workplaces: one can go and see them, because the same workshops and the same home-workrooms of outworkers, many of them dangerous fire-traps, are also still there, virtually unchanged.

Hours of work were very long, and the workers sweltered in the high temperatures (hence 'sweatshops') generated by the stoves and the gas rings that heated the 28-pound irons. The workplaces were even damper than the houses and the 'mansion' flats because of the steam generated by the pressers running the hot irons over damp-cloths.

The air was fetid. A report in *The Lancet* in 1884 of a study tour of East London workshops described how the workers were 'surrounded by mounds of dust and chips from the cut cloth, breathing an atmosphere full of woollen particles containing more or less injurious dyes', and concluded that 'it is not surprising that so large a proportion of working tailors broke down from diseases of the respiratory organs'.

The State provided very little protection against these savagely oppressive conditions. The factory inspectors didn't have, as they still haven't, a complete list of the workplaces, and there were then, as there are now, too few of them to maintain anything like continuous and thorough surveillance. Before the Factory Act of 1901, the inspectors had no jurisdiction over the conditions of adult males. That Act did improve matters just a bit; but the only substantial improvement, especially in raising the beggarly wages, came with the setting up of trade boards (which later became wages councils) after the passing of the Trade Boards Act in 1909. During the second Thatcher government the factory inspectorate was cut, and the Wages Act 1986 narrowed the scope and reduced the powers of the wages councils, doubtless as another return to the Prime Minister's Victorian values.

In the smaller tailoring workshops of the East End, especially those doing only cut-make-and-trim, the livelihoods of both the 'master' and his workers were precarious. The merchant clothiers who gave out the work would play off one small-scale entrepreneur against another, and thus exercise a constant downward squeeze on the piece price, out of which the master had to run his workshop, buy his trimmings, and pay his workers. The trade was, and still is, highly seasonal, with two busy seasons a year and slack times in between; and even the widespread casualisation of labour failed to protect many small employers from running out of money in the slack. (In those days they didn't have any computerised cash-flow projections.) So there was a good deal of role reversal: a cutter who had saved up a bit would start up on his own account (the capital requirements of straight-through hand-tailoring were very small), and find himself employing his former employer who had been forced to give up and was going back to the cutting-table or the machine, at least for a period, to earn a living. On one occasion, after the tailors' strike of 1889, the employers and workers got together in a joint effort, which didn't last long or have any success, to squeeze a bit more money out of the merchant clothiers.

To the immigrants' travail of bad housing conditions and bad working conditions was added the further pressure of condemnation, abuse, discrimination and violence at the hands of growing numbers of racists. Life was full of hardships for all the people of the East End, and it was tempting and easy to make the Jews the scapegoat for those hardships.

I've been right in the thick of racism at both ends of my life – from schooldays up to and through the Mosley eruption, and after 1964 as a Member of Parliament trying to cope with racism in what was probably the most ethnically mixed constituency in the country. Those experiences have taught me to distinguish between two types of racists, separated from each other by differences of outlook and purpose.

Making the Jews the scapegoat for everybody's hardships was a formula that came to be used as a recruiting-agent by the fascists in the 1920s and 1930s, in both Britain and Germany. But the politically-motivated racism of Hitler and Mosley rested on a different concept from the personally-motivated racism that existed in the East End in my father's time and still exists to this day. Political racism is based on the *Herrenvolk* concept, namely that every *Volk* (people) except your own (e.g. Jews or gipsies or blacks) is inferior to your own and therefore carries the danger of diluting the quality of your own. Personal racism, commonest amongst the most exploited sections of the working class, is based on pure xenophobia, which literally means, from its origin in Greek, fear/hatred of another not because he's inferior but merely because he's *different*: that's enough to condemn him, enough to ensure that when he moves into your street or your housing estate you throw a half-brick through his window and daub his front door and shove nauseating things through his letter-box.

The pejorative description of the Jews in the pubs and canteens and street-markets of the East End a century ago was (as it is, word for word, of the Bangladeshis today) that they're different – they look different, they dress different, they talk different and (most heinous of crimes, and most common of neighbours' complaints) their cooking smells different.

That sort of racism is spread by word of mouth, which accounts for the plethora of disparaging slang names for the hated groups: yids, sheenies, kikes; niggers, coons, wogs, monkeys and the less printable jeers of the hooligans on the football terraces.

The two brands of racism, though starting from different points, have three features in common. The first is that some racists not only supported statutory limitations on the number of immigrants, as in the Aliens Act of 1905 and in the anti-immigration laws and regulations of the 1970s and 1980s, but went further and urged, as some of them still do, that immigrants should be sent back to where they came from: as long ago as 1885 the then rector of Spitalfields called for forcible repatriation.

Second, the racists' prejudice had a regular and enthusiastic medium of amplification in the lower levels of the popular press – the tabloids, as we call them today. And third, the Conservative Party adopted anti-immigrant activity as part of their official policies, and in later years the loony right in the Tory Party gave a good deal of support, sometimes covert and sometimes overt, to Mussolini, Hitler and Mosley.

Countervailing forces against those of racism were few and weak. There was open opposition to the racists from socialists, liberals and some Christians: for example, the rector of Spitalfields' call for repatriation was vehemently rejected by the Whitechapel Board of Guardians to whom he addressed it. The great disappointment for the immigrants was that there was not enough support from the one quarter from which they were most entitled to expect it, namely the existing, longstanding Anglo-Jewish community.

Some members of that community set up and supported charities and charitable institutions to help the newcomers, but that was all. Beyond that, the native oligarchs of the Anglo-Jewish establishment were conservative, and they felt embarrassed and worried by the large influx of poor, unskilled and mostly illiterate Jews. They were also Conservative, and didn't like the presence amongst the immigrants of so many socialists. Sir Samuel Montagu MP and some of his friends succeeded in stopping publication for a period of the left-wing Yiddish journal, *Arbeiter Freint* (Worker's Friend), by threatening sanctions against its printers, and they also pressured the owners of halls not to let them for political or trade-union meetings. Chief Rabbi Adler, receiving a deputation of starving tailoring workers on strike, sided with the employers: it isn't only the Church of England which is the Tory party at prayer.

At the Annual General Meeting of the Jewish Board of Guardians in 1884, a certain N. S. Joseph told his colleagues that he would support government measures to restrict immigration, and the same attitude was taken by a number of Jewish Conservative MPs for East London constituencies: H. S. Samuels, MP for Limehouse; Harry Marks, MP for St George's-in-the-East; and, most unctuously, Benjamin L. Cohen, the honours-seeking MP for Islington, who was a vehement supporter of the anti-alien lobby in Parliament. He told them that he and some of his Jewish colleagues were in favour of anti-immigration regulations; and, in a burst of nauseating populist sycophancy, told his fellow-Jews 'to make it clear not to endeavour to oppose any action which the responsible advisors of the Crown may deem necessary for the national interests which we are as desirous to protect as our fellow-citizens'. He voted for the Aliens Act in 1905, and duly got his baronetcy. (In my own recent years in Parliament I have faced, across the floor of the Chamber, a few of his spiritual successors – people who were born Jews but devoutly wished they'd been born something else.)

There was one more pillar of the Establishment which opposed the working-class immigrants and their political and trade union institutions, and that was the *Jewish Chronicle*, which called (and still calls) itself 'The Organ of British Jewry' but which, at least in those years, was the voice of only the anti-socialist elements in British Jewry.

The immigrants, for the main part, tended to reciprocate the unenthusiastic attitude towards them displayed by those they came to call 'the princes of Anglo-Jewry' or 'the nabobs'. They were grateful for the philanthropic assistance they got from some of the Anglo-Jewish families, but they resented the fact that the benefactors were invariably paternalistic, patronising and condescending. They didn't like being told that the best way for them to become accepted was to become less obviously Jewish. Those who were deeply religious condemned the diluted religious observance and the low incidence of hebraic learning amongst the Anglo-Jews; and those who were socialists saw the nabobs as well-heeled supporters of employers against the working class. This strained relationship persisted for quite a long time: I recall that in my own childhood in Portsmouth the leadership of the local Hebrew Congregation was in the hands of a few long-settled families, until, in the 1920s, some of the bolder spirits among the newer settlers began to rebel against the oligarchy and gain some authority of their own.

These complex characteristics of a social and economic order made up of slums, sweatshops, racism and communal divisions were, of course, little known and less understood by my father and his fellow innocents abroad as they made their way into the slow and painful processes of initiation and acclimatisation. Some years after my father had settled in, and could therefore be proud that he was no longer a *greener*, he and his friends, roaring with laughter, would swap stories – and pass them on to their children – of the blunders they made, the clangers they dropped, in the first few weeks of their clumsy, groping initiation.

One of those stories sticks in my memory. It was Morris's description of his first meal in London.

He and two of his friends, wandering northwards from Aldgate, found a cheap eating-house. From his description I identified it, and in 1922 went to see it. I vaguely recall, though I could be wrong, that it was in Brick Lane, opposite Shefsik's Steam Baths. It was a converted shop with a low doorway and two steps to go down into the steamy, noisy café. It was laid out in the traditional pattern of the carmen's pull-in, the ancestor of the present-day transport caff: oblong three-a-side tables with a bench on each side backing on to a partition, so that each table and its benches formed a sort of cubicle.

Morris and his companions went into one of these cubicles and sat down. The *carte du jour* was chalked up on a board, in Yiddish of course, but they couldn't read it. Instead of asking the aid of the waiter (*greeners* were hypersensitive about their ignorance and helplessness), they decided to eavesdrop on what was being ordered by the customers on the other side of the partition, and order the same meal. They did; and many years later my father was able to remember, and tell me, what it was. It began with a penny *zoop* (soup) *mit* a member (a marrow-bone: the regulars called it a member as a joke because they reckoned that the same bone was dished up every day); then followed a penny *lingnleber* (mixed offal) *mit* a penny potatoes *begossen* (literally 'poured on', i.e. with gravy), and a ha'penny *broit* (bread). Good peasant food, not very different from what they were used to back home.

Morris was in London four months before he discovered that he wasn't in New York. That sounds incredible, but it happened, not only to my father but to quite a number of other immigrants I got to know in my teens.

The explanation is simple. There they were, in the Pale, saving up enough money to escape from it. The tour operators who arranged that escape (some of them of dubious honesty, like some of their Asian and Filipino successors in our own day) told each young client that he would be put on a train and travel on it for most of a day or night, and then he would be put on a ship (it was generally at Hamburg or Bremen or Rotterdam), and when he got off the ship he would be in *die goldene medina* (the golden land – Eldorado, the mecca of prosperity-seekers throughout the ages). By implication *die goldene medina* was the United States, but it was only by implication: there wasn't any contract, with or without small print.

A while later Morris decided to go to New York to see what he had missed (a few pounds paid for a passage in steerage), but he found the sweatshops were worse there than in London, and so he came back.

Such were the simple, unlettered, vulnerable, exploited people that made up that generation of refugees. They stood up to everything that was thrown at them, and welded themselves into a decent and stable self-help community.

Their religion was one of the cohesive forces that kept them together. At first they would meet for prayer in a *stiebl* (literally 'little room'), the Jewish equivalent of a bethel; but later they put together enough money to build synagogues. They set up benefit and mutual-aid societies, some with colourful grandiloquent titles (one that I remember was the Brethren of the Covenant and Shield of Abraham and another was the Grand Order of Israel and the Sons of Jacob): there is a record in 1898 of more than a hundred of them in London alone, and there were many more in the larger provincial cities. They set up a number of Yiddish newspapers – the first Yiddish socialist paper was *Der Poilishe Yidl* (The Little Polish Jew) – and Yiddish publishing-houses, several Yiddish theatres and a Yiddish opera company.

Somehow or other, out of their meagre, skimpy resources, they managed to sustain the London Jewish Hospital; they sent money to the families they had left behind, and paid for relatives to come and join them; and they even contributed to charities in the old country and in Palestine. (Many of their present-day children and grand-children do the same, supporting both the cause of Soviet Jewry and social developments in Israel.)

Above all, they saved and scraped to make their children better informed than themselves. The Jews are the People of the Book, and they have always treated learning as an object of reverence. The Jewish immigrants were determined to give their children the education that they themselves had largely or totally been denied. Their communal life was centred, to no small extent, on the high-quality mixed-sex schools they set up. The oldest and biggest and most important of those schools was the Jews' Free School in Spitalfields, a large compre-hensive school founded long before local-authority comprehensives were thought of: by the turn of this century it had over 4000 pupils. Among the others were the Stepney Jewish School, which my Mary and some of her brothers and sisters went to, and the Spanish and Portuguese School, as well as some infant schools.

Perhaps the most outstanding feature of the Jewish East End of those years was the busy, bustling ferment of its political and quasi-political life. While the great mass of the immigrants were unlettered, there were a few among them who were politically conscious and poli-tically informed to a high degree, some with a history of opposition, including revolutionary opposition, to the tsarist government back in *der Heim* (the Homeland). They ranged across a very wide spectrum of the Left: communists; democratic socialists; anarchists propagating by the word, like Rudolf Rocker; anarchists seeking to propagate by the gun, like Peter the Painter, the anti-hero of the Sidney Street siege; freethinkers; syndicalists (syndicalism, advocating workers' direct seizure of control, was imported from France about 1910, and made a lot of converts from the anarchist groups); *Poale Zionisten* (Worker Zionists); *Linke Poale Zionisten* (Left ditto); *Bundisten* (anti-

Zionist socialists); and almost enough breakaways to make up 57 varieties.

From the 1920s onwards I met many of them and saw and heard at first hand the conviction and dedication of their political struggles and the effervescence and sharpness of their multiple disputations. Much later, in 1975, it was all brought back vividly in Bill Fishman's masterly study, *East End Jewish Radicals, 1875–1914*. It was a minor miracle that this flow of political activity quickly exploded beyond the coteries of the cognoscenti and developed a large following, including many women, amongst the general mass of the immigrants who hadn't any previous contact with this side of life or even any knowledge of it, and most of whom could learn about it only from the spoken word. Rudolf Rocker, a German gentile who came to London in the 1870s, and learned enough Yiddish to edit the *Arbeiter Freint* and to become the great teacher and inspirer of East End revolutionary (but non-violent) politics from 1875 till he was interned as an enemy alien in 1914, recorded the deep impression which this mass movement made on him. 'What amazed me,' he wrote, 'was the thirst for knowledge amongst those ordinary working people who had received so little general education, yet had so much natural intelligence that they could easily grasp things about which they had been completely uninformed before.'

The most important division running through this conglomerate political mass was the line between the democratic socialists-cum-trade-unionists, who sought to ameliorate the workers' lot through party, parliamentary and industrial pressure, and the anarchists, who sought the revolutionary overthrow of the State, some by violent means but the mainstream by other forms of anti-State agitation and activity.

The democratic wing involved themselves in organisation, in meetings and in demonstrations. They set up many political clubs and societies (the most notable was the Workers' Circle, founded in 1903) and over thirty trade unions of Jewish workers, some of which had short and chequered lives. Although in the earlier stages some British trade-union leaders were opposed to the immigrants, whom they saw as competitors to their own members, the Jewish trade unions eventually established good fraternal relationships with the other unions in the East End. Those relationships were sealed by the substantial support given by Jewish workers to the dockers who were suffering hardship during their strike in 1912: they subscribed money, shoes and clothing, and took in 300 children from dockers' homes that were short of food.

The most active adherents of their main rival group, the anarchists, were based, most of the time, on a club in Berner Street (now Henriques Street), just off the Commercial Road. Their outlook is mirrored in that of many of today's trotskyist factions: they preferred a grievance to a victory, since any improvement in workers' lives would lessen the impetus to revolution. They even condemned the tailoring workers who joined with their employers to press for higher piecework rates from the merchant clothiers.

This, then, was the Jewish East End in which my father, apart from the short New York interlude, spent the first years of his life in Britain. What took him from there to the South Coast was the First World War's casting its shadow before. In the years before 1914 Great Britain and Germany were engaged in a race to build a dominant naval force. The rapid expansion of the Royal Navy led to the recruitment of many more officers and ratings, and they all needed kitting out. So the naval ports, notably Portsmouth, sprouted workshops to make naval uniforms and caps, and the main catchment area for manning up those workshops was the East End of London.

Some master tailors would travel up from Portsmouth to a sort of open-air job-centre, called the *chazir mark* (pig market), on a stretch of pavement on the north side of Aldgate High Street which later became the site of one of the East End's most noted tourist attractions, Tubby Isaacs' jellied-eel stall. Immigrants looking for work would gather there, and the master would look them over and take his pick. Sometimes, following the practice of the slavemasters of ancient times, he would take his newly acquired 'hand' back to Portsmouth with him and put the man to work immediately, leaving him to sleep his first few nights under the cutting table until he could find bed and board.

So that's how Morris, my father, came to move to Portsmouth; and that's how I came to be a Hampshire hog instead of a cockney, and from earliest days a follower of the Hampshire instead of the Middlesex County Cricket Club, and a fanatical supporter of 'Pompey' instead of Clapton (as it was then) Orient or Tottenham Hotspur. Those childhood loyalties get into one's blood and stay there: that's why I am able to understand (though of course I can't approve of) Michael Foot's consuming passion for Plymouth Argyle.

# Chapter 2

PORTSEA is the part of Portsmouth adjacent to the harbour, the dock-yard and the naval barracks, and so it became the natural centre of the trades of naval tailoring and outfitting. People in those days lived as near to their work as they could get, and most of the workers recruited into those trades found or set up homes in Portsea, and continued to live there for at least their first few years in the town.

The spine running through Portsea is Queen Street, and it was there, and in the smaller streets on the south side of it, that the Jewish quarter developed, with its synagogue, its community centre and its *kosher* butcher and poulterer and fishmonger. The ghetto-like huddling-together of the immigrants in Queen Street and its environs was almost a carbon copy of that same phenomenon in the Commercial Street area of Spitalfields in East London, though in much smaller numbers and more thinly spread. (Later the area was almost totally flattened by Hitler's *Luftwaffe*, and I now find it difficult to identify some of the most familiar landmarks of my childhood days.)

At the harbour end of Queen Street, on its north side, the houses almost back on to the dockyard wall, and it was in one of them that my parents set up home in 1907 and brought me into a much-troubled world a year later.

Like the dockside areas of other great ports it wasn't a very salubrious place for kids to be brought up in. The houses along that stretch all had cellar-kitchens which were invaded every night, and sometimes even visited during the day, by rats which were presumed to have come to us by some subterranean route under the dockyard wall. One

21

of my earliest memories, and a most vivid one, is of my sister Hetty, then a toddler, climbing on a chair and opening a drawer in the dresser to get a spoon, and screaming wildly as her finger was bitten by a rat.

The war against the rats took up a lot of the effort and ingenuity of the people in that row of houses. If you put out a wire cage-trap at night there was always a rat in it in the morning, but you can't repulse an invading army by taking them prisoner only one at a time. Somebody had a brainwave, which all the rest followed: at night we put out a suitably baited tea-chest, and in the morning we would find four or five rats in it: they could jump into it easily enough, but then couldn't climb up the smooth plywood inner walls of the tea-chest to get out. By trial and error we discovered that the most effective bait (and the least wasteful) was the head and tail of a salt herring. The morning disposal of the captured enemy was a difficult and unlovable task: Geller the cobbler, a swarthy, tough man whose little shop was just across the road from us, had to be pressed very hard before he accepted the office of public executioner.

There was a high incidence of infectious disease amongst Portsea children, and the ambulance of the Isolation Hospital – the fever-wagon, as we called it – was a frequent visitor to our streets. Popular belief was that the rats were responsible for these visits, but I never heard whether there was any evidence for this charge or whether it constituted unfounded character-assassination of the rodents.

The rats were by no means the only environmental hazard which we kids had to face. Sailors coming ashore after a long stretch of crowded and uncomfortable imprisonment aboard ship are not the gentlest and most fastidious of men; and visiting foreign sailors experiencing the adventurous excitement of first acquaintance with a new country tend to slip off the safety-catch, rather like football fans going abroad to an away game. So Portsea was rife with drunkenness, violence, prostitution, gambling (mostly in the game of Crown and Anchor) and petty crime, and nearly all of us kids were streetwise, in a smattering of three or four languages, before the age of ten.

At night we would watch the four-man naval police patrols, tall and erect and smartly gaitered, frogmarching drunken or brawling sailors back to the naval barracks. We knew all about the red light district located in the area between Queen Street and Flathouse and centred on two unsavoury alleys. One of them was named Rorke's Drift, after a British military outpost which was held by a tiny force against the enemy at the beginning of the Zulu War in 1879 (the locals, who didn't know that, called it York's Drift, and the name has survived as York Place), and the other, incongruously, was called Blossom Alley (now Blossom Square). Both of them are now fully converted to respectability. We knew the names of the most famed of the streetwalkers and their madams: two of them, Big Jean and Scotch Maggie, still stick in my memory.

By the time I was old enough to know what was going on around me, my parents had got on a bit out of two wage-packets and had launched out for themselves in a little shop doing alterations and repairs to uniforms and other clothing, and selling outfitting requirements of sailors and marines; but at the beginning of their new life together they were very hard up.

A couple of months after the marriage there wasn't enough money in the house to buy what was needed to celebrate the Jewish New Year properly, and Bluma, my mother, pawned her wedding-ring (there were almost as many pawnshops in Portsea as pubs and fish-and-chip shops) to buy a chicken and a bottle of *kosher* wine and the ingredients for baking a honey-cake and other delicacies. I can still remember the break in her voice when she told me, years later, how triumphantly happy she was on the morning she walked up the road to get her ring out of pawn.

The language of the family in those early days was, of course, Yiddish. My grandmother, who did most of the running of the house because mother and father were both working, never acquired, to the day of her death, a single word of English. (She had a few words of Polish, most of them unsuitable for polite conversation, which she taught me and which I've still got.) She had a special soft spot for me because I was her official interpreter in her dealings, such as shopping, with the world outside our front door. Gradually my parents began to learn English from contacts with their customers and their neighbours, but their vocabulary was limited, and sometimes the English and Yiddish were mingled in the same sentence. My mother, in particular, invented words of her own consisting of Yiddish suffixes added to English roots. (Much later I discovered the same philological phenomenon in a mixed German-English language called Pennsylvanisch, which was developed by the steelworkers who left Germany to settle in and around Pittsburgh.)

When I went to school at the age of three I had only a few words of English, and that put me instantly at a disadvantage in relation to my classmates. Fifty-three years later, when I became a Member of Parliament for a constituency containing many Bangladeshi families whose young children had only a few words of English, and saw them harassed by having to study the usual range of school subjects whilst they were unfamiliar with the language of their teachers and their textbooks, I well understood what they were up against because I could remember, as I still do, the agonies I suffered as a child going through that same process.

In fact we were, in one important respect, much worse off in my generation than the parallel children of today. The teachers I have met in the primary schools of my constituency are all deeply conscious of, and warmly sympathetic about, the special difficulties facing immigrant children. They have acquired, to use the current jargon, racial awareness, which in plain English means that they understand and they care: if that were not so, they would presumably have chosen to teach in a less ethnically mixed area than Tower Hamlets.

Not so those teachers of yesteryear who worked in the (far fewer and smaller) areas of ethnic diversity. Racial awareness had not been a subject in any teacher-training course they had gone through, and the term 'multiethnic and multicultural community' was not included in the vocabulary of the time. Moreover, a teacher with fifty or sixty in his class was idiotically overworked, and his hands were much too full to enable him to cope with the special separate needs of any child or any group of children in his class. It is understandable, however unfortunate, that some of them would feel not too well disposed towards any child in the class whose linguistic poverty added to their burdens.

My first school was popularly called the Beneficial School, though its full title was the Beneficial Society's School. The Society was founded in 1754 as a mutual aid society, and its rules provided that any surplus left after paying out sick, funeral and widows' benefits 'may be applied to putting out poor children to school'. At first the charity boys were educated privately, but in 1784 the Society built its own school. By the time I went there in 1911 the school, though still independent, was virtually part of the public education system because it was very closely monitored by the schools inspectorate. (When the Society dissolved itself in 1933, the school was taken over by the Local Education Authority.)

In my class there were the children of two sets of immigrants, Jews and Maltese. The Maltese community in Portsea doubtless originated

24

from workers in the Malta dockyard who had come to seek better-paid and more secure employment in Portsmouth dockyard. They had more English than the Jews, though in some cases it was eccentrically accented.

My memory still recalls that my first teacher was Mr Thomas, and my memory's eye still pictures him as he stood, a remote Jehovah-like object of fear, between his blackboard and his desk. He was a racist bully if ever there was one. He delighted in picking on, and ridiculing, the boys who 'couldn't talk properly'. Some of the kids followed his lead, in the way that children can be very cruel and hurtful to other children. Years later, after many other experiences of discrimination, the still painful memories of those childhood days helped me to think about and understand and hate antisemitism and all other forms of racism. Those who go through that harrowing experience become either haters themselves or internationalists, and I had the good fortune to come out of it right side up.

So it was that, for my first ten years, my life was confined within a few overcrowded acres. Our playground was the Camden, an open space at the harbour end of Queen Street. The local park, Victoria Park, didn't attract children to play in it, since its main features were railings, 'Keep Off the Grass' notices and formidably disciplinarian park-keepers. (Maybe it had been better when it was first opened, long before my time: it was then called the People's Park, which suggests that it was originally designed for the enjoyment of the people rather than for the orderly veneration of Her Majesty.)

Our nearest point for sea bathing (and we could all swim almost as soon as we could walk) was ten minutes away at Sally Port, where, in 1545 Henry VIII sent out to sea the navy he had proudly built, and soon after, together with many of his loyal subjects, watched the *Mary Rose* being sunk; and from where, in 1587, Walter Raleigh despatched a hundred men, women and children to found the second colony in North Carolina; and where, in 1642, Colonel George Goring was besieged in the Square Tower by the parliamentary forces; and where, in 1775, Captain Cook made his landfall when he got back from his world tour; and from where, in 1787, the first fleet to Australia set off on its eight-month voyage; and from where we could see, up the High Street, the George Hotel in which Horatio Nelson spent his last night ashore and parted from his Emma. We boys knew only fragments of this history; and certainly we could not foresee the next landmark, which was in 1956, when a policeman walked into the Sally

25

Port Hotel and tore a page out of the hotel register in order to eliminate from history a Secret Service spook named Commander 'Buster' Crabb who frog-dived into the harbour to take a surreptitious look at the hull of the cruiser *Ordzhonikidze* which had brought Khrushchev and Bulganin on an official visit to Britain, and who was never again seen alive.

Ventures further than that were few and far between. Sometimes we walked from Sally Port along the top of the sea wall to the Clarence Pier, and watched the holidaymakers and the day-trippers getting on and off the paddle-boats that crossed the few miles of the Solent to Ryde in the Isle of Wight. On Wednesday afternoons the penny ferry from the Hard across the harbour to Gosport was half-price, so we would go across and spend the afternoon in an open space called the Horse Fields (some real horses were generally grazing in it). It had a lot of grass and no notices telling us to keep off it. Some Sunday mornings in summer, two or three of us would be sent to take the threepenny tram to Horndean, a few miles to the north of the town. In a nearby wood, the Holt, we had to collect, from under the trees, a basketful of what my mother called *shtyuv*, from which she made a slightly bitter but epicurean *borsht*. I didn't discover until years later that its name in English is sorrel.

Every springtime, when the Passover festival came, there was a ritual excursion to the other end of the town. My grandmother, interpreting the Passover dietary laws at their strictest, insisted that she could drink her milk only from a receptacle that had never been used before. So just before the festival each year we bought a quart-size oval milk can with a wire handle, and each day of the festival I walked across the town to Copnor, where there was a little farm with a few cows, and they milked a cow straight into our can, and I bore it back triumphantly to the old lady, who would reward me with a stick of liquorice, which she thought was good for me.

The expansion of the navy, and hence the dockyard, provided Portsea with a higher standard of living than it had ever had before; but even so there was a great deal of poverty, decay, hardship and avoidable disease. When, in my teens, I began to read and listen and learn about the role of socialism in the elimination of poverty, that concept quickly became meaningful, indeed vivid, to me because it sharpened into focus against the backdrop of the poverty I'd encountered, a few years before, at first hand.

And particularly against one very special memory which burned itself deep into my consciousness. I made my first non-Jewish school friend, Harold, when I was about nine or ten, and one day I went with him to his home to play in his back yard. After play we went into the kitchen, where Harold's mother was doing some household chores. The place bore all the hallmarks of severe deprivation. Harold's father was disabled from an accident at work, and it was several years since he had brought home a pay-packet. The family were just about keeping their heads above water.

Harold and I were sitting at the kitchen table playing Ludo when I looked up and noticed, on the top shelf of the dresser, a large Toby mug with a chipped nose and a broken handle. For some reason I was curious about it and asked Harold what it was.

'It's called the Umbrella Cup,' he said.

'Umbrella Cup?' I asked. 'Why?'

This time it was Harold's mother who answered. 'Because it's there,' she said, 'to protect us against a rainy day. There's one in most houses in this street.'

And so, as I later discovered, there was, and I grieved, and still do, for the desperate waste of human resources and human spirit that was represented by the Umbrella Cup.

Into the Umbrella Cup went every extra uncovenanted bit of money, every sixpence or penny, that came unexpectedly into the house. If it ever got filled, it would represent a pathetic little reserve fund; but it never did get filled because it had to be dipped into every now and again for some emergency expenditure or other, generally for Dr Cashin, who charged a shilling if you went to his surgery in Queen Street and one-and-sixpence for a home visit.

There were all those fine, worthwhile people blacked out, throughout the whole of their lives, from developing their aspirations and talents and creative potential by the great gloomy cloud hanging over them with its threat of that rainy day coming to wash them away. Just as a man with an intense, torturing pain is incapable of thinking about anything else because the pain fills the whole of his mind, so those people in Portsea were incapable of thinking about anything else because their minds were totally and exclusively possessed by the evil spirit of insecurity, by the ever-present fear of a rainy day.

Nearly thirty years later, in 1945, on the day after I was selected as parliamentary candidate for Reading, I was interviewed by a reporter for a local newspaper. One of the questions she asked me was 'What made you become a socialist?' I answered, almost automatically, 'The

27

Umbrella Cup,' – and then, of course, had to explain.

One day in 1984 I called on one of my constituents in Poplar whom I was helping to claim an allowance for constant attendance on her chronically sick and disabled mother, and I noticed on a shelf in her kitchen a dented cocoa tin with a few coins in it. I caught my breath sharply with the realisation that, with all the advances we've made since the beginning of the century, we still haven't got rid of the Umbrella Cup, and I felt a twinge of shared guilt for the failure.

By the time I sat my eleven-plus exam for entry into the Portsmouth Southern Secondary School for Boys, we had moved from Portsea to Somers Road, in the borderland between Fratton and Southsea (though we later moved back to Portsea). Whilst we were there I went to Omega Street school, where we were crammed for the eleven-plus. That examination was fiercely competitive, with over a thousand entrants for a hundred or so places, and the pass-lists, in which the names of the successful entrants were set out in the order of the marks they'd received, were published not only to the schools and the parents but also in the *Portsmouth Evening News*. That list was scrutinised all round the town, by the parents, relatives, friends, teachers and schoolfellows of the entrants, as though it were the roll of those to be admitted to the top storey of the Mansion of Heaven.

In my year, 1919, I was top of the pass-list. In Omega Street School that created an all-time sensation: for the head and the staff, if not for the boys, that was a bigger success than winning the Junior Schools Football Cup. In the local Jewish community, too, and especially among the new immigrants, I was hailed as something of a hero: they looked on me as carrying their banner, as lifting them up a step from their lowly place in the social scale.

My headmaster invited my parents to the school for a little celebration. My father, whose intense natural shyness was compounded (though he would never admit it) by being sensitive about his limited and erratic English, wouldn't go; but mother, a strong matriarch typical of her generation of Jewesses, accompanied me proudly to Omega Street, and her pride was enhanced by the congratulations showered on her, notably by my class teacher. He was a tall, handsome Channel Islander named Le Rossignol, and he must have stayed on beyond retiring age, as a lot of teachers did during the war, because I remember him as having white hair and a waxed military-style white moustache. He said to Bluma, my mother, 'That boy of yours is a very clever boy. He will go a long way. I wouldn't be at all surprised if he finished up as a Member of Parliament.'

It would have been natural if Bluma had glowed with pride and pleasure at this forecast. The archetypal Yiddishe *Momme* is fiercely ambitious for her sons, and of course a *Momme* who could talk about 'My son, the MP' would always have one up on her neighbours who had to be content with 'My son, the doctor' or 'My son, the lawyer'. But Bluma was noticeably cool and unmoved, and I couldn't understand why. It was only later that I discovered the reason: it was that she had already made up her mind about the position I was to achieve, and it was one at a level much above that of a mere Member of Parliament.

# Chapter 3

MY MOTHER'S soaring ambition for me was that I should become
a rabbi, no less, and it was the accident of our being in Portsmouth
that opened a door to that career.

In the first half of the nineteenth century a Portsmouth Jew named
Lewis Aria made a lot of money in tea, and when he died in 1858
he left a large legacy to set up a trust fund 'for the training and maintenance of young men, natives of the county of Hampshire, as Jewish
divines, on orthodox principles'. The original trustees of the fund
set about establishing a seminary for this purpose, and Aria College
was opened in 1874.

Over the years the age of entry was lowered to eleven plus, and
the requirement that the collegians should be natives of Hampshire
was dropped, doubtless because there weren't enough boys offering
from within the county to make up a class, even though the class
number was limited, both by finance and by the size of the college
house, to eight lads at a time.

There was an arrangement between the Trustees and the governors
of the Portsmouth Grammar School under which the Aria collegians
attended the Grammar School for their secular studies. When I went
to the College, I was excluded from this arrangement because it was
thought that I was doing so well at the Southern Secondary School
that it would be wrong to disturb me. I came to realise, a couple
of years later, that that was a mistake. The curriculum of my school
was vocationally oriented, and tightly so: it was designed to produce
not educated, thinking men but only competent apprentices for the

Royal Dockyards and competent artificer cadets for the Royal Navy. Moreover, my being in a different day-school from the other seven robbed me of a part of the benefit of intellectual exchange with them. I have a feeling that if I had spent all my time with these school-friends instead of only evenings and weekends my life after seventeen might have followed a very different course.

There was a break in the functioning of the College during World War I, but soon after the end of the war it was reopened with a new Principal and an intake of eight new boys, including me.

I was the only one of the eight whom the late Mr Aria would have welcomed *ab initio*, since I was the only native of Hampshire amongst them. The others came from all over the country: from the North-east, from Liverpool, from London and from Plymouth. In fact the late Mr Aria would have strongly disapproved of the lot of us and would have considered that his trust fund had been wasted on us, because our 'training and maintenance' on which it had been spent didn't produce any great harvest of 'Jewish divines, on orthodox principles'.

One of the eight of us did become, after a somewhat chequered career, a rabbi of sorts in the United States; two others went into lesser synagogue-based vocations, one as a *chazan* (cantor) and the other, who had a delicate ear and a silky tenor voice, as a choirmaster; one became a pharmacist in his native Liverpool; two were high-flyers in the Civil Service; and the other two, including me, made careers as management consultants. (The last four of us on that list kept in touch with each other, often over a bridge table, right through our lives.) My mother would have shared the late Mr Aria's disapproval of this wholesale departure from the vocation of the cloth: when, on 26 July 1945, I went back to our home from the election count in Reading Town Hall to tell her that I'd just been elected to Parliament, the joy she expressed was by no means unconfined, because she still thought that I'd made only second best.

The newly appointed Principal of Aria College was the Reverend Doctor (or at least that's what he called himself) Jacob Samuel Fox (anglicised from Fuchs). He resembled in many ways the only other man calling himself Reverend Doctor who has since crossed my path, and that is the Reverend Doctor Ian Paisley MP, each of them being a booming-voiced demagogue, a propagandist, a word-spinner, an intriguer, a lot larger than life, and a lot less than he cracked himself up to be.

I can't describe Dr Fox adequately because I haven't the talent and the pen of a Dickens or a Maupassant or a Dostoievsky. He was Russian-born and German-educated, with a rabbinical diploma acquired in Berlin. By profession he was a journalist: he wrote for, and sometimes edited, Hebrew-language journals, and only later took up teaching. He was a large man, round-faced and Vandyke-bearded and potbellied, speaking English with a germanic accent, and with a presence that was overwhelming until you got to know him and saw through him, rather like the Wizard of Oz.

At Aria College he fulfilled a double function: he was the teacher of a wide range of subjects, and he was also the manager and caterer of the hostel which housed himself, his wife, a maid and his eight pupils. He was very much better at the second of these functions than the first, and the boys had no doubt at all that he made a handsome profit out of the capitation fee he got for feeding each of us. He did all the shopping himself, mostly in markets, and he had a keen eye for a bargain. We were healthy, growing lads, and we could have eaten more and better forage than we got.

Our curriculum was so wide as to be beyond the ability of even a great scholar to teach the whole of it. It included the Hebrew languages, both classical and modern, and their literature; the Bible and the biblical exegetists (and they're not easy); Hebrew theology; the Talmud; the history of the Jews; and one or two less weighty subjects. Dr Fox was no great scholar: that wide curriculum was well out of his range, and we discovered after a while that he had a small library of cribs which he used to dive into before facing us round the class table. We were mystified by this, and couldn't reconcile this manifest lack of scholarship with his rabbinical diploma and the academic qualifications which were on his record. We finally came to suspect that the solution to this mystery was that Dr Fox was not the man he purported to be, that the qualifications belonged to a brother of his, either dead or left behind in Germany, whose persona and identity he had purloined for himself – and he got away with it.

When I look back on those years I can't imagine how we managed to cram into each week all the things that we did. Our regimen was by no means an easy one. Five days a week we were at school till four, and brought back the usual solid slab of homework, which grew bigger each year as we moved towards matriculation. But before the evening's homework there was a class in our wide-ranging 'Jewish divine' studies, and those occupied Saturday afternoon and most of Sunday and a part of the normal school holidays. Friday evenings, Saturday mornings and the Jewish Holydays were devoted to synagogue attendance.

That's a full enough programme in all conscience, but we crammed a long list of additional interests into our congested schedule. In the early 1920s, three newish recreations became fashionable and spread like wildfire: ping-pong (which later became table-tennis); auction bridge (which later sophisticated itself into contract bridge); and cross-words. We didn't have a ping-pong table (both the Trustees and the Principal would have considered that a waste of money), but we managed quite well on one of the enamelled-top class tables with a row of books on their edges across the middle of the table doing service for the net. It was one of our standard jokes that after the evening's Hebrew class we would toss up what to do first: heads for bridge, tails for ping-pong, and if the penny stood on its edge we would do our homework.

Over breakfast we religiously did the *Times* crossword; and in any daytime breaks we had we would do the natural boys' thing and play football or cricket in the large yard behind the house. There was a telephone-pole in that yard, and we painted stumps and bails on it.

Another burden on our time was that the Principal used us, quite improperly, as his amanuenses in his guerrilla warfare with the leaders of the Portsmouth Hebrew Congregation. We never really discovered what was the ideological or other significant *casus* of this particular *bellum*, and indeed the war was probably based on no more than mutual personal antipathy and jealousy between the parties. Fox was an inde-fatigable operator of political intrigue, a poor man's Herbert Morrison: he spent a lot of time on the telephone, forging petty alliances with his cronies and others, and he got us boys typing, with two fingers, letters to all sorts of people seeking support for his various abstruse campaigns. I can still remember the typewriter on which we did this work: it was an ancient clattering German machine with two cylinders of characters, like the 'golf-balls' of today, one with English and the other with Hebrew characters, and a lever to reverse the carriage travel for the typing of Hebrew from right to left. After a while I became very bolshie about this exploitation of us (already very busy) boys on unpaid labour which had nothing to do with our studies, and I led a deputation of protest to the Trustees. They were a bunch of ageing establishment figures who showed no understanding of, or sym-pathy for, or even much interest in, the boys in their charge, and I suspect that the only effect of this first venture of mine as an activist was to get me marked down as a troublemaker and give me a black mark to start a collection of them that I added to later. Thus, quite unknowingly, I joined the century-old ranks of ten thousand shop stewards and other trade-union activists whose reward for speaking up for their fellows was to get themselves into the black books of the authorities.

An additional burden descended upon us when Dr Fox's machiavellian intrigues finally resulted in the College's breaking off all diplomatic relations with the Portsmouth Hebrew Congregation. In 1924 a conservatory at the side of the college house was built over and converted into a small synagogue, in which were held the regular Jewish services, partly to relieve us from attending the Portsmouth synagogue which was the object of Fox's obsessive phobia, and partly as a competitor to it. The competition turned out to be successful and we attracted a full house from Jews living nearby, in some cases because it saved them the walk to Portsea and for others because our services were more interesting and literate, and less samey, than those of the older foundation.

It was a part of our 'Jewish divine' training that the services were mostly conducted by collegians. We formed a little choir, and one of our number, who was an untrained but naturally talented musician, developed the skill of adapting classical musical passages, in three-part harmonies, to the words of some parts of the prayers – a notable improvement on the standard turgid tunes.

On special days Dr Fox would preach the sermon, but for the rest of the Sabbath morning services that task fell to the boys in turn. One or two of my own sermons got me into further trouble: I remember one in particular in which I took as my text a dictum from the Ethics of the Fathers which may be freely translated as 'If you're judging a man, give him the benefit of the doubt.' I used it to suggest that we ought to take a fresh look at some of the baddies in our biblical and post-biblical history, and try to understand them even if, in the end, we continued to condemn them. (I had been reading Byron, and I may have been led into this train of thought by his *Cain*.) Later I suggested that we might apply a bit of the same objectivity to some of the goodies: for example, the patriarch Jacob, who by tradition is considered to be a successful and admirable asset-accumulating capitalist, was in fact a common crook. Instead of being rewarded, I opined, with a birthright for cheating his brother and two wives for cheating his father-in-law, he ought to have been brought before the courts and compelled to make restitution to the victims of his cozenage. These unspeakable heresies brought down the wrath of the righteous on my boyish head so fiercely that I felt fortunate that there was no Jewish equivalent of Torquemada around at the time.

I cannot leave the Rev Dr J.S.Fox without acknowledging one debt that I owe him. Though he was, as I've said, no great scholar, he was a linguist and a littérateur of the very highest order. When he wrote or spoke in English his phraseology was, at best, eccentric. But when he launched into a sermon or a speech in Hebrew, and even more in Yiddish, he was reborn as a Demosthenes or an ancient Hebrew prophet, inspired and inspiring; the flood of his oratory rolled on like a cascade, lit at intervals by a strikingly colourful phrase, and he always chose the precisely apt word. I listened to him in rapt wonderment, and I think I owe to that experience such capacity as I have for extempore speaking and such fastidiousness as I have for the choice of the right word in the right place.

Fox was a keen Zionist, and, in common with many others, he experienced a fillip to his Zionism on the promulgation of the Balfour Declaration in 1917. Perhaps because his devotion to this cause was one of the few things he was sincere about, his oratory when he spoke of it rose to new heights. It also changed in style: the thunder of the ancient Hebrew prophet mellowed into an almost poetic evocation of the Land of the Fathers rebuilt, of deserts reclaimed and fields resown and forests replanted by hands selflessly devoted to the creation of a haven from the sufferings of two millennia of Jewish dispersal.

We boys were infected – perhaps we could not fail to be – by this evangelical inspiration: it was the only part of Fox's campaigning that we joined in of our own volition, and enthusiastically. In the early part of 1922 there was a meeting called one Sunday evening in the Vestry Rooms, a classroom and meeting-room annexe to the Portsmouth Synagogue, for the purpose of setting up a Portsmouth Zionist Society. An audience of a hundred or so turned up, mostly of the fairly recent immigrants of the Portsea ghetto. We boys had written a lighthearted playlet for the occasion; and, after a dull chairman's introduction by one of the local bigwigs, we produced it, amidst much laughter and applause, to warm the audience into receptiveness and curiosity. Then came the speakers, and I was one of them. Soon after I began, my feeling for the reaction of my audience led me to switch from English into Yiddish, and most of them loved it. I was thirteen years old, and it was my first-ever public speech, and I'm not sure

I have ever made a better one, or at least a more effective one.

When I look back at those days and marvel, as I've said, at how much we boys crammed into our crowded life, the biggest marvel is how we found time for all the extracurricular reading we did. Half of us or thereabouts had insatiably enquiring minds, and we read voraciously and sharpened our minds on each other's reading. Understanding schoolmasters helped. Dr Parks, headmaster of the Secondary School, gave me a lot of encouragement and guidance, but the man to whom I owed much of my later development, especially of my political thinking, was my English master. By coincidence he had the same name, Thomas, as the racist horror who had been my first infant-school teacher, but this one was a lover of his fellow-men, and not least of the growing-up fellow-men who were in his care. He had the great teacher's capacity to get his pupils to think for themselves: challenge the premises, he said; tackle every problem, every new departure, from a blank sheet of paper. Looking back, I think he understood the mental turmoil I was going through in challenging the premises of the religious dogmatism which was being pumped into me at Aria College and in applying to it the blank-sheet-of-paper methodology.

The seminal event in my reading was stumbling on R.H. Tawney. *The Acquisitive Society* left me as wide-eyed and breathless as Keats told us he was on first looking into Chapman's Homer:

> 'Then felt I like some watcher of the skies
>    When a new planet swims into his ken;
> Or like stout Cortez, when with eagle eyes
>    He star'd at the Pacific – and all his men
> Look'd at each other with a wild surmise –
>    Silent, upon a peak in Darien.'

What I could see from that peak in Darien was a whole ocean of books waiting to be explored, and I dived into it eagerly. I remember that my first dive brought up *Fabian Essays in Socialism*, edited by G.B. Shaw: little did I dream that thirty years later I would be one of the authors of the next volume, *New Fabian Essays*.

Over the first year or two of this feverish exploration of my new world, I found myself testing all the political material I read and heard against the criterion of how it related to Tawney. I linked what he had written to the impression made on me by the Umbrella Cup in Portsea: in reading him I began to understand what had created the

Cup, and that its existence was no accident but the product of the hand of Man, and that therefore it could be got rid of by the hand of Man. I managed, somehow, to fit even the fiction I read into this pattern: two novels that I found particularly relevant to the development of my thinking were Dostoievsky's *The Idiot* and Hardy's *Jude the Obscure*.

I sometimes wonder whether my outlook would have developed differently if I had chanced upon Marx and Marxism before my discovery of Tawney and the other democratic socialists: in fact, my introduction to Marx's thought, and the incentive to read him, came a couple of years later when I listened to an exposition of Marxism in a Yiddish-language discussion-group in Stepney.

So there I was, living in two conflicting, clashing cultures at the same time, one based on unquestioning acceptance of received doctrine and tradition, and the other on thinking things out for oneself. There was never much doubt about which, for me, would come out on top. I think it was Clemenceau who said he was congenitally incapable of accepting anything not susceptible to either physical or logical proof, and that became my way, too, from a quite early age. Somebody suggested to me that Spinoza had produced a logical proof of the existence of a God – 'a Being', as he put it, 'with infinite attributes and modifications' – and so I threw myself hopefully into the *Ethics* and the *Tractatus Theologico-politicus*, but found no salvation or even comfort in them. It was years later that I discovered that many of the Jewish socialist thinkers and leaders from 1870 onwards had reached their political/philosophical position from the same starting-point as I did, namely from reaction against, and escape from, education in religious institutions, in their case in Eastern Europe.

My confusion and frustrations were compounded by an increasing inability to get on with my parents, especially my would-be domineering mother. When I went home to them from Aria College for a visit or a holiday, there was very little we had in common, and therefore very little we could talk about. It became inevitable that when I reached the stage of dropping out, or being dropped out, of Aria College I would want to get away not only from the College but also from my home, and that meant from Portsmouth. That did happen; and though from time to time I went back, between my peregrinations, sometimes for quite a period, and lived in my parents' house, it was always as a visitor and not any more as a settled member of the family.

The process of sallying forth into the wider world was made easier for me by my lighting upon another brave new world, one teeming with fresh and exciting and challenging perceptions. It was the world of the Jewish East End, which I discovered, and was drawn into, some twenty years after my father discovered it and became part of it.

For some years before, I had made short trips to the East End, often with my mother, and had been fascinated by the sharp contrast between its colourful liveliness and the grey conformity of my home town. I delighted to hear Yiddish spoken in the streets, I enjoyed reading the Yiddish posters on the hoardings, and I loved the noisy, babbling Jewish eating-houses and their Yiddish-speaking waiters.

Later on I took every opportunity of going up to London, sometimes for a day, sometimes for several days, sleeping on the floor of my Aunt Betsy's cramped, poverty-stricken but ever-welcoming home; and later still, when I had taken the road to an independent existence, I would always get back to the East End whenever I could from where-ever I was.

Aunt Betsy was one of the world's natural losers. She was homely in appearance and guttural of voice. Her husband had deserted her, leaving her with three small daughters to live as best she could in two small shabby rooms in Goulston Street, just off the Petticoat Lane market. But she had a heart as big as a football, and an enquiring interest in the world around her. Poor as she was, and without any formal education, she nevertheless hosted a political salon. Two or three evenings a week, at about nine o'clock, there would turn up at her living-room half a dozen middle-aged men, each bearing a screwed-up tissue-paper cone containing an ounce or two of coffee. Aunt Betsy would put the kettle on a gas-ring; the coffee was poured; and then they all settled down to a long session, in Yiddish of course, of political analysis and disputation. For me it was a grove of Academe: I sat there with my ears flapping, sucking it all in, asking an occasional timid question, wanting to know more and more, and to understand better.

From these classes I moved on to other lecture-theatres in this homespun university: clubs, societies, discussion-groups, the Workers' Circle, and the open-air university of Mile End Waste.

Mile End Waste is the name given to the stretch of wide pavement on the north side of Whitechapel Road between Vallance Road and Mile End Gate, including the entrance to Whitechapel underground station and facing the London Hospital. On weekdays it is a busy street market, but on Sunday mornings in the 1920s it became a speakers' corner like the one in Hyde Park, though in a different language and with much more serious, and better informed, political content.

On this speakers' corner there were no rostrums representing named lobbying organisations; indeed there were no rostrums at all. All that happened was that a couple of Jews, acquaintances if not friends, would stop each other and start an argument, and then a passer-by would stop and join in, and then another and yet another, and in a few minutes there was a *dredl* (a little circle) all going at it hammer and tongs. By midday there would be half a dozen *dredls* spread along the Waste, with participants and listeners often moving from one to the other, ever seeking a livelier discussion than the one before. I did exactly that, and it was my greatest pleasure of the week; and after a while I became one of the debaters rather than a mere auditor. At the end of the morning some of the citizenry (not many, because Jews are not great drinkers) would adjourn to one of the pubs on the Waste, where the Sunday lunch-time nibbles on the counter were not crisps or nuts but slices of salt herring and onion, which was good business for the publicans because it created a thirst for more beer and schnapps. (There is a Yiddish saying that the reason Jews like eating salt herring is that it makes water taste like champagne.)

By the time of which I write, some major changes had taken place in the political make-up of the East End Jewish radicals from that of twenty or thirty years earlier, which Bill Fishman described so well in his book, whose story ends in 1914. These changes had come about for four reasons.

First, the Jewish population in Spitalfields, Stepney and Mile End had thinned out considerably. Some few had gone on to the United States or to South Africa, but many more had moved northwards into Hackney, Clapton, Stoke Newington and Stamford Hill. (The further moves north-westwards to Hampstead, Cricklewood and Golders Green, and then even further to Hendon, Finchley, Stanmore, Edgware, Elstree and Radlett, and eastwards into Redbridge, came later.)

Second, the great battles of 1880 to 1914 between the revolutionaries and the democratic socialists/trade unionists had been virtually settled by the revolutionaries being forced into a way-back second place. The anarchists never recovered from the loss of the leadership of Rudolf Rocker when he was interned in 1914, and syndicalism proved to be no more than a passing phase. Almost all the residual revolutionaries moved into the Communist Party, and although that Party had some success in the East End, and even made some progress amongst bourgeois Jews, it was always a declining force, and its success in electing a Communist MP for Mile End in 1945 was the last flicker of the candle before it began to gutter towards near-extinction.

Third, immigration had virtually ceased, and the outlook of the settled immigrants became modified, indeed diluted, by their children, who were British educated, in English, and were expressing themselves in the wider community beyond the specifically Jewish milieu, and carried some of the parents with them. Many joined, and were very active in, the Labour Party, especially in local government. While some of the specifically Jewish trade unions lingered on for a while (the longest survivor was the London Jewish Bakers' Union), the great majority of the Jewish workers joined, and took an active part in, the national trade unions, notably in the needle trades and in cabinet-making.

Finally, there were three seminal phenomena between 1914 and 1918 which precipitated some serious rethinking among the Jewish radicals: (i) the collapse of the hopes of international working-class solidarity at the beginning of the War; (ii) the Balfour Declaration of 1917, which changed the concept of a Jewish National Home in the Holy Land from a pious utopian, almost messianic, aspiration into a practical possibility; and (iii) the Russian Revolution, which settled some of the arguments between the pre-war socialist factions but at the same time opened up a lot of new ones.

These radical changes did not lower, indeed in some cases they raised, the volume and intensity of political disputation throughout the Jewish East End, from which I was learning so much. Was the way forward for the working class along the paths of political organisation and industrial agitation, or along the path of revolution? If revolution, was it along the menshevik path or the bolshevik, and was it to be sought in one country, or many, or all? Did improvements in living standards, however hard-won, blunt the struggle for social justice? Does economic oligarchy negate political democracy, i.e. can the worker ever acquire the full fruits of his labour while the ownership of the tools of his trade passes into the hands of an ever-concentrating economic oligarchy? Does the control of the media by a few defenders of the Establishment make it impossible for the worker and the socialist to get their case widely heard and understood? How far, if at all, does Zionism provide hope of a solution to the age-old Jewish problem; or is it, as a nationalist concept, a barrier to the spread of international socialism throughout the world? It's depressing, in a way, to note how many of these questions are still before us today, and still looking for answers.

These boyish excursions of mine into the political scene were not the only part of my East End education. In addition I got into, and became fascinated by, Yiddish-based culture and tradition and Yiddish literature. (A few years later I wrote, after much painful research, a study of the philological development of Yiddish and its influence on the thought and the social structure of East European Jewry: it was published in 1932, and I still find a lot in it that's valid, even though its style is unsophisticated and a bit pretentious.)

There is often a close interrelationship between a growing language and the outlook and life-style of the people on whose lips it develops. The Jews who moved, from the thirteenth century onwards, from the ghetto cities of the Rhine into Eastern Europe spoke, and took with them, *Mittelhochdeutsch* (Middle High German), and they developed that language into Yiddish separately, and indeed cut off from, those left in Germany who developed *Mittelhochdeutsch* into modern German.

The Yiddish language has two outstanding characteristics. First, it is pre-eminently the language of the family and family relationships: it has more diminutive and caressive forms, a few of them borrowed from Slavonic languages, than any other tongue. Secondly, it is essentially the language of the working class: whilst the few Jews in the Pale who had got on a bit learned and spoke the vernacular of their gentile neighbours and associates, and whilst the religious hierarchy stuck to Hebrew and resisted, as hard as they could and for as long as they could, the spread of Yiddish, the working-class rapidly adopted it for all their everyday needs. The linguistic division among the Jews was somewhat similar to that among the British in the period after the Norman Conquest, with the bosses, the landed hierarchy, speaking Norman-French and the workers, the peasantry, speaking Anglo-Saxon.

This linguistic evolution created among the East European Jews two social phenomena which they carried with them when they emigrated to the West. The first of these was the erosion of the power of the ruling priesthood as a result of the translation of religious texts and works of religious scholarship into a language that the man in the street could understand. (Christianity, of course, went through the same process with the translation of the Bible into English and other vernaculars, and its greatly increased accessibility after the invention of printing.) The rabbis lost the power to keep their congregants in thrall, which had rested for centuries on their monopoly of contact with God and his words.

Yiddish changed the attitude of the mass of Jews towards their religion and their God. In the Yiddish-speaking family, just as father was *tatenyu* and mother was *mamenyu*, so God became *gotenyu* – not the distant awe-striking deity of the Hebrews whose very name it was blasphemy to pronounce, the jealous god who visited the sins of the fathers upon the children unto the third and fourth generation, but instead an ever-present counsellor and friend, a member of the family one could talk to across the kitchen table, as he was talked to by *Tevye der Milchiger* (the milkman) who became popularised in the musical *Fiddler on the Roof*.

The other great social characteristic of Yiddish is that it is not only the language of the working-class but it is also the language in which the workers pursued the class struggle. Every one of the tales of Yiddish folklore – two great long sagas of them – invariably ends with a poor man achieving a putdown of an establishment bigwig – either the local plutocrat, or alternatively the *parness* (president of the congregation) or the rabbi. The hero of the outstanding Yiddish novel *Stempenyu* is a poor, crippled itinerant fiddle-player. The best of the modern Yiddish poets, Morris Rosenfeld, wrote of the tyranny of the sweat-shops. The oldest, and to my mind the best, of the songs of the class struggle – long before Joe Hill and the songs of the Wobblies (IWW) and of 'Pins and Needles' – is a sad little Yiddish ditty in which a small boy seeks to discover the meaning of the Hebrew words for bread and meat and fish and tasties, and finds that what they mean to the wealthy is very different from what they mean to the pauper. The first time I heard that song it took me straight back to the Umbrella Cup. Indeed, the whole of my absorption into the culture and literature of Yiddish meshed very closely into all my explorations – near-sighted and fumbling as they must have been – into the political facts of life.

I was to have (though, of course, I didn't know it at the time) two later sojourns in the East End – one in the 1930s, when I lived there, and did my courting there, and married there, and both my daughters were born there, and the other from 1964 to 1987 when

I represented a part of it in Parliament. But it is the education, especially the socialist education, which it gave me in my teenage years that, at all times and wherever I am, keeps me bound to that bit of London between the Aldgate Pump and Bow Bridge.

# Chapter 4

THE NEXT dozen or so overs in my long innings were a dull patch, with the batsman tied down by threatening bowling and tight fielding, scratching round the crease and settling for mere survival; and there were few highlights worthy of a turn of the camera. The times were hard, and they got steadily harder all the way through the 1920s and into the early 1930s. I drifted from one boring dead-end job to another to seek a few shillings more in the pay-packet, thankful to have a job at all, and occasionally topping up the money with a bit of evening and weekend work, teaching or translating or bookkeeping or occasional writing.

I joined the Labour Party and, at the same time, *Poale Zion*, the Zionist Workers' Movement, which is affiliated to the Labour Party; but for most of the time I engaged in little political activity because, as with so many others during the Great Depression, the mundane grind of earning a living left little time or energy or resources for anything else.

It wasn't only political activity that was sacrificed: it was only rarely that I could rake up the turnstile-money to go and watch my beloved Pompey playing football.

In 1930 I met my Mary, and found a new family in hers. It was a large family, and those who weren't married crowded together in a rambling old house in Bow, a few doors from George Lansbury's, mucking in together and sharing both the chores and the money and squeezing every drop of fun we could get out of life: we were an anything-can-happen-next horde, rather like Sanger's Circus in

Margaret Kennedy's *The Constant Nymph* or the equally eccentric family in *Brother of the More Famous Jack*. For me it was a great, heart-warming experience: it filled the gap left by my not having had that sort of close-knit kibbutz-like relationship in my parental home.

During that time I did make one excursion into politics, and it foreshadowed some of my future political activity because it was a departure from, indeed a protest and a revolt against, the Labour Party's mainstream.

That mainstream, between 1929 and 1931, was represented by the Labour Government. The leaders of that Government took office in the midst of an economic crisis, which deepened every month they were in power. They hadn't the knowledge required to understand the causes of it; and because they didn't understand its causes they couldn't work out a remedy; and because they couldn't work out a remedy for it they accepted, indeed seized on, the remedies pressed on them by their opponents – the Conservatives, the City, the industrialists and the newspaper magnates.

Their policy – if indeed blind gropings can be dignified with the name of policy – was exactly the opposite of what the circumstances demanded. The body politic was anaemic, so they applied leeches to it. They were arch-deflators, seeking to cut the purchasing-power of the low-paid and the unemployed – those with the least purchasing-power to cut. They were arch-monetarists, putting financial 'rectitude', including even the maintenance of the exchange-rate, before any attempt at economic recovery. At the first whiff of difficulty, all they had preached before 1929 vanished into thin air: Hugh Dalton has told us that the Government 'ran away from its programme from the first day'. The Ministers were like convinced republicans becoming overnight *plus royaliste que le roi*. When capitalist depression came in at the door their socialist aspirations flew out of the window.

The ignorance and incompetence of the Party's leaders, and their arrant betrayal of all that the Party had stood for and fought for, blotted out our sun and left us in deep darkness – until, in 1930, a thin shaft of light broke through, bringing with it the realisation that there was a way out of the gloom, and an indication of what that way might be.

The man who lit that torch was Oswald Mosley. From the moment he estranged himself from the other leaders of the Party he began to develop and propagate, in speeches and articles, an alternative economic strategy – one which had a great deal in common with the economic strategy put foward by the Left in the Party, some decades later, as the alternative to the deflationary, monetarist and regressively-distributive practices of the Wilson and Callaghan governments.

The main thrust of this strategy was an attack on mass unemployment, then rising above two millions. That thrust was to be promoted by stimulating industrial growth, over the long term through increased demand arising from increased purchasing-power and immediately by a programme of infrastructure building and improvement (the terms used in those days were 'public works' and 'relief works') and by planning and controlling the economy, and not least our external trade, and integrating it with that of other Commonwealth countries, partly through bulk-purchase contracts. Further, there should be higher taxation of the rich, and an acceptance of the principle that 'it is far more important to have industrial recovery than to balance our Budget'. (Sadly, that principle had to be fought for all over again under later Labour governments.)

The many members of the Party, both in the Commons and out in the sticks, who were in despair at the supine passivity of the Government, would have seized on almost any manifesto for action: anything was better than nothing. But the Mosley programme was more than just anything: it made real sense not only to the employed who were being squeezed into pay-cuts and the unemployed who were being squeezed into benefit-cuts but also to those of us who had the wit to see that the arch-deflators were aggravating the disease they claimed to be curing.

The outstanding member, by far, of the group of Labour MPs who supported Mosley's concepts at this stage was Aneurin Bevan. Michael Foot has recorded that 'to Bevan the Mosley programme appeared as ... one well suited to the urgencies of the hour'. Bevan got sixty MPs to sign a petition demanding that the Government should take more urgent action to combat the rise in unemployment.

Within my own little grassroots circle there were sharply different views about Mosley. Some felt their Party loyalty strained by one who attacked the leadership so vigorously, and indeed intemperately; some were illogically put off by Mosley's upper-class background ('He's not really one of us, is he?'); but quite a few, and I was one of them, shared Bevan's view that what Mosley was advocating was what the needs of the time demanded. This sort of argument simmered for a while, and then boiled over at the Annual Party Conference in Llandudno in October 1930.

The centrepiece of Conference was a long debate on unemployment, opened by Ramsay MacDonald. Most of the debate was pretty colourless: there was some criticism of the Government from Nye Bevan amongst others, but it didn't really strike home. It was mid-afternoon when Mosley went to the rostrum, and it took him only a few minutes to electrify his audience.

Robert Skidelsky, in his painstaking though perhaps overindulgent biography of Mosley, records the main themes of that great speech. It 'started off,' he writes, 'quietly enough with a sober account of the differences which had arisen between him and the Government.' Mosley said that £122 million had been allocated to public works – an impressive sounding total until it was realised that this was to be spread over four or five years, offering a maximum employment in any year of little over 100,000 men and women. 'In other words, the 'ambulance work' only put one man in employment for every ten put out of employment since they came into office.'

The long-term programme of reconstruction had been left largely to the banks. The conference ought to realise that rationalisation would inflict great hardship on the working class unless it was subject to Government control. The home market, the 'purchasing power of their own people', alone offered any real hope for permanently absorbing the unemployed. But the market had to be insulated from the shocks of world conditions by a combination of tariffs and import boards which might be extended to embrace the whole Commonwealth. 'The principle was to have an organism planning, allocating, regulating their trade rather than leaving these great things to the blind force of world capitalist competition ... Unless the Labour Party did it, capitalism would undertake it with all the chaos and suffering that would follow.'

It is a matter of history that when he ended his speech the whole Conference rose to him in a great wave of relief and thanks for this promise that all need not be lost. It is equally a matter of history that the resolution which Mosley was supporting was thrown out by the trade union block vote. *Plus ça change* . . . .

The enthusiasm of those Conference delegates who gave Mosley his great ovation was equally felt by many of the younger members of the Party at the grass roots. I was caught up in a ferment of discussion which the speech activated. Even though some of us had detected, in certain of Mosley's earlier activities, indications of an authoritarian attitude at odds with the *mores* of the Party, and were disturbed by it, we didn't allow that concern to deflect us from supporting the socialist programme which Mosley was advocating.

I went to a few meetings, and took part in some discussion groups, and wrote one or two pieces which were published in *Action*, the journal which Mosley established to get wider support for his views. *Action* was a surprising paper: it had a very mixed bag of contributors and an equally mixed bag of contents: politics and economics, including an unexpectedly sympathetic account of the Soviet system; the arts and sciences; the environment; the generation gap (this by Christopher Isherwood); and much else.

When, not so long after, Mosley went off the rails and turned off all the young socialists (and many others) who had supported him, there were some wise-after-the-event sages who told us that if we had looked hard at Mosley we would have seen clear enough signs, even as early as 1930, of where his authoritarianism and élitism would finally take him. There was a substratum of truth in that charge – enough to make it hurtful.

[*Digression*. Over the last two or three years I've been struck by some similarities in the careers of Oswald Mosley and David Owen.

Of course there are great differences between the two men. I've always found David Owen to be a kindly man (certainly he was very kind to me when I was taken ill one evening in the House of Commons), and Mosley was not at all kindly. I can't envisage for a moment David Owen strutting around in a paramilitary uniform surrounded by a bodyguard of similarly-uniformed moronic bouncers, or his ever being tainted by racism.

But there are nevertheless some close similarities. Both of them came from privileged backgrounds divorced from the working-class trade-union base of the Labour Party, and neither ever really bridged the gap. Beatrice Webb described the early Mosley as 'entangled in a smart set and luxurious habits ... he cannot get on terms of intimacy with working men ... [he] will be a great success at public meetings – but will he get round him ... the national leaders ... of the proletariat?' That wouldn't be too far out as a comment on David Owen. On the other side of the coin, David Owen is described in Andrew Roth's *Parliamentary Profiles* as 'brilliant; able; hardworking; vain; impatient; arrogant,' and that wouldn't be too far out as a description of Oswald Mosley.

Mosley was, and Owen is, a tall, attractive man, at once publicly charismatic and privately charming, ready to challenge the orthodox ideas of others, and with a considerable gift for expounding his own.

Each left the Labour Party in order to break the mould of politics and each subsequently set up another party of which he would automatically become leader – and which had orange-marigold as its official colours. Each of them, on a critical occasion, ignored the views of members of his party – an example of the authoritarian, élitist kink which is a characteristic of both of them, though I'm sure David Owen will never let it run away with him in the way Mosley did.]

The horrendous result of the 1931 general election, followed by MacDonald going over to the enemy and Mosley going round the bend, knocked the political stuffing out of many of my generation, and it took a while for us to recover. In the next few years I did little more than go to some of the outdoor fascist meetings in Bethnal Green and Stoke Newington to heckle the speakers, and at other times collect a bit of money for the republican victims of the Spanish Civil War.

I married in 1931, and by 1935 had acquired two daughters, both born in Stepney. Even before 1931 I had started to face up to the fact that I needed to acquire some skills that were more readily marketable than those I had, and marketable at a better price, and was trawling for opportunities. The break came for me when I stumbled on an advertisement for a seminar on what was then called 'scientific management'. I had already seen enough, in my various jobs in factories, warehouses, and marketing and distribution agencies, to satisfy myself that there was plenty of room for improvements in industrial and commercial organisation and management, and I was curious to discover whether or not there was, as the term 'scientific management' implied, an established corpus of knowledge, a tested discipline, which laid down criteria for devising those improvements and methods of applying them.

So I enrolled for the seminar, and received a pre-seminar reading list. I worked through that list and some other material suggested in it as optional extras. My reaction to this material was mixed: I readily saw the advantages of line-and-staff organisation, but at the same time I recognised that the effects of what was called Taylorism, after one of the American founding fathers of time-and motion-study, could at one end of the scale produce greatly improved work practices but at the other end could result in no more than exploiting the shop-floor workers whilst leaving much of the managerial process unchanged and unimproved.

So I approached the seminar with a mind wide open to explore

49

and to learn, but a bit critical, and even sceptical, round the edges. I digested all I heard at it, and afterwards I read furiously every book on the subject and every tract and study-guide that I could lay hands on, and went to every lecture and every class I could manage. Within a few months I had evolved my own variant of 'scientific management', my own formula for improving organisational method and practices.

It was a formula founded on what I had learned, and on how my thinking had developed, way back at school. It rested on the habit drilled into me by my second Mr Thomas of starting every problem-solving effort from a blank sheet of paper, sceptical of received wisdom, always ready to challenge the premises, and also on my own obstinate refusal to accept any proposition until I was satisfied that there was a logical justification for it.

I ought not to be able to claim any originality for that approach, since in theory everybody with managerial responsibility behaves in that way. But in practice only a minority do. Too many deceive themselves into believing that they have an infinite capacity to make the right decision off the top of their heads. One too-rapidly-promoted managing director once claimed to me that he could run his company successfully by playing his hunches, and I told him that if his hunches were consistently so good he could have a much easier life and make a lot more money as a professional horse-race punter than as a managing director. A few years later his company was insolvent.

Outside the ranks of these self-deluders there are too many managers who are so pressed by day-to-day problems, so harassed by the three telephones and the intercom and the visual display unit on their desks, so absorbed in the constant losing battle to keep down the contents of their in-trays (and in most cases the other papers littering their desk-tops) that they have no time to sit back once in a while and see the wood for the trees. That's the justification for bringing in, once in a while, a consultant or some other outsider who, because he isn't responsible for the care of the trees, can examine the wood through fresh, wide-vision eyes.

Most organisations are initially constructed specifically to fulfil their defined objectives, and therefore they are designed and structured in clean lines and simple shapes. But with the passage of time the initial structure has grow'd like Topsy, because new bits are added without considering, or at least adequately considering, the effect of each of them on what is already in place, and consequently the clean line develops kinks and the simple shapes become convoluted, and

50

that distorts the movements between parts of the machine and slows down many of its operations.

During World War II, when I spent a lot of my time in aircraft factories, I saw a close parallel to this situation in a different context: aircraft designers were always complaining (maybe they still do) that they started out designing a machine in beautiful, simple, aerodynamically perfect lines, and then the bigwigs at the Air Ministry would demand, even before the prototype took off on its maiden test-flight, hundreds of additions and modifications, each of which created a bump or a projection or an appendage, breaking up the streamlining and lowering performance and leaving the final product hung around like a Christmas tree or, like Bardolph's face, 'all bubukles, and whelks, and knobs'.

This process of gradual erosion of a well-conceived, clean-line structure is a characteristic of all man-made organisations, both public and private government departments, local authorities, public corporations, quangos, the churches, large businesses of all types, legislatures, charities and many others. The process of erosion comes about in a number of different ways: department A is temporarily shortstaffed and therefore overloaded, and so the managing director decides to transfer one of its functions to department B just for a few months, and since *c'est seulement le provisoire qui dure* this arrangement goes on after the need for it has expired; or department C acquires a new head who is an empire-builder (we all know the type) and who, perhaps because he's an achiever, succeeds in persuading the managing director to put in his charge some functions which properly belong elsewhere; or a new range of functions is transferred into a factory or a branch from another which has been shut down and the transfer is made without any adequate examination of the effect of the additional workload on the structure of the receiving organisation. (That's the process by which all the political empires in history have been built, and the reason why, in the end, they all declined and fell.)

One physical consequence of this process of erosion is a build-up of superfluous paperwork – the phenomenon which in popular shorthand is called bureaucracy. This, too, comes about in a number of different ways: an additional set of statistics is required for a one-time purpose, for example, a specific piece of market research or a three-month check on quality control to test the effect of a new set of guidelines, and nobody remembers to cancel it when the one-time purpose has ceased to apply, and so it goes on being compiled, unnecessarily and wastefully, to the end of time; or the empire-building department-head decides he must have a separate stock record in his own department so as to avoid having to go to another for information (in this age of computers the central data-bank has reduced the incidence of this disease, but not completely cured it); or the closed-down factory or branch brings its own paperwork with it into the one to which its work is transferred, and some of that paperwork is merely added to, instead of being absorbed or integrated into, the existing paperwork of the receiving unit.

After I set up as a management consultant on my own account (this is jumping ahead a bit, but I'll come back to the chronology in a minute), some of the first assignments I undertook were in the form of what I called the paperchase. I would go through an organisation listing every single form that was compiled and probing rigorously why it was compiled; and in how many copies; and where each copy went; and what, if anything, the recipient of each copy did with it; and whether that copy was permanently filed; and if so who, if anybody, ever consulted that file; and why.

That repeated question 'Why?' evoked some responses that recurred over and over again: 'Well, I've been here twelve years and that's the way we've always done it'; or 'If I didn't have this index in our own office, it would take me some time to get the information from another department' (which might be in the office next door); or 'I don't know what the reason is but there must be one, because otherwise we wouldn't be doing it'; or 'I like to keep everything I need under my own hand'; or any one of half-a-dozen other reasons which weren't reasons at all but only rationalisations.

This paperchase function brought me not fame and fortune but some modest acclaim and some consequent recommendations from one client to another.

There was one occasion on which I used it to political advantage – a very small-scale advantage, since its result was to get for some Labour candidate in the 1945 general election one, only one, vote he would not otherwise have won. At the time when that general election was announced, I was carrying out a reorganisation of the production-control functions in a company manufacturing vibration-reduction equipment. The company's managing director was a man I liked very much: he was a retired brigadier who combined a sharp business acumen with a wide range of social and cultural interests and a genuine, not just a cosmetic, concern for the people who worked for him.

On the day the election was announced I drove over from Reading to tell him that I would be missing for a month while I was campaigning and would be back on the job full time immediately afterwards because there was no possibility whatever that I could win a majority in the safe Tory constituency I was contesting.

We sat in his office and drank coffee and talked. He wished me well in the election campaign even though he was a lifelong Conservative and had never voted any other way. 'Mind you,' he said, 'I've been thinking about possibly voting Labour this time, but I'm put off by your plans for economic control because of my wartime experience of industrial controls and having to fill up lots of government forms, all in triplicate.'

I leaned across the desk and asked a sharp question: 'When you buy something in this company, how do you do it, and with what paperwork?'

'I've no idea,' he confessed.

'So ask somebody,' I said.

He flicked a switch on his intercom, and asked, and the somebody at the other end said, 'If it's not more than ten shillings, we buy it out of petty cash and fill in a petty cash docket, but if it's more than that we make out an official order form.'

'In how many copies?' I asked over the intercom.

'Six,' came the answer, 'unless it's Aeronautical Inspection Directorate material, in which case we have to make out two extra copies to send to them.'

My friend and client smiled at me across the desk. 'OK,' he said, 'you win'.

'Splendid,' I said, 'and to reward you I'll come back in the week after polling-day and we'll go round the place together and see what happens to each of those six copies and whether every one of them is necessary.'

Notwithstanding my unexpected success in the election, I did go back in the first week of August, and we spent a day and half together following through the five retained copies of the order form, and our research ended by getting rid of three of them and the bulky files in which they were stored.

But, as I've said, I've jumped ahead a bit, so let me go back to the point at which I satisfied myself that I knew enough about management science to become a practitioner in it. At that point I got a junior job in a small consultancy organisation specialising in revamping distribution and sales departments, and then went on to a slightly better job in a somewhat bigger group, but I wasn't satisfied with them because I felt that their investigations were a bit superficial, and I began to think about starting up on my own account so that I could put to use all the ideas on organisation and management which had crystallised in my mind and were screaming out to be tested in practice. My switch, when it came, from employee to self-employed was the result of pure accident. (Although we are loth to admit it, the majority of the entries in the *curriculum vitae* of most of us, including even our marriages, are the product not of pre-planning but of an accidental encounter or some other chance occurrence.)

I was taking a week's holiday, and one sunny afternoon I stopped to watch a schools cricket match in a North London park. I walked out of the park, crossed into a long residential road and had to jump a bit to avoid a laundry van which was pulling up at the kerb. I noticed the name of the laundry on the side of the van: it was not altogether unfamiliar to me because I'd come across it somewhere described as a large and growing firm. The driver picked up a parcel from within the van, and walked up to the door of a nearby house to deliver it. It was a familiar scene, and I didn't give it a second thought – until, a moment or two later, another van of the same laundry pulled up at another house a few yards along the road and its driver also got out and delivered a parcel. I walked along thinking about that, and just as I got to the end of the road a third van of the same laundry pulled into the road, and its driver delivered yet another laundry parcel.

The following morning I presented myself at the laundry's head office and asked to see the general manager, and after a bit of difficulty and delay I was ushered in to him.

I came straight to the point. 'I can save you a great deal of money,' I said, 'on your transport costs, and I can do it in a few months and without a lot of trouble.'

'What makes you think that?' he asked.

In reply, I told him, in detail, what I had seen the previous afternoon.

'Well, you can't avoid that sort of thing happening,' he said, 'though I didn't realise it was as bad as that. What's your proposition?'

I told him that I was prepared to work in one of his offices for a few days in order to carry out a pilot study to establish the potential for reducing mileage and costs. 'I don't want to be paid for those days and I'll provide myself out of my own pocket with any aids I need. All I want from you is a chair to sit on, a desk to work on, and a copy of the round-sheets [the list of customers and their addresses in running order] of three contiguous rounds.' The manager – he was a tall ascetic-looking man with a northern accent – hesitated a moment and then called in two of his colleagues, and we went over the ground again, and again I spelled out my offer of a free pilot study.

They were clearly a bit sceptical. While they hesitated I threw in a question: 'Does any of you ever have a bet on the horses?'

Getting over his surprise one of them answered 'Yes, I bet regularly, though I don't get much out of it.'

'In that case,' I said to him, 'you should know that no punter with his wits about him ever turns down the chance of a bet to nothing, which is what I've just offered you.'

That clinched it.

They put me in a little office in an outbuilding with a chair, a desk and a blank wall, and gave me three round-sheets. I bought a large square of cork sheet and fixed it to the wall. I also bought a street map of the area which included those rounds, had it enlarged, and drawing-pinned it up on my cork sheet. My final purchase was three boxes of pins with coloured heads, one black and one white and one red, and three reels of thread of the same colours.

It took me two long days to pin the three lots of customers on the board, with thread of the same colour marking the travel from each customer to the next. At the end of that process my pin-board looked like a splodged painting in a toddlers' play-group; but I could estimate from it how long it would take me to clean up the mess and how much would be saved in transport costs. I asked the management to come across the yard to my little office. This time there were five of them: they took one look at what was on the wall and didn't need a second look. I handed them a report with my findings, and they accepted it on the spot – though they were surprised at my saying that I didn't think the job could be done, and wouldn't want to do it anyway, unless we got the consent and the ready co-operation of the drivers.

That operation, by the time I completed it, was a great success for the company, and in addition it did me personally a power of good because I learned a lot from it and because I used it as a base to extend the scope of my work. Before I left that company I had instituted a staff-training scheme for the vanmen which turned them into salesmen instead of mere collectors and deliverers, and increased their earning power; and I had gone into the plant and devised and instituted improvements in the processes of receiving the soiled linen, marking it, and then laundering, drying, ironing, re-assembling, packing and despatching it. By that time, too, I had acquired a number of other clients for similar work, dividing my working-time and increasing my capacity by using some of their employees as assistants.

As time went on I became more interested in working on the planning and control of production than on the ancillary departments and I developed some ideas on loading work on the shop floor, especially in engineering, and progressing it through its operations – ideas which stood me in good stead later in my wartime work in aircraft and armaments factories. For the next ten years the greater part of my work was in this field.

My first major wartime assignment arose from the shortage of high-performance light alloys which began to be felt even before the war broke out. So there was a search for possibilities of finding substitutes for light alloy to use in some of the products made from it. A factory in Trafford Park, Manchester, which had been a successful producer of standardised doors and window-frames was converted to the manufacture of airscrew-blades out of reinforced laminated wood. It was a hideously complex process, and full of unquantifiable difficulties arising from the fact that we were trying to make an organic living material behave like an inorganic static material. We succeeded; and the time I spent there was one of the most satisfying experiences in the whole of my professional career.

Nevertheless, my warmest memory of that factory is not related to the work we were doing: it is related to a brilliant, eccentric Australian aircraft designer who was our top boffin. Every now and again he would go AWOL, and we would send out a search-party for him, and they would find him sitting on a park bench watching birds alighting on, and taking off from, the boughs in the trees, because he reckoned that we wouldn't build the perfect airframe until we discovered precisely what enabled a bird to land precisely on a chosen spot and to take off without a runway. We all thought he was a bit cranky, but he was wiser than the lot of us because what he was doing was to anticipate both the vertical-landing-and-take-off and the variable-geometry aircraft that were to come a lot later.

After one or two more short assignments in war factories, I undertook a major one in the Miles Aircraft factory on Woodley Aerodrome, just outside Reading. It was to occupy most of my working time and to last for quite a while, and so I moved with my family to Reading. We spent a few weeks in a private hotel and a few months in digs, and then we rented a house in Tilehurst from a man who joined the RAF and was posted overseas.

My acquiring that work at Woodley and therefore moving to Reading was another of those accidents that shape the *curriculum vitae*. In this case my *vita* was revolutionised, no less, by the move, because it resulted in my becoming, for the first time, deeply and passionately and dedicatedly involved in the Labour Party and the trade union movement and in putting my feet on the path that led to a career as a professional politician.

# Chapter 5

As soon as I settled into Reading I transferred my Labour Party membership to that Constituency Party and became closely involved with the people who were running it. Not that there was much running to do: the agreement between the political parties to forego contested elections till the war was over (this armistice was later broken by the formation of Common Wealth, which contested parliamentary by-elections) did away with the function which, more than any other, is the focus and motivator of party activity. Moreover, the Constituency Party, like all the others, was missing some of its best members who had gone off into the forces. But we were nevertheless a lively crew: we had some good oldsters and quite a number of younger ones who were in reserved occupations (mostly in aircraft and component manufacture), and a joyous bunch of teenagers, some of whom I still meet now and again.

We decided to fill the gap created by the loss of the electoral function by engaging in two types of activity. The first was to make the Constituency Party a forum for political education, and the other was to increase our work in the trade unions, particularly by making an input into them which was specifically political, and for us that meant socialist.

We had the good fortune to have a little monthly paper, *The Reading Citizen* (a title which can of course be construed in two different ways), as a base for our education work. It was produced by a husband-and-wife team whose dedication to socialism and internationalism owed much to the Quaker tradition that for a long time had had a strong presence in Reading: the wife edited the paper and her husband printed it. It was a little paper because the supply of newsprint was limited and strictly controlled, but the standard of its contents was at least up to that of better-known and larger-circulation socialist journals.

Even during the war there were some resources available to those who wanted to learn and to help others to learn. We made use of the Workers' Educational Association, the Workers' Educational Trade Union Committee, the National Council of Labour Colleges and the Oxford Extramural Delegacy. When all else failed we fell back on ourselves: we organised our own reading-groups and discussion-circles and seminars. One of the courses we arranged for a dozen enthusiasts was a series of lectures on the organisation of war industries to be given by an Extramural Delegacy tutor, and when he had to withdraw before the first lecture I undertook to do them myself. (I rather fancy that some of the votes I got, a year or so later, in the selection of the parliamentary candidate came to me as a thank-you from members who had been my pupils on that course.)

Later still, when the psephologists and the other pundits were analysing the reasons for Labour's landslide victory in the 1945 general election, they reckoned that one of the major contributors to that highly unexpected result was all the political education and discussion that had gone on amongst the uniformed forces through such instruments as the Army Education Corps, the Army Bureau of Current Affairs and the Forces' Parliament in Cairo. (Bill Davidson, one of the creators of that Parliament and its Foreign Secretary, later became chairman of the Reading Constituency Party, and presided creatively over its most fruitful years.) That analysis was undoubtedly right: one could see the outcome in the overwhelming Labour majority in the separately-counted forces' vote. In addition a great deal of the home vote was influenced by what servicemen had written to their families and what they had said when they came home on leave. All that is received wisdom: what is not so generally understood is that there was also a great deal of discussion/education activity on the home front – in factory canteens, in queues, on home guard patrols, on chilly roofs during firewatching, in the educational work that was done by many Constituency Labour Parties like ours in Reading, and later by Common Wealth. Everybody was keen to think and talk and argue about the sort of Britain we wanted to create after the war, and about how we could carry forward into the peace the wartime solidarity of sacrifice and the willingness to subordinate our individual interests to those of the community as a whole. As an example, my own course on the organisation of war industries was basically an introduction to the creation of a planned economy when the war industries eventually came to be converted to the production of civilian goods.

The armistice in the formal war between the political parties didn't stop us from engaging in guerrilla action. We politicised every one of our May Day rallies (at one of them the speakers were the men who had been shortlisted for the parliamentary candidature, and you couldn't get more political than that), and we even politicised our social get-togethers. We were making sure that when the truce between the parties came to an end and the battle was resumed, we wouldn't be short of weaponry and our powder would be dry.

The publication of the Beveridge Report at the end of 1942 gave us another open door to break out of the purdah of the party truce. We organised a series of public meetings in support of the general thrust of Beveridge's proposals (we were critical of some details, not least his acceptance of too high an estimate of postwar unemployment), and we extended the discussion beyond his plan for a social security system into the broader need to narrow the gap between rich and poor and the mechanism by which that change in the distribution of wealth and income could be brought about. The meetings attracted large and thoughtful audiences: the two highlights of the campaign were first, Beveridge himself explaining his proposals from the stage of the Palace Theatre, and second, an overflowing meeting in a large hall at which the star speakers were Barbara Betts and Ted Castle, who soon afterwards were married and became a great political partnership.

In the same way we were able, now and again, to use the trade unions as a political platform. The Government, with the support of the TUC, were strongly encouraging the establishment of joint production committees in war factories (I was myself responsible for creating the committees at two aircraft factories, and was a member of one of them), and in the discussions on setting up the committees and on how they were to function we extended the agenda to cover the whole area of management/worker relationships and examined the potential for a meaningful industrial democracy. In the same way, whenever there was some action by the Government which affected trade unions, like the promulgation by Ernest Bevin, Minister of Labour, of the notorious Regulation 1AA, which criminalised some of the hitherto legal trade union activities, we used it as a basis for examining the whole area of Government/industry/trade union relations.

In the latter part of the war the TUC, looking forward to the peace, mounted a substantial campaign of trade union recruitment. Again that gave us a basis for arguing about how industry was to be run after the war, and certainly that was politics if ever anything was.

[*Digression*. It was in the course of that campaign that I got my first grounding in how to deal with heckling. The Reading Labour Party's secretary/agent was no public speaker himself, but he had sat at the feet of some of the great orators of the time, and very soon after I met him he gave me a mini-lecture on dealing with hecklers. The first time one bobbed up, he said, you take no notice of him, nor the second time either. If he is really serious – and only a few of them are – he'll come back a third time, and then you've got to deal with him because otherwise he may get too much sympathy and support from the audience.

I was invited to be one of the speakers (the other was Gordon Sandison, general secretary of Equity, the actors' trade union) at an open-air meeting in Bedford in support of the recruitment campaign. That Regulation 1AA of Ernest Bevin's was being very widely discussed at the time, and very widely opposed throughout Labour's political and industrial wings alike. Notwithstanding Bevin's very strong position in Government and Parliament, only a third of the Labour MPs voted against Nye Bevan's prayer to annul the regulation, and a motion in the Parliamentary Labour Party to discipline Bevan for his tough criticism of the Minister of Labour failed to carry. Equally, notwithstanding that the General Council had given its blessing to 1AA, a large number of rank-and-file trade unionists (including me) – probably a majority of them – were strongly opposed to it. The chairman of the Bedford meeting told Gordon and me, before the meeting started, that some people in the audience might give us a rough time over the regulation.

There was a great crowd packed in a semi-circle round the rostrum. As soon as I got up my eye was caught by a man right in front of me who was a lookalike of Old Bill, the cartoon soldier of World War I – corpulent, round-faced with a drooping moustache over a hard-sucked pipe, a battered tweed hat, and a silver chain across his ample waistcoat with a medal hanging off it that I guessed was a reward for prowess at darts or pigeon-racing.

The audience was attentive, receptive and quiet – until, when I had got into my stride, Old Bill looked up at me and asked, in a stentorian voice, 'Wot abaht Ernie Bevin?'

No response from me: I ploughed on regardless. Ditto a couple of minutes later when he repeated the question a bit more vehemently. But soon afterward I saw him take his pipe out of his mouth, and I knew that was going to be serious. This time his voice filled the square with reverberating challenge: 'Wot abaht Ernie Bevin?'

I leaned forwards towards him and shouted back 'Wot abaht 'im?'

This answer, rich in factual information and profound analysis, appeared completely to satisfy my persecutor. A slow, beatific smile spread over his face, indicating that I had made him happy by giving him all the information he was seeking. When I finished my speech, he applauded more vigorously than anyone else.

It was a lesson I never forgot.]

When I joined the Reading Labour Party its prospective parliamentary candidate was Margaret Bondfield, who had been a junior Minister in the 1923 Labour Government and who in 1929 became the first woman Cabinet Minister. She wasn't well, and she lived some distance away in Surrey and hadn't been to Reading for some time. In 1941 she decided that the war wasn't going to end quickly and that by the time it was over a general election campaign would be beyond her.

To be frank, there wasn't much regret in the Reading Labour Party at her decision. We entered avidly into the process of selecting a new candidate, not only for its own considerable interest (nothing else in the life of a Constituency Party creates so much lively argument and campaigning as choosing a parliamentary candidate) but also because it provided us with one more opportunity for educating, politicising and activating our members.

The Reading constituency was no snip for a Labour candidate. We had won it only in the large pro-Labour swings of 1923 and 1929, and then only by very narrow majorities. At all other elections the Conservatives had gained victories which were always comfortable and sometimes overwhelming. There was, and had been for a long time, a substantial Tory majority on the Borough Council; and the Conservative parliamentary candidate, William McIlroy, had been a member of the Council for a long time and was the Mayor right through the war: he was also the owner of the town's department store, and in general a respected local figure. (He eventually got some consolation for the defeat of his parliamentary ambitions by being appointed chairman of the Oxford Regional Health Authority, and a very good job he made of it.)

In spite of this unattractive prospect for a Labour candidate, our vacancy attracted an array of talented applicants and nominees. We were delighted with that, because it ensured that we'd have a candidate good enough to inspire our troops into a strong campaign.

Just before the closing date for nominations the chairman of the Party, Charlie Gill, asked me to meet him at the Labour Club for a talk. Charlie was an archetypal dedicated Labour man, a lifelong socialist and trade unionist who devoted almost all his leisure time to the Party and his union branch – a natural leader with the authority that came from winning the affection and respect of his followers.

When we met at the Labour Club his first words were such an earthquake-shock to me that I almost spilt my beer. 'I want you,' he said, 'to stand for the candidature.'

When I got my breath back I asked 'Why? – we've already got a sufficient number of good nominees.'

'That's right,' he said, 'but there's not a local man on the list, and I think we ought to have one – otherwise our opponents will be able to say the Reading Labour Party can't amount to much if it couldn't find even a single one of its members good enough to be put into the ring with people from outside the town.'

'I see that, Charlie,' I said, 'but I've no desire whatever to become a Member of Parliament, and that's not just assumed diffidence or modesty – I really mean it.'

This time it was he who was surprised. 'Why,' he asked, 'don't you want to be an MP?'

I spelt out the answer patiently and in detail. I told him of the struggle I'd had through the nineteen-thirties to make a decent living for my family, and that I felt I had now got into an area of work as a management consultant which I enjoyed very much, which I thought I was pretty good at, and which I was sure I could make a success of after the war and thus do more good for both myself and my fellow-citizens than sitting on the back benches of the House of Commons where I might not be all that good anyway.

Charlie's answer to this apologia rested on two arguments, one of principle and the other of practicality . The first of these arguments was that any member of the Party who was of parliamentary calibre had a conscientious duty to provide the Constituency Party with the widest possible area of choice of its candidate. 'But anyway,' he added, 'if you accept nomination I don't think you need worry too much about the danger of becoming an MP. In the first place you might not even get shortlisted; and if you do get shortlisted you're certainly not going to be favourite to be selected against the other nominees, who are a very good bunch; and if you do get selected you're not at all likely to win the seat against the pro-Churchill euphoria which will sweep the country in the postwar election, whenever it comes.'

I could see the force of both those arguments, but it wasn't only because of them that I gave way – it was also because I was so fond of Charlie that I just couldn't refuse to go along with a project he was keen on. I was satisfied by his presentation of the case that I had nothing to lose and that there was no danger of my professional career being interrupted for more than the month or so of the actual election campaign.

In fact I did get shortlisted, together with four others: Rennie Smith, who had been MP for Penistone; Austen Albu, a man of great quality who was later dropped from the list and who subsequently became MP for Edmonton and an active colleague of mine in our trade union, the Association of Supervisory Staffs and Engineering Technicians (ASSET); Christopher Shawcross, brother of the more famous but less lovable Hartley, who subsequently became MP for Widnes; and my fellow-Portsmuthian James Callaghan, who in 1945 became MP for Cardiff South and eventually Prime Minister of Great Britain.

The selection conference was memorable for one particular incident. It is the regular practice for every Labour selection conference to be attended by a member of the Party's regional staff whose function is nominally to represent the National Executive Committee but actually to ensure that the proper procedure is followed and to report on it to the National Agent.

So there turned up at our selection conference a certain Hinley Atkinson, one of the officers of the London region. He had a mandate, though we provincial innocents didn't suspect it at the time, to secure the selection of Jim Callaghan, who was one of the group of young men perennially being promoted by Hugh Dalton. (Jim didn't actually appear at the selection conference because he was in the Navy and away at sea, but the friend he sent to speak for him was a competent and effective substitute.)

As soon as Charlie Gill, from the chair, had opened the meeting, Hinley Atkinson got up to speak. 'Mr Chairman ...' he began, but he got no further before the chairman stopped him. 'Mr Atkinson,' said Charlie, 'you can't speak at this stage of the meeting.'

Atkinson was shaken rigid. 'But Mr Chairman,' he said, 'I'm here to put to the meeting the views of the National Executive....'

'Yes, I know,' said Charlie, 'and when we've completed our selection we'll be delighted to hear from you. But before that, this is the Reading Labour Party selecting its candidate, and we'll do it in our own way and on our own say-so without any interference from outside.'

As far as I know, that was the first time that an attempt by the Party machine to influence, and even to decide, the outcome of a selection conference – attempts which were common practice in those days and for some years after – was totally frustrated. The Labour Party could have done with a lot more Charlie Gills.

So I won the selection, and at the end of the meeting one of my friends amongst the delegates remarked, most uncomplimentarily but quite truthfully, that the result was a turn-up for the book like a selling-plater winning the Epsom Derby.

Though I had absolutely no vision of my making a postwar contribution to the Labour Party as one of its Members of Parliament, I did think I had some experience and expertise to offer in the formulation of the Party's postwar policies on the relations between government and industry within the framework of a planned economy. The Party had, of course, a lot of members with industrial experience at the level of the shop floor, but very few (there are a lot more now) with industrial experience at the level of higher management and at the interface between industry and the government machine. My work in a variety of aircraft and munitions factories was giving me a close insight into both the benefits of government planning and control and the many defects of the system through which they were operated. (Many of the glaring and expensive errors in public procurement during the war, notably in arms purchases, are still with us today.) When I talked to people, as individuals or in groups, about these matters I found keen and interested listeners.

I wrote up a lot of my thoughts in this area in a pamphlet, published by ASSET, called *Centralised Control of Industry*. Its core argument (oversimplifying it a bit) was that a planned economy was an extension to the national scale of the practices of corporate planning and control carried out in an efficient large company, and that the relations between a planned economy government and the country's major industries and enterprises, as well as with the separate departments of State, was a large-scale projection of the relations between a factory's top management and its various departments. It was a natural extension of this argument that, since no efficient modern manufacturer would tolerate *laisser-faire* competition between the departments with his factory, he couldn't reasonably justify *laisser-faire* competition between government departments, industries and large-scale enterprises within the whole economy.

[*Digression*. I was to return to this theme in 1947 in *Keep Left*, which I co-authored with Dick Crossman and Michael Foot. The chapter in it entitled 'The Job at Home', which was based on a background paper I had written, pursued this argument and derived from it a sharp criticism of the shadowy and ineffectual interdepartmental planning mechanism which the Government, belatedly and half-heartedly, had established only a couple of months earlier. We wrote:

'The recent setting up of an overall planning mechanism shows that, for more than a year and a half, we have been without an adequate overall planning mechanism. Even now, there is room for some doubt whether this task is being taken seriously enough. Such a planning mechanism, to be successful, needs to be able not merely to co-ordinate the work of the departments of State but also to reconcile conflicts of view between them, and even to override them when the need arises. For this purpose, it must be headed by a Minister who can give the necessary time to the job, and who has a position and prestige above those of the departmental Ministers. We haven't got that yet.

'But even more important is the relationship between the overall planning machine and the individual departments of State. This is a problem in management which is by no means confined to the business of government: it is the standard problem of every organisation which has both planning and executive functions. In individual businesses the relationship between "staff" departments, who determine the methods, and "line" departments, who put the methods into operation, has been the subject of continuous and intense study over the last fifty years or more. All that study has led to conclusions which are violated by the new planning mechanisms announced by the Prime Minister a few weeks ago, which is based on the principle of departmental autonomy. This is simply trying to eat your cake and have it, to plan without interfering with preconceptions; and its result is not to integrate the planning machine into the executive machine, but to make it a superstructure which adds to the weight without supplying a compensating increase in power. Departmental autonomy never works in practice, as any managing director knows who has had to resolve conflicts of view between the sales manager, the works manager, the personnel manager, and the accountant; and as the Prime Minister discovered when, in the fuel crisis, he had to set up a special organism which overrode the normal interdepartmental machinery.'

That was a lesson which neither that Government nor any of the later Labour governments had the perception to understand or the political will and courage to apply. There was some hope of it in 1964, when the newly-formed Wilson Government set up a Ministry of Economic Planning and chose the robust and able George Brown to run it; but even his robustness and ability didn't suffice to break the stranglehold which the Treasury has always exercised over almost all the functions of government, like the accountant in a company arrogating to himself all the authority and powers of the Board and the managing director. There was a moment again in 1975 when the introduction of the Industry Bill promised a radical intervention by the Government into the control of large-scale industry, but that hope vanished when the Prime Minister, probably with the consent of his Cabinet, succumbed to the blandishments or pressure of the CBI and carried out a vasectomy on his own Bill.]

Now back to the 1940s, when my interest and researches in industrial planning and management led me into one more branch of political activity, the Fabian Society.

G.D.H.Cole, in some respects the greatest of the great Fabians, was among those who were thinking hard about the sort of society we should be seeking after the war, and how we should go about creating it. He trawled for people to join a number of research groups which he was setting up. One of them was specifically on relations between government and industry. He heard – I don't know how – of this fellow in Reading who was working in the same field and who knew a bit about it from being involved at the sharp end. He invited me to join his group, and very soon I was up to the neck in it. Before long Cole's informal get-togethers became formalised into the Fabian Society's Industrial Group: I was one of its founder members, and chairman of its civil aviation subcommittee. This was my first experience of deep political discussion and painstaking, detailed research: it was an experience that enriched and rewarded me hugely, and I think I gave something in return.

As soon as I joined Douglas Cole's group I became a member of the Fabian Society, and for the next few years I was very involved in a lot of its activities. Mary and I went regularly to the Fabian weekend schools and summer schools, and at some of them I was the director or one of the lecturers. I took some classes in public speaking; on the lighter side, Mary and I taught ballroom dancing (it sounds incredible to me now, but we were a high-class dance team, notably in the Argentine tango), and I composed some wickedly acid sketches and lyrics for the end-of-school revues which were the fore-runners of the revues we now have at Labour party conferences.

There was one of our summer schools which my elder daughter, Ruth, will never forget. It was in 1949, in the charming milieu of the Royal Agricultural College just outside Cirencester. The partici-pants were a very mixed bunch, from unfledged teenagers like Ruth and her cousin Barbara to the veteran prestige figure of James Griffiths, the Minister of National Insurance.

We decided to introduce a nitty-gritty practical lesson into our theor-etical studies and take the students out for a mass canvass in the nearby constituency of Stroud, which Ben Parkin was holding by the skin of his teeth. A busload of us descended on the picturesque village of Painswick, and emptied ourselves out into a group of adjacent streets and started knocking on doors house-to-house. The very first door Ruth knocked on was opened by a very old lady who said she was glad somebody had called on her because she was having some trouble over the pension and couldn't find anyone authoritative to talk to about it. 'Oh, that's all right,' said Ruth, 'hang on a minute and I'll bring the Minister himself to talk to you.' The old lady stared incredu-lously, but Ruth nipped off into the next street, found Jim Griffiths and brought him back to the old lady: 'Tell him your problem and I'm sure he'll fix it.' You can imagine the astonishment of that old lady at a slip of a girl producing a Minister of the Crown in two minutes flat like a conjurer fetching a rabbit out of a top-hat.

I was one of the participants in the annual Fabian Autumn Lectures, and I contributed to *New Fabian Essays* (1952) a study of trade unions in a full-employment economy. (The only other survivors of that group of eight essayists are Denis Healey and Roy Jenkins. I wonder whether Denis still thinks that 'America is closer to Britain than is Western Europe,' and whether Roy still believes that 'a substantial extension of public ownership is . . . an essential prerequisite of greater equality'.)

Eventually I became treasurer of the Fabian Society and at one point rescued it from near-insolvency. But I resigned that office and left the Society when Hugh Gaitskell, suborning its tradition of non-involvement in inner-Party affairs, turned it into a leadership power base for himself by using the Executive's right of co-option to stuff it with his cronies. I was succeeded in the treasureship by Jack (later Lord) Diamond, who in the fullness of time did what came naturally and joined the SDP. But I still went occasionally to a Fabian school, and as late as 1972 was the director of a summer school in Bulgaria at which all the participants, except the poor couple whose luggage the Bulgarians managed to lose, had a whale of a time, with nothing to remind us of our Stalinist surroundings except the painfully slow service of meals.

It was my selection as parliamentary candidate that led, indirectly, to my transforming myself from a passive, merely card-carrying trade unionist into a deeply involved activist in the Association of Supervisory Staffs and Engineering Technicians (which later changed its title, but so as to preserve the acronym ASSET, and still later merged with the Association of Scientific Workers to form ASTMS, the Association of Scientific, Technical and Managerial Staffs, which in its turn merged with TASS to form the present MSF, Manufacturing Science Finance). The Association had started life over twenty years earlier, when a small number of foremen, mostly on the railways, got together to form the National Foremen's Association, and for all those twenty years it had stuck at about the same level of membership and of somnolent inactivity.

A change of general secretary brought a metamorphosis. The new incumbent was Tom Agar, a big bold bluff brazen Barnum for whom salesmanship – what we now call PR – was all and don't worry about producing the goods, much less about delivering them. Compared with Tom, Elmer Gantry and L. Ron Hubbard were fumbling apprentices. He had a National Executive Council consisting mostly of worthy but unworldy deadbeats: one of them always amused me because whenever any controversial matter was before the Council he would remain silent throughout the discussion but as soon as the vote was taken and the chairman was moving on to the next business he would launch himself into a passionate speech in favour of the decision we had just taken. The General Secretary had little regard for this lot, and he told them no more than he thought they needed to know, which wasn't much. The tail wagged the dog.

Tom judged, rightly, that the rapid wartime growth of the engineering industries provided an opportunity for his Association to expand. He set out on a recruitment campaign, which was less successful than the claims he made for it, and I was one of the fish he netted. One of his most cherished objectives was that the Association should get a presence in the House of Commons and thus achieve the same political status as that of older and larger trade unions. So he set out to recruit as many parliamentary candidates as he could lay hands on, and I was the first he enrolled. He didn't think, as I didn't, that I was going to win the Reading seat, but at least I gave him a first political foothold, and so he looked on me as a valuable catch. Little did he suspect that within a couple of years he would come to regret, deeply and bitterly, that he ever set eyes on me.

(My election to Parliament in 1945 gave me many opportunities of giving some political help to ASSET. In February 1947 the Association set up a parliamentary committee, and I was its first chairman. By then we had acquired eight MPs, but the number grew steadily, and was especially boosted by the ASSET-AScW merger, until the committee became, as it still is, the largest and strongest of all the parliamentary trade union groups and a most effective lobbying instrument.)

I also became chairman of the Reading branch of the Association, and was soon in demand as a speaker at other branches. A few months of this process was long enough for me to discover that there were many things seriously wrong in the management and operations of the Association. The general secretary was a frog who wanted to be an ox, and blew himself up until he burst: his bigheadedness got him into an interunion confrontation in the steel industry which he couldn't possibly win, and his capacity for self-deception prevented him from recognising that hard fact. The handling of the Association's finances was, to put it most charitably, slipshod. The National Executive Council was totally inexecutive. The more I saw of this, and the more I guessed at what lay behind what I saw, the angrier I became. Very soon I took up the role of the Association's Elijah chastising the prophets of Baal.

In order to do my chastising, as Elijah did, from the top of a mountain, I stood for election to the National Executive Council and won the seat. My colleagues on the Council welcomed me with the enthusiasm of a vegetarian lighting upon a caterpillar in his salad. Most of the time any motion I moved fell for want of a seconder. Although I was quite used to being in a minority (and was to be so many more times later), I thought that was a bit much, and after a year of this pariahdom I resigned from the NEC in order to demand an enquiry into the administration of the Association. I canvassed, and acquired, enough support to convene a special delegate conference which did set up an inquiry committee of four lay members, of whom I was one.

The committee's report hurled more thunderbolts than were ever dreamed up by Elijah and all the other ancient Hebrew prophets put together. We found that the accounts were riddled with irregularities, that the general secretary deliberately withheld information from his Council, that ballots had been conducted in breach of the rules, and much else besides. At the Association's annual delegate conference in Southport in 1945 our report was accepted, and I moved a vote of no confidence in the National Executive Council which was carried. The members of the Council then resigned en bloc, and at the subsequent election I was returned to the NEC.

This time I remained on it for more than thirty years. There are few things in my life which have given me more satisfaction than my work in my trade union. In those thirty-odd years I saw its membership grow from a few thousand – the actual figure was obscure – to over 400,000. I was the union's president for five years, and presided over the ASSET-AScW merger.

In 1947 I chaired a three-man selection committee which appointed as assistant divisional officer in the Midlands a young and somewhat innocent lad, just up from the Welsh valleys, named Clive Jenkins. I think I was the first to recognise in him the outstanding and unusual talent that he is – as organiser, as negotiator, as publicist – and later I pushed hard to have him appointed general secretary. Clive is by no means the best-loved man in the Labour movement: amongst some of our colleagues originality arouses suspicion and intellectual superiority provokes resentful envy; but it is also a fact, truth to tell, that he can be abrasively, and even arrogantly, intolerant of opposition. It isn't merely that he doesn't suffer fools gladly – he also doesn't suffer gladly wise men who won't follow where he seeks to lead. But that can't detract from his monumental service to both the trade unions and the Labour Party.

I described the early Clive as a somewhat innocent lad. When I first knew him he was not only – as he still is – a fervent non-smoker, indeed anti-smoker; he was also a teetotaller and an almost pentecostal scorner of the fleshpots. Today he is an epicurean and bon viveur;

and I must confess that it was I who started his rake's progress, because it was I who bought him his first alcoholic drink.

I remember the occasion well. We two represented ASSET on the trade union side of the National Joint Council for Civil Air Transport, and we negotiated the wages and conditions of our members in that industry: we were a pretty good negotiating team, because before each meeting with the employers we would decide between ourselves which was going to be the tough bastard and which the emollient compromise-seeker.

There was one meeting of the trade union side at which all the unions received a substantial concession from the employers, and after the meeting a few of us went into St Stephen's Tavern for a celebratory pint. When the round was called Clive hesitated loud and long. 'Go on,' I said to him, 'be a devil: have a half of lemon-and-bitter shandy.' He did, and from that he moved over the years to an educated passion for champers – an aberration which I fail to understand but am prepared to forgive.

So it was, then, that I served my busy but unremarkable political apprenticeship in three separate little classrooms – in a Constituency Labour Party, in a Fabian Society group, and in a small and struggling trade union. It wasn't really an apprenticeship, because an apprenticeship is a preplanned course of study and work-experience carried out under guidance and supervision, whereas I had taught myself to swim by diving in at the deep end and trusting to nature and luck to save me from drowning. It's not the best way to learn, because it wastes energy and risks error: the French proverb *En forgeant on devient forgeron*, is, like many other proverbs, the colourful expression of a sweeping inaccuracy: if you become a blacksmith by doing no more than forging, you acquire on the way a whole bodyful of burns and bruises, and at the end of it all you're liable to have it wrong.

But in 1944 there turned up one more in the chain of accidents that had so far shaped my life, as indeed most people's lives are shaped. It was a chance encounter with destiny that transferred me at one go from the obscurity of a local arena into the floodlights of the big time, like an unknown lad playing for his works team who suddenly and unexpectedly finds himself signed up by Manchester United. The man of destiny who was responsible for this revolution in my political career was Wilf Cannon, a railwayman on the Great Western who worked in the marshalling-yard at Scurrs Lane, just to the west of Reading General station.

# Chapter 6

IN 1944 the Government asked the political parties and other organisations which normally held their annual conferences in mid-year to postpone them for some months so as to keep the railways and roads as clear as possible for the movement of men and materials engaged in the invasion of Normandy. Among those conferences that were postponed (many were not) was the forty-third Annual Conference of the Labour Party, which convened in mid-December in the Central Hall, Westminster.

During the months before the Conference there was a lively discussion, in constituency parties and trade unions throughout the country, about the postwar policies of the Party which had been adopted by the National Executive Committee (NEC). Most of this discussion centred on a paper which was entitled *Full Employment and Financial Policy* but which went beyond that title and covered the whole sweep of economic policy, industrial and commercial as well as financial. That paper was in many respects an impressive statement. It analysed accurately and described forthrightly what had gone wrong in the inter-war years, and why it had gone wrong. In some areas, notably in exchange and import controls, in regional policy and in overseas aid, its proposals went further than subsequent Labour governments were prepared to go and were more radical than the Party's present stance more than forty years later. Nevertheless it left many members of the Party with the feeling that the NEC, which clearly was to provide the core of the next Labour Cabinet, was stronger on diagnosis than on prescription, clearer on ends than on means: in particular the document suggested only a lukewarm, partial and defensive commitment to the use of public ownership as a tool of economic management. In one of our discussions in Reading on this statement I recalled my school motto *Suaviter in modo fortiter in re* (sweetly in style, strongly in content), and suggested that there was a danger that our leaders might reverse that formula and prove to be strong in the word but overgentle in the deed.

Worse was to follow. In the run-up to the Annual Conference the NEC published a revised statement for submission to the Conference as the centrepiece of the Party's manifesto for the postwar general election, whenever it came. The new text was much shorter than the policy paper on which it was based, and much more timid and conventional. It made no mention whatever of public ownership, and raised enhanced doubts about whether our leaders had the political will to carry out the radical reconstruction of the national economy which they themselves had asserted as being essential if we were to cope with the sharply changed conditions of the postwar world. Those leaders of ours, grossly miscalculating the mood of the Party members throughout the country, expected that they would have no difficulty in getting this new policy statement adopted at the Conference.

In the preparation of the Conference, the constituency parties and affiliated organisations were asked, in accordance with standard practice, to submit resolutions (not more than two each, later reduced to one) for the conference agenda. When that invitation arrived at the Reading Labour Party it was, again in accordance with standard practice, sent out to the ward parties (we now call them branches) and the locally-affiliated organisations, one of which was the Reading No 1 branch of the National Union of Railwaymen (NUR).

When that branch met it decided to submit a resolution to the Constituency Party for consideration as one of the two to be submitted for Conference. Wilf Cannon went to that meeting straight from the end of his shift and still in his working clothes: as his contribution to the war effort he was working on past retirement age. I remember him as a lean, vigorous, silver-haired, patrician-looking man, a good talker, a good listener and a discriminating reader, an intensely political animal.

At that meeting of his branch one of his fellow-members put up a resolution for conference on the need to reorganise the railway system, and argued that this was a natural and proper resolution for a railwaymen's branch to sponsor. But Wilf Cannon opposed him on the grounds that the railways were just one element in the national economy and that we should all aim, at the forthcoming conference, to get policies adopted which would put the whole economy right: we would get an expanding and efficient railway system, he contended, only within a total economic system which was expanding and efficient. Accordingly he proposed a resolution which had the effect of correcting what he saw as the defects of the NEC statement, and in particular spelling out a programme for extending the public sector. There was a debate on which of the two resolutions should go forward to the Constituency Party, and on a vote Wilf's was chosen.

When that resolution came before the Management Committee of the Reading Labour Party it was one of six which had been submitted and from which we had to choose not more than two. Wilf Cannon was one of the delegates to the Management Committee from his branch of the NUR, and he argued strongly for his resolution to be chosen. The delegates representing the sponsors of each of the other five resolutions argued their respective corners equally strongly, but in the end Wilf got his way and his resolution was submitted to Party headquarters for inclusion in the Conference agenda.

In the upshot there were no fewer than twenty-two resolutions on the same theme submitted by a variety of constituency parties and affiliated organisations. They all sought an explicit commitment to extending the publicly-owned sector. Most of them listed some industries and services to be nationalised: not all the lists were identical, but they had a lot in common.

The delegates responsible for these resolutions were called together, as always, in a compositing group. By this time the Party leaders had begun to understand that they had a potential revolt on their hands, and unprecedentedly no fewer than three NEC members turned up at the compositing group to mollify the rebellious delegates and turn aside wrath. They sought to do that by telling us that there was no need for us to attack the NEC statement since that statement implied all that we were seeking, even though its wording said something entirely different. That was about as convincing as the sales-patter of a street-market auctioneer – 'Never mind the quality, feel the width.' I listened carefully to the three NEC members and whispered to my neighbour the classic words of Damon Runyon, 'If that is not a lie, it will do until a real lie comes along.'

We ignored the blandishments of those on high, and got on with the job. Out of the twenty-two original resolutions we produced three composite resolutions. Most of the delegates subscribed to one of these composites which was closely based on the Reading resolution, and I was chosen to move it.

I am by nature a pretty tough self-confident imperturbable character, much more likely to be underawed than overawed in any situation. But I must confess that when I walked into that great packed hall on the first morning of Conference I felt very small indeed. I had been to a couple of previous conferences as a visitor, but this was the first time I had been a delegate, sitting in the body of the hall, amongst all the other delegates, a humble unknown first-time candidate for a safe Tory seat, surrounded by people who had been active in the Party a lot longer than I had, many of them household names as Ministers or MPs or trade union general secretaries, including, in the chair, Harold Laski, who had become for me a second revered Tawney. If L-plates had existed in those days I'd have been wearing one.

It was even worse – much worse – when I entered the Central Hall on the Thursday morning because that was the session in which the NEC's economic statement was to be debated and in which I would have to go to the rostrum and make a maiden speech to an audience of a thousand sophisticated, experienced critics. I didn't have butter-flies in my stomach – I had a whole flock of whacking great pterodactyls flapping about in there.

The debate was opened for the Executive by Manny Shinwell in a long and skilful speech which was clearly influenced by his realisation of the opposition he was facing and which was therefore more serious, more directly relevant and better structured than his speeches generally were. (At other times he couldn't resist the temptation to tangle the thread of his argument with a witty parenthesis and sometimes a sub-parenthesis within that parenthesis.) His speech was designed to conciliate the critics and defuse their opposition, but he was in a no-win situation because he couldn't squeeze any inspiration out of the flat, uninspiring NEC statement which he was defending.

I then moved my resolution in a short speech which argued that 'We have got to show the people that we mean what we say and say what we mean' – an argument which clearly won the support of most of the delegates. Almost all the other speakers in the debate took up the same theme. Evelyn (later to become Lady) Dennington, who seconded my resolution, said, 'We have to convince them [the electorate] of our sincerity'; Dr Monica Felton (later to chair one of the New Town Corporations) said, 'It is a very curious point that the

Government White Paper and the Labour Party's statement are very much alike'; Jack Blitz of Portsmouth said, 'Let our Report on full employment be a sincere one'; Jim Callaghan (who by then had become candidate for Cardiff South: he owes me a debt for beating him to the selection of the candidate for marginal Reading because he then got his safe seat in Cardiff) said, 'I think it is high time that we should restate our fundamental principles'; and Bessie Braddock, (then a rabble-rouser of the far Left who was later to become a *tricoteuse* of the far Right) said, 'I cannot for the life of me understand how we are going to fight a general election when we are in practically complete agreement with the Conservative Party': what they were all arguing was the inescapable fact (to which I shall return) that what is most needed by a political party, and not least the Labour Party, in its appeal to the electorate is not smooth talk but credibility.

The debate was wound up from the platform by Philip Noel-Baker. In his first sentence he urged me not to press my resolution to a vote. At the end of his speech, Harold Laski, from the chair, asked me if I was willing to remit my resolution to the NEC, and I told him I had no mandate from the parties supporting the resolution to do other than press it to a decision. So a decision there was, and the resolution was carried on a show of hands by such a large majority that no-one dared to call for a card vote. I sat there in a daze.

As I moved out of the hall at the end of the morning's session, I was still in a daze at the revolution I had unexpectedly wrought, like one of the trumpet-blowers at the walls of Jericho. On the way out of the hall, at the foot of that expansive twin staircase which makes the sedate Methodist Central Hall look like an ornate Hapsburg palace, I was caught up in a press of delegates milling around, all talking excitedly about the events of the morning. A moment or two later along came Herbert Morrison, and he walked straight towards me. He didn't know me, of course – indeed he had never set eyes on me until I had got on the rostrum a couple of hours earlier. He stepped up to me and put a friendly hand on my shoulder. 'Young man,' he said, 'you did very well this morning. That was a good speech you made – but you realise, don't you, that you've lost us the general election.'

That howling misjudgement came not just from anybody – it came from the man who was accepted throughout the Party as by far our greatest and most authoritative electoral strategist. How could such a man be so outrageously wrong?

[*Digression*. I will tell you, on the basis of all my subsequent experience of fighting a dozen elections of my own and of taking part in more than a hundred other election campaigns, how such a man could be so outrageously wrong.

What Herbert was enunciating in that remark of his was the received wisdom, shared by many of his successors in the leadership of the Party, that the best formula for electoral success is to move to the 'respectability' of the middle ground and thus blur the policy differences between us and our opponents.

The history of the two decades following that 1944 conference blows that theory sky-high. As a result of that conference we fought the 1945 election, against the wishes of our leaders, on a radical and defiant manifesto, and we won a landslide victory. For each of the next four general elections – 1950, 1951, 1955 and 1959 – we produced a manifesto considerably watered down from the previous one, and in each of them we returned fewer Labour MPs than in the previous one (though in 1951 we did poll the highest popular vote). The next election in which we had a manifesto that was widely distanced from that of our opponents was in 1964, and we won.

There were two events connected with the 1959 general election which reinforce this point. The first was the gratuitous and foolish undertaking given by Hugh Gaitskell a few days before polling day that a Labour government would not increase taxation; the electors, understandably sceptical, said, 'Oh yeah, tell us another,' and turned away from us in droves: in Reading we saw the effect clearly in our canvassing on the very next day. The second was the reaction of Gaitskell and his coterie to the election defeat. He asserted that Labour would never again win an election as long as we had Clause 4 in our constitution, and therefore we had to get rid of it; and his close associate, Douglas Jay, added that Labour was unelectable (the term thus preceded its use in 1987) as long as we were called the Labour Party, and therefore we had to change our name. We had the good sense to ignore both of these panicky panaceas, and we won four of the next five general elections.

During a general election campaign the leading figures in any party spend almost all their time in large meetings, press conferences and other media events, and in travelling all over the country. So they don't get the chance, as lesser mortals do, to go canvassing on the doorsteps of their prospective constituents, and therefore they don't get a first-hand insight into what electors are thinking and feeling.

The analyses and conclusions of pollsters and other advisers are a poor second-hand substitute for straight talking across a couple of thousand thresholds. Those of us who do have that first-hand experience know very well that the most damaging thing a Labour candidate can hear across the doorstep is not 'I won't vote for you because I don't agree with your policy on this or that', or 'I won't vote for you because I'm not impressed with your leaders': the most damaging thing a Labour candidate can hear across the doorstep is 'I won't vote for you because when you get in you do much the same as the other lot.'

To put it another way, the most important factor deciding whether people will vote for us is not whether they approve of our policies (not all that many electors know clearly what our policies are), and not whether we've put up a good show in an election campaign (1987 proved that): the most important factor deciding whether people will vote for us is our credibility; and nothing so undermines our credibility as spending years decrying our opponents and then adopting policies which make us look a bit like them.]

Long afterwards I learned that Morrison left that Conference with the firm intention of securing an election manifesto based solely on the NEC's original economic statement. He urged the Campaign Committee, when it met to draft the manifesto, to ignore the Reading resolution: in particular he was totally opposed to any commitment to public ownership in the iron and steel industries, on the grounds that the City wouldn't like it. He got some support in the Committee, notably from Arthur Greenwood, but Ellen Wilkinson and Hugh Dalton said it would be dangerous and damaging to flout the decisions of Conference, and Morrison was defeated.

When I got back to Reading the first man I sought out was Wilf Cannon. I congratulated him on having been the initiator of a radical change in the policy of the Labour Party and in our forthcoming election manifesto. 'Initiator, yes,' he said with a smile, 'but hardly sole begetter.' We laughed at that, and agreed that the whole episode had been an encouraging demonstration of the ability of an individual rank-and-file member of the Party, if he cared enough and were persistent enough, to claim an input into its policy-making process. 'If that ever ceased to happen,' Wilf added, 'it won't be the same sort of party, and it won't be our sort of party, will it?'

By the beginning of 1945 the war in Europe was moving visibly towards its end, and people were thinking and talking more than ever

79

before about what was to follow it. In the Reading Labour Party we began to prepare for a general election in case there should be one after VE (Victory in Europe) Day: I say 'in case' because it was well known that some of the Labour Ministers in the wartime coalition (notably Morrison again, though he changed his mind later) favoured keeping the coalition going, and hence postponing the general election, until the end of the war in Asia, which at that pre-Hiroshima time was generally expected to last another eighteen months to two years.

My agent and I began planning our election campaign. Neither of us thought we had any chance of winning – a miscalculation which we shared with most people throughout the land, because the name of Churchill carried magic and it seemed inconceivable that, in the relief of war-end and the euphoric glow of victory, the nation would turn its back on the man who had led them to that victory – the same sort of sentiment that had determined the result of the khaki election in 1918. Two notable dissenters from this widespread error were Aneurin Bevan and George Strauss, who had drawn their conclusions largely from the surging anti-government votes in by-elections, notably Charles White's victory, as an Independent Labour candidate, in West Derbyshire; but I knew only two men who correctly forecast the huge Labour landslide that was to occur. One was Sir William Beveridge. On the day he came to Reading in March 1944 to speak at a meeting on his Report, he and his wife Janet came to tea with us. Over tea the two of them carried on a lively argument about the political outlook, which I thought Janet won hands down, and at the end of it Beveridge made a confident forecast that in the postwar election, whenever it came, the Tories would suffer a slump like the one in 1906 – and he added that he thought the Labour Party wouldn't be as ready and able to cash in on it as were the Liberals in 1906. (I realised from this addendum that the attempts that were being made, notably by my friend Stewart Cook, to persuade Beveridge to stand as the Labour candidate for London University were a waste of effort.)

The second successful tipster of the 1945 election result was a swashbuckling character named Lord Strabolgi, who before inheriting his title was Lieutenant-Commander Kenworthy and had sat in the Commons as MP for Hull Central. He was offered 33–1 against Labour getting an overall majority of more than a hundred. He had a bet of £250 on it, and spent part of his £8000 + winnings on a joyous victory celebration in the Savoy Hotel, no less.

Of course my agent, John Douglas, and I didn't give our troops the least hint of our pessimistic private estimate of the election in the Reading constituency. We talked victory loudly and vehemently – perhaps more loudly and vehemently than we would have done if we'd really believed what we were saying. The centrepiece of the campaign we planned – and in this we were a bit ahead of our time – was intensive door-to-door canvassing and getting an accurate-as-possible list of those who, if they voted at all, would vote for me. This campaign fell far short of the standards we subsequently achieved when we developed and refined what has come to be called the Reading system, but in its day it was a good deal better than most.

Those first few months of 1945 subjected me to a pretty good test of mental and physical stamina. Besides planning the election campaign, I was busy in my consultancy work, organising it always with an eye to being able to interrupt it for a month (I didn't expect to need more) whenever the election came: very often I drove through the night from one factory to another. On top of that, a lot of my time was taken up by the ASSET Committee of Inquiry already described, and by all the shenanigans that went with it. I was getting many requests to speak to constituency parties and trade union district councils and branches in different parts of the country. But there was enough interest and excitement and fun in it all to keep the valves pumping and the adrenalin flowing.

Mary and I spent the second week of May, the week before the 1945 Party Conference, at a Fabian summer school at Abergele in North Wales. We made a lot of new friends there, amongst them Maurice and Tilly Edelman, a warm attractive sparkling couple of whom we saw a great deal over the next few years. Maurice was a man of classic handsomeness and captivating charm, and he very much knew it: sometimes I thought he was quite consciously modelling himself on the young Disraeli. He was an elegant and perceptive writer, as much at home in French as in English, and as knowledgeable about French politics as about our own. (Later he wrote a parliamentary column for the *New Statesman* and much else, but he never became fully committed to the political battle, and finally disengaged himself from it in order to write a number of novels.)

One thing I remember most vividly about the week of the school: on the Wednesday it became finally and completely clear that the coalition Government was breaking up and we were to have a general election. We were all wildly elated at the news, and celebrated it with a midnight party on the beach. It was a balmy, moonlit summer night, and our hearts were young and gay, and we celebrated good and plenty with a bonfire, a little food and a lot of bottles, in and out of the water, singing at the top of our voices, and occasionally couples wandering off into the darkness for a bit of offhand private celebrating of their own.

At the end of the week a dozen or so of us travelled together to Blackpool for the Conference: some of us were delegates, and others were going as visitors to see history being made. We stayed in the same boarding-house just round the corner from the Winter Gardens, and virtually carried on our Abergele celebrations for another week.

On the first morning of Conference I was buttonholed by an expansive, lively woman who introduced herself as Pearl Hyde, the delegate of the Coventry West (as it then was) Constituency Party, which was desperate, she said, to find a candidate, and did I know anybody who was both good and available? I suggested Maurice Edelman, and that afternoon fixed a meeting between them. Maurice was duly selected, won the seat and held it for many years.

It is hard to recapture now the bubbling excitement of that 1945 Conference. We resembled Henry the Fifth's troops before Harfleur, 'like greyhounds in the slips, straining upon the start'.

I spoke twice during the week, once in the general economic debate and once on postwar policy for civil aviation. I had written, in partnership with Will Arnold Forster, a pamphlet called *Frontiers in the Air*, in which we argued that civil aviation should be organised not in cut-throat-competing national airlines but through international co-operation, at least throughout Europe. I took up the same theme in my conference speech: how, I asked, could we hope to build friendship in Europe across frontiers on the ground if we began by drawing frontiers in the frontierless air? Alas, it is only now, nearly half a century later, that this dream of mine is starting to be fulfilled – and it's a timid, hesitant, tentative start at that.

And so back to Reading for the election campaign. If I don't remember it too clearly, it's because when you've fought a lot of campaigns they tend to blur into one another. But there were two events during that 1945 campaign that are indelibly memorable, and each of them gave me the uncovenanted benefit of a substantial propaganda advantage.

The first arose out of a meeting in the canteen of the Miles Aircraft factory at Woodley, just outside Reading. There were about 6000 people working in that plant and its subsidiaries, and they were all witnessing the virtual end of the construction of military aircraft. Not unnaturally they were worried about how and where they were going to get new jobs. They invited all the local candidates to a meeting to describe their policies and answer questions.

It was a sultry evening, and sultrier still in that canteen filled with a bursting-at-the-seams audience of enquiring, hopeful but anxious men and women, determined to squeeze all they could out of the first opportunity they'd had for ten years to put some aspiring politicians through the hoop. It was an occasion of real basic old-time hustings.

The first question each of the candidates was asked was the obvious predictable one: 'If your party forms the Government, will it guarantee to maintain full employment, and how will it do that?'

It was my Conservative opponent, William McIlroy, who answered first. When he got up I wondered interestedly what he was going to say: I knew that all political issues beyond the borough boundaries, and certainly all economic issues, were a closed book to him, but I assumed that he would have got some briefing from somewhere on the one question he was certain to be asked.

He hadn't. 'A Conservative government,' he said, 'will certainly guarantee a job for everybody. If need be we shall build battleships, tow them out to sea, sink them, and come back and build some more.'

For a few moments the audience sat in a total stunned silence, like the people in one of those dear old Bateman cartoons, and then they broke out into a mixture of derisive shouts and mocking laughter. I didn't join in. I was honestly sorry for the chap; he was a nice guy who had made the single but fatal mistake of diving into water out of his depth.

Unluckily for him there was a local reporter in the audience who was also a stringer for the *Daily Mirror*, and the next day that paper ran the story. For the rest of the campaign poor McIlroy wasn't allowed, wherever he appeared in public, to get away from battleships.

My other propaganda advantage derived from the fillip which every Labour candidate got – but especially those with the wit to exploit it fully – from a monstrous blunder committed by Winston Churchill. In his first election broadcast on the radio he warned the country that if they elected a Labour government they would find themselves under the jackboots of a socialist gestapo. The British people just wouldn't take that. They looked at Clem Attlee, the timid, correct, undemonstrative, unaggressive ex-public-schoolboy, ex-major, and couldn't see an Adolf Hitler in him. They recalled how often Churchill had praised and thanked the Labour leaders for the support and loyalty they had given him as members of his War Cabinet, and they couldn't believe that in two short weeks those Ministers had metamorphosed from decent Britons into operators of concentration camps equipped with gas chambers. Writing of this 'gestapo' accusation, the historian Kenneth Morgan records that 'following the recent uncovering of the horrors of Belsen and Buchenwald, this observation might be considered tasteless in the extreme' – an understatement if ever there was one –, and he recalls that both *The Times* and *The Economist* – neither of them rabid red revolutionary rags – condemned it roundly.

I don't believe Churchill the war leader would have made such a howling error; but when he became not the leader of the nation but only the Leader of the Conservative Party his judgement deserted him – or maybe it was warped by the electoral 'expertise' of the wide boys in Conservative Central Office. For the remaining four weeks of the election campaign everybody who chaired one of my meetings was instructed (and was taught the correct pronunciation) to introduce me as Obergruppenführer Ian Mikardo, prospective Gauleiter of Berkshire, Buckinghamshire and Oxfordshire. That always got us off to a good start.

But better was yet to come. John Douglas decided that at our eve-of-poll rally in the Town Hall we would have, amongst the speakers, a soldier and a sailor and an airman. We found a local lad who was an army corporal (Brian Bastin: he's still around, and still a keen Labour Party activist), and another who was a naval lieutenant; but we were stuck for an airman until there providentially turned up in our committee-rooms a young pilot officer in the Royal Australian Air Force, Russ Kerr. Russ had been a member of the Australian Labour Party before he joined up, and indeed had helped to elect the then Australian Labour government led by Joseph Curtin. But he had never made a public speech, and the idea of facing an audience of 1300 terrified him much more than all the flak he'd faced in umpteen bombing sorties over Germany. We had to twist his arm to get him on the platform, and when he saw that packed audience he sat there petrified. When he was called to speak he stood up, shaking all over like a badly-tuned engine, walked to the microphone at the front of the stage, and in a deep Australian accent that crackled like a present-day commercial for lager he said, 'Good evening, sports. I am a refugee from Joe Curtin's socialist gestapo in Australia.' The audience erupted:

I never heard such applause in my life, not even for the greatest ovation of the greatest orator; and I wished Churchill's gestapo-speechwriter could have been there to see the counter-productive effect of his smart-aleckery.

(Russ and I were soon the closest of friends. He became a parliamentary candidate, and eventually a Member of Parliament. He was a multifaceted man of beguiling witty charm and boiling-over joie-de-vivre; a thoughtful socialist; a good judge of a political situation; a master of scintillating quick-fire repartee, both in conversation and across the floor of the Chamber; a notable cricketer, with a fine arm; at the bridge-table a hard trier but no more; an all-round good companion. There were several successive summers in which he and I and a couple of friends would go off every month or so on a long weekend hike during which we reckoned to walk forty miles, play thirty rubbers of bridge and drink, between us, eighty pints of ale.)

The rest of the campaign consisted of the regular daily slog, largely repetitive and often boring. It wasn't till the Sunday before polling-day, 1 July, that I got a taste of something different and a foretaste of what was to come.

I was dragged out of bed very early that morning by a persistent telephone-bell. Behind it was a regional party organiser. 'We'd like you to go to Swansea to speak at a meeting there this evening. It will be a big night: Clem himself is addressing a rally there.' 'I don't get it,' I said. 'If you've got Clem Attlee, why on earth do you need me?'

'Because,' came the answer, 'we've had four times as many applications for tickets for the rally as there are seats in the hall, and we need a toughie with a good loud voice to take what will be a large open-air overflow.'

I agreed to go; and Mary's brother Sidney, who was on leave from Germany and staying with us, offered to drive the 350-mile round trip. (Being driven by a major, I felt a bit like a field-marshal.) The overflow was held in an open space called the Forum, and when I reached its outskirts I had difficulty getting through the crowd of many thousands making their way to the meeting: the scene was like Villa Park on the day of a cup semi-final. I made the last two hundred yards to the rostrum by courtesy of a mounted policeman who inched his horse through the masses with me walking behind its tail, my field of vision restricted to its ample but not particularly prepossessing hindquarters.

I think I did pretty well at the meeting (certainly I had a much bigger audience than Attlee's), and after a drink and a bit of food Sidney and I set off home. It was after three in the morning when we got back to my house in Tilehurst, and I was astonished to see a light on in my front-room. When we got in we were greeted by the sight of John Douglas sitting on the floor submerged nearly halfway up in a sea of paper. The paper was canvass returns: there were canvass returns on the table, on the chairs, on the floor, on the furniture, on the mantelpiece, on the windowsills, and John was clutching a clipboard with sheets of figures all over it. He was never a very cheerful customer at the best of times, but at that moment his eyes were blear and his face grey, drawn and haggard.

Not a word was spoken while I poured him and us a quick drink, and then he gave tongue. 'Mik,' he said, 'I've got something to tell you which you're not going to like.'

'Go on,' I said, 'tell us the worst.'

'I don't at all think it's the worst. I'm more than glad about it, but I know you've got different ideas. The fact is that you're going to win this election.'

I thought he was wrong, but we agreed to differ about it because we were both too tired to start an argument. John finished his drink, got to his feet and handed me a small sealed manila envelope. 'In that envelope,' he said, 'there's a bit of paper, and I've written on it what your majority is going to be. Bring it along with you to the count, and we'll see who's right.'

Three days later was polling day, and the count was three weeks after that, on 26 July, to allow time for the services' votes to come in. We began the count at nine in the morning, and by midday I had been announced the winner with a majority of 6390 over the Conservative candidate. At the first opportunity I opened John Douglas's little brown envelope and took out the bit of paper on which he had written his forecast of my majority: it bore the figure 6500: in a total vote of 62,384 he had come within 110 of a precise forecast, an error of just over one-sixth of one per cent.

I led a small army of wildly enthusiastic supporters across the market place and into the Labour Club for some celebratory drinks, though truth to tell we were all already hilariously drunk with unexpected triumph. But in the midst of all the euphoric backslapping I was conscious of the fact that we hadn't won an overall majority, because the combined Tory and Liberal votes exceeded ours by 1400, and

I realised that we were always going to have a difficult job to hold the seat at subsequent elections. It was that realisation that led me, over the next few years, to start rethinking from scratch and challenging, in discussions with some of my colleagues, the regular, accepted, conventional methods of running an election campaign – a basic reassessment which led, a few years later to the evolution of the Reading system. But before I come to that there is much to tell about the emergence and growth of disillusionment with the Labour government amongst a small but growing number of our backbenchers, and about how that disillusionment sowed the seeds of the bitter, hard-fought Left-Right controversies of the next two decades.

# Chapter 7

So THERE I am, after that fateful election, making my way into the Palace of Westminster as one of the record intake of 324 new members, 244 of them Labour; a lot of us scarcely believing we were there because in truth we were there against all expectations; some of us, in political terms, with our mothers' milk still wet on our lips. I still recall vividly the new-boy excitement as I stood with a group of friends to watch the royal procession on the opening day of the Session – the King at the head, walking hesitantly and shakily, his Queen a pace or two behind him telepathically giving him support and strength: Tom Driberg, in awed admiration, whispered, 'Look at her – every inch a king!'

Our history over the next few years – the euphoric romantic belief that we were about to break out of the constraints of past practice and create a brave new world (sacrilegiously singing "The Red Flag" in the lobby as we voted to pass the Second Reading of the Coal Industry Nationalisation Bill); the enactment of the first major elements of that brave new world – the National Health Service and universal secondary education and the ending of four centuries of a degrading Poor Law; the nationalisation of some essential industries and services by a Government which didn't really believe in public ownership and which therefore organised each of those publicly-owned industries and services as a faithful copy of a large privately-owned company, and thereby lost much of the value of the change of ownership; the failed attempt to oust Attlee; the growing disillusionment of the socialists in the Labour Party and their consequential revolt against our pragmatic, and therefore non-socialist, leadership which led to the bitter Left-Right split of the 1950s – all this has been recorded in the closest detail by many writers, including some of the participants. There would be no point in my retelling familiar history, and therefore I shall write only of some events in which I was involved at first hand and which haven't been recorded or which I saw in a perspective different from that of previous reports.

My entry into Parliament opened for me two fresh windows on the world. The first of these was getting to know personally, face to face and word to word, the leaders of the Party who for me had previously been only names, almost legendary names, and finding that some of my gods had feet of clay. My first encounter on this one-to-one basis was a renewal of the experience I had had at the previous December's Party Conference of incurring the displeasure of Herbert Morrison. It happened at a party given, in July 1945, by George (later Lord) Archibald, who was in film production and distribution, and his wife Dorothy, who had been our candidate in Bath and was sore at not having been swept in by the landslide.

The adoption of the Reading resolution was still rankling with Morrison, even though (or perhaps because) his forecast that it would lose us the election had turned out to be such a monumental miscalculation as to damage his standing as the Party's expert on elections. As I walked in, Herbert was holding forth acidly on this theme to a small knot of people, including David Stark Murray, the secretary of the Socialist Medical Association, and Ellen Wilkinson, and he broke off to greet me, as unkindly as he could, which was plenty: 'Oh, well,' he said, 'you're all right now – you can nationalise everything in sight, even iron and steel.' It transpired later that that was the one industry whose proposed nationalisation was bugging him more than any other, and that he spent five years, on and off, quarrelling about it with some of his Cabinet colleagues. Yet at the same time he argued strongly in Cabinet that we should nationalise iron and steel in the British zone of Germany: I suppose his reasoning was that whereas the press would strongly criticise steel nationalisation in Britain they couldn't care less about it in occupied Germany.

But after a while Morrison abandoned this theme in order to launch into an acid tirade on the most acute of all his obsessions, which was his belief that he had been unfairly robbed of the chance he ought to have had of becoming leader of the Party. He had expected that Churchill would delay handing in his resignation until after the meeting of the Parliamentary Labour Party which had been called for 28 July, that the meeting would be given an opportunity of holding an election of Party leader, and that only then would the King send for the man so elected and ask him to form the new Government. Herbert was so paranoiac on this subject as to accuse Churchill of resigning early for the sole purpose of keeping him (Morrison) out of the top spot, and so self-deceiving as not to realise that if there had been an election at the PLP meeting he would have been beaten by a distance.

Whenever, to this day, I read or hear about problems in prison management I remember a remarkable woman I met at that party, Charity Taylor, a handsome, flashing amazon who swore and drank beer like a docker and who had just been appointed the first-ever woman prison-governor in Great Britain. Her account of her first few days in Holloway was riveting: the most difficult inmates to cope with, she said, were the sixteen-year-old prostitutes because they began every conversation by reminding her that they earned a lot more than the Governor of Holloway Prison. (They were operating in a market made buoyant by the large number of United States soldiers stationed in and around London.)

My second new window on the world was the educating, invigorating, uplifting experience of daily contact on the back benches with minds that were superior to and better-stocked than mine.

In those days the Members' Smoking Room, which is the most *recherché* of all the bars in the Palace of Westminster, was used by Labour members much more than it is today; but a sort of invisible curtain across the middle of it separated the Labour members occupying the northern half of the room from the Tories in the other half. (In the Members' Dining Room the division is the other way round.) In one corner of our end was a large round table which became the regular watering-hole of a score or so left-wingers, plus two or three on the right, like Reggie Paget and Dick Stokes, who clearly found our company more amusing and interesting than that of their political allies. The seven or eight of us there at any one time would bubble over with animated talk and pointed argument not only on politics but also on history and literature and the arts. Around that table were forged many friendships and many comrades-in-arms partnerships (they're not always the same thing), some of them later broken by the estrangement of changing views or of a move to the front bench, but many remaining lifelong.

Of those drinking-pals of mine, only six remain, alas: Michael Foot, whose friendship has been one of the most precious things in my life; Donald Bruce, now translated into the Lords but otherwise unchanged; Barbara Castle, who in her heyday moved mountains but finally exiled herself to Strasbourg; Julius Silverman, a quiet-spoken lawyer always worth listening to, the best chess player in the House, whose strongest tipple was (and is) orange-juice; Richard Acland, a devout Christian and socialist, almost too pure and gentle for the rough and hurly-burly of politics, which he eventually left to go back to teaching; and Woodrow Wyatt, who has undergone a sea-change, or maybe several successively, each bringing added kudos (of a sort), enhanced prosperity and a fresh title.

My memories of some of the others are as warming as a brazier on a January picket-line. Dick Crossman, a towering intellect but also a towering intellectual élitist; Sydney Silverman, incomparably courageous in espousing unpopular causes and facing down a hostile audience (but he never forgave me for the occasion when I said of him, truthfully, as Shakespeare's Brutus said of Cicero, that he would never follow in anything that other men began); Tom Driberg, the first 'William Hickey' columnist, a strange mixture of a man who could be at one moment hypersensitive and vulnerable (as many homosexuals are) and at the next boorish and bullying, and who was a grandmaster at rewriting recondite, stilted papers into English pure and undefiled. I recall with glowing pleasure that lively, entertaining and controversial threesome of George Wigg, Harold Davies and Stephen Swingler: they all came from the same adult-education background in Staffordshire, and for a while shared a flat in Bloomsbury and were forever doing petty-cash sums on the backs of envelopes about who had paid how much for what. But they were as mixed as liquorice allsorts – Wigg earnest and chronically conspiratorial, Davies a gushing fountain of Welsh rhetoric, Swingler going for years without the recognition he deserved and then flowering late into a most effective and successful Minister but dying tragically young.

Then there were the two Mancunians, the Lancashire Mancunian Will Griffiths and the Irish Mancunian Hugh Delargy, who were delightful companions at the beginning of an evening but liable to become overvehement when they'd had a drink or two; and John Baird, a hedonist Scot who was a superb raconteur of tales of the Highlands, most with a sharp political point in the dénouement. Konni Zilliacus ('Zilli'), polyglot and encyclopaedic, was, until his expulsion in 1949, sometimes among us but never totally with us: he often

91

accused us of pulling our punches. Leslie Hale, the most fluent and the fastest speaker I ever heard (he was the bane of the Hansard writers, who in those days had no Palantype or electronic recording), could always break a moment of tension by recalling one of the law's asininities that he had experienced in some provincial police court. Bill Mallalieu, 'Curly' to his friends, a delightful writer on politics and sport and the navy and much else, became over the warring years a sort of counterweight to me in that whenever I proposed some course of immediate action he would counsel caution and a pause for reflection. Another of the same quiet temperament was Tom Williams, a lawyer and lay preacher who had won a hard-fought by-election in Hammersmith.

There were two who, with Richard Acland, had come back to Labour from Common Wealth: Millington and Mackay. Ernest Millington was a tough Royal Air Force officer who had won a seat at Chelmsford in a by-election before the general election. Kim Mackay, an Australian company lawyer with irons in many fires, became my running mate when the Reading constituency was split into two: a man of boundless energy with a mind of unlimited fecundity, he was amongst the first and strongest supporters of the European Community because he believed it would eventually be constrained, notwithstanding the market-oriented Treaty of Rome, to move Western Europe towards socialism. And another lawyer, the sometimes mysterious, always inventive Geoffrey Bing: after 1951 he used his unparalleled expertise in parliamentary procedure to organise the Midnight Hags, a small group of us who harried the new Tory government by day and night, but mostly night; after he lost his Commons seat at Hornchurch he became legal adviser to Kwame Nkrumah, the first president of Ghana, and subsequently attorney-general in Nkrumah's government.

I shared weight-losing campaigns, though more in word than deed, with Frank Bowles, a wealthy bachelor of unproletarian mien and tastes, only mildly political but a lover of all mankind. He subsequently married, late in life, and then went to the Lords and was drawn into the aristocratic embrace; the last time I saw him he looked positively archaic in the court dress of the Captain of the Gentlemen-at-Arms. Mary and I used to play bridge with Benn Levy and his lovely actress wife, Constance Cummings: Benn, a noted playwright and one of the most dedicated of socialists, was nevertheless an aesthete who loved the fleshpots (he and Mary used to swap esoteric recipes).

Those were the men who formed our coterie of the Smoking Room round table. In those days women rarely ventured into that room: later it was Lena Jeger and Patricia Hornsby-Smith who first struck a blow for equal rights by invading this hitherto all-male sanctuary. It was only seldom that we were joined by a Minister, but we had Nye Bevan and Hugh Dalton and George Strauss as occasional visitors. There was even one evening when, uncharacteristically and surprisingly, Clem Attlee came and sat with us.

I remember the occasion well. It came about as an indirect result of the Attlee Must Go campaign in 1947. (George Brown canvassed me on the Terrace to support it, and got an earful of short sharp words of four letters.) After that campaign collapsed Ernie Bevin told Clem that he ought to get around more amongst the backbenchers. He should drop into the Members' Tea Room or the Smoking Room now and again, and have a cup of tea or a drink with different groups of his backbench supporters.

There were half a dozen of us sitting round our table listening to a lively disputation between Michael Foot and Dick Crossman, with an obbligato by Leslie Hale, about some recondite point of eighteenth-century history: I suspect that Michael was at the time doing some early reading for his study of Swift and Marlborough, *The Pen and the Sword* (1957), which I still think the best thing he ever wrote. I was sitting opposite the door: I saw it open and, to my astonishment, in walked the Prime Minister. For a moment or two he looked round the room, blinking helplessly like an owl in sunlight, till I called out to him, 'Clem, come on over and have a drink.'

He shuffled over and we moved round to make room for him, and someone called up a drink. The conversation sank like a stone: one or two valiant attempts to refloat it were broken on the rocks of the staccato monosyllables which were all we could get out of our guest. There was a period of awkward uncomfortable silence until it was broken, in a lightning-flash of inspired genius, by Wesley Perrins, an NUGMW (as it then was) officer who had won the seat of Birmingham Yardley, and who happened to be sitting with us that evening. Wesley turned to Clem and gave voice in his ripe Black Country accent: 'I see,' he said, 'that Worcestershire are beating the daylights out of Yorkshire at Headingley.'

This innocent remark had an effect on Attlee like an action-shot in a commercial for Duracell batteries. In an instant his eyes lit up, his speech became polysyllabic and fluent. He analysed expertly the state of the Yorkshire-Worcestershire match: the wicket, by all accounts, was wearing, and the morrow might well witness a complete turnaround.

Clem came into the Smoking Room again a couple of weeks later, and this time, without preliminaries, Will Griffiths plunged straight into cricket. (Will was a cricket fanatic who sent his wife, when she was about to have their first child, to Lancashire so that if it was a boy he would be qualified to play for the county.) But this time Attlee stayed for only five minutes, and left, and never came again. His visits to the Tea Room faded out in the same way. He just couldn't mix.

Every single one of us in that round-table group had come into the Commons bursting to help our leaders to carry out, against all the mountainous obstacles resulting from the war, the programme on which we had been elected, and as long as they were doing that they had no better or more loyal foot-soldiers than our little lot. We charged enthusiastically into the battles for the National Health Service, the advances in public ownership, the housing programme, the radical reforms in education and in the social services. But as the months wore on we began to develop some concern about, and criticism of, several of the Government's policies and actions. There were, in particular, three elements which worried us.

The first of them was the lack of boldness and urgency in the Government's economic planning: we felt that the impetus towards maintaining a planned economy was blunted by the tendency of Ministers to run away from any serious confrontation with vested interests. We applauded their pushing ahead with the agreed programme of nationalising the basic industries and services, but we could see that the public corporations they were setting up were not the instruments of socialist planning that had been promised, since they had much the same structure, objectives, operational methods and men at the top as the companies they were replacing.

Secondly, we thought the Government wasn't doing enough to enhance the interests of workers. In particular Stafford Cripps, whose life-pattern had kept him away from any close acquaintance with workers and their work and their attitudes, was putting forward one-sided policies which placed solely on the workers, and not at all on entrepreneurs or financiers, the responsibility for economic expansion: he was arguing for restraint on earned incomes without any restraint on unearned incomes or prices or profits or capital gains. (We were to live through the same experience in two later Labour governments, between 1968 and 1970, and again between 1977 and 1979.) Nor was the Government doing anything, or even seriously thinking, about any first-stage moves towards industrial democracy to improve the position of the worker in his workplace.

But the area of government policy which caused us deepest concern was external relations. We could see the looming danger of the wartime alliance splitting into two hostile blocs arming against one another. We believed Britain ought to have no part in that and therefore should not be tied to the coat-tails of either Washington or Moscow; but we could see Ernie Bevin's negative, sterile anti-communism, with the wholehearted approval of the Tories, turning our Foreign Office into a subsidiary and subordinate branch of the State Department, which it has been more or less ever since.

We saw no necessity for that. Britain, we argued, bargained too weakly with the Americans: the support they gave us was given principally with their interests in mind, not ours, as witness their sudden, damaging withdrawal of Lend-Lease, and their even more damaging insistence on our making sterling convertible; and if we needed their goods, they needed our market.

One particularly noxious effect of the Government's self-imposed subservience to the United States was that Britain was undertaking commitments beyond its strength and capacity. To do that we were, at a time when our industries were crying out for labour, conscripting too many men into the armed forces, and for too long: even when the rundown was completed, we would still have a million men under arms, which was proportionately twice as many as the United States itself.

Some of us suspected that conscription was being continued for such a long period because some of our Ministers were too weak to stand up to the generals and admirals and air marshals and their civil service equivalents, or at least were too heavily influenced by them. I had these suspicions dramatically and amusingly confirmed one evening towards the end of 1946 when Fred Bellenger, the Secretary of State for War, invited a number of Labour Members to a reception in the War Office to meet their top people. I went along, and at one point I was chatting in a large crowded room with the Quartermaster General when Bellenger buttonholed me and said that he would particularly like me to meet Sir Eric Speed, the Permanent Secretary. We were introduced, and Speed took me off to his office where he was closeted with a brigadier and a few MPs, including George Wigg

95

and Raymond Blackburn, having a much better party than the Secretary of State's. I tried not to be too shocked at this spectacle of a Minister acting as personal assistant to his Permanent Secretary.

Speed turned out to be a caricature of an archreactionary, a burlesque of cartoonist David Low's Colonel Blimp. He hoped, he said, that conscription would be continued permanently, because every young man benefited greatly from a period in which he had to do as he was told and ask no questions. After about twenty minutes listening to this stuff I had to ask Sir Eric to excuse me for leaving early because I was booked to speak at a meeting of the No Conscription Council. He kept his cool, but only just.

Of course our little circle of lefties were not the only people who were feeling increasing doubts about where the Government was going. There were thirty or forty backbenchers who, in varying degrees, agreed with us, and in addition there were a number of members of the Trade Union Group who, though far to the right of our general views, were worried about the possibility of wage control. Moreover, we heard some loud whispers to the effect that two or three members of the Cabinet had opinions similar to some of ours and argued those opinions with their colleagues. There were, as I've said, Ministers who challenged Morrison's deep-dyed opposition to public ownership; there were three Ministers – Nye Bevan, Hugh Dalton and Manny Shinwell – who challenged Ernie Bevin's Palestine policy; there were some Ministers who were much less keen on extended conscription than others; there was, as always, a battle of wills between the Chancellor and the spending Ministers; there were differences of opinion about some of Stafford Cripps's economic concepts; and doubtless much else.

These battles were of course kept under the wraps of Cabinet confidentiality, but there was (there always is) the occasional hint, the occasional indiscretion, the occasional leak. I particularly remember the day (it was later, after the formation of the Keep Left Group) when Manny Shinwell sent for Kim Mackay and me because he wanted to talk to us about Cripps's attitude to the economic situation as expressed sharply in the White Paper on wages and prices and even more sharply in a speech he had made in Edinburgh the previous weekend. Manny's opinion of Cripps's general economic ideas was exactly in line with the Keep Left Group's, and he criticised the White Paper in terms almost identical with those of an article I had written for *Tribune*. But the one thing that worried Manny most was Cripps's assertion, in the Edinburgh speech, that if the Government didn't do something radical about the economic situation the country might be faced with the threat of a totalitarian régime: he suspected that this was Cripps's clearing the ground for a coalition government with himself as Prime Minister. Both Kim and I pooh-poohed this suspicion as fantasy, but Shinwell was convinced it was sound. He told us that he was thinking about resigning in order to be able to say these things out loud; but I wrote that off as empty talk. I couldn't see Manny ever giving up office of his own volition, as was demonstrated by his behaviour when he was sidelined during the 1947 fuel crisis.

But it was the Government's foreign policy, not home policy, which caused us round-tablers most concern, and induced us to make representations to the Prime Minister; but he just wouldn't listen. Some of us tried to get into a dialogue with the Foreign Secretary, but Bevin was not the easiest man to talk to and the last man in the world to suffer dissent gladly. There was one point at which Dick Crossman made an impression on him which resulted in Bevin's choosing him to be a member of the Anglo-American Committee of Enquiry on Palestine; but Dick was firmly erased from Bevin's good books when that Committee, with Crossman's support, produced a recommendation that Bevin and his Foreign Office didn't like. My own single attempt to have a talk with Bevin was a disaster, and I came away from it with the discovery that he was not only anti-Zionist but also anti-Jewish.

Ernie's great power of personality derived from his being an elemental, visceral man whose attitudes were inspired by empathies and antipathies rather than by assessments, and whose policies derived from gut reactions rather than cerebral analysis. That's a sure-fire formula for making a successful populist.

His trade-union career, before he left it to go into government, was a long unbroken chain of outstanding successes. His high-level skills in negotiation and organisation and his dominant personality had enabled him, over the years, to build and rapidly expand the Transport and General Workers' Union (TGWU) into supreme size and influence amongst the unions. The only continuous opposition he met throughout those years was from his communist members, who were a part of the Rank and File Movement, and they didn't get very far, except on one occasion – but that exception rankled bitterly in his memory for the rest of his life.

It was in 1937. The Union's Central London Bus Committee, led by a driver named Bert Papworth (who also later became a leading figure in the Communist Party), and with strong support from the Rank and File Movement, put in a claim to the London Passenger Transport Board to reduce the working day of central London bus-drivers to seven hours, on the indisputable grounds that increasing traffic congestion and two successive rises in the speed-limit had increased the strain on those drivers to the extent that a large proportion of them contracted chronic gastric diseases.

The Transport Board rejected the claim; and though Bevin negotiated strongly, there was no settlement and a strike was called. Bevin went along with it, though he wasn't really in favour and tried to delay it, perhaps because at the time London was crowded with visitors, including some distinguished visitors from abroad, for the celebrations of the coronation of King George VI. Maybe Ernie didn't want to be seen as putting a damper on the Rule Britannia jollifications. After a few days of the strike the Board agreed to reopen negotiations, and Bevin urged that this offer should be accepted, but Papworth and his drivers turned it down and continued the strike.

It was the only time in Bevin's trade union career that anyone had defied him so openly and so successfully, and it stayed with him. I've always had the feeling that when Ernie became Foreign Secretary and found himself, a few days later, in Potsdam for the peace negotiations, he looked across the table at Molotov and saw behind the full-moon face of the communist Foreign Minister the more rugged features of the communist Bert Papworth, and said to himself, 'Lest We Forget'.

The similar fanatical hatred he developed for the Jews in Palestine became an obsession which finally led him into the humiliation of having to give up the Palestine Mandate because his operation of it had become a miserable, abject, irredeemable failure.

Ernie's first contact with Jews had been some fifteen years earlier at a parliamentary by-election in the Whitechapel and St George's constituency, which resulted from the death of the sitting Member, Harry Gosling, president of the TGWU. That constituency was a Labour stronghold – in the previous election Gosling had polled, against two opponents, 63.2 per cent of the vote – and the first thought of the Labour leadership was to use it to provide a seat for Stafford Cripps, who had been appointed Solicitor General. But they had second thoughts about that because there were many thousands of Jewish electors in the constituency and it was feared that most of them would desert Labour in the by-election and therefore the seat might be lost.

The reason for that fear was that a year or so earlier the Colonial Secretary, Lord Passfield (Sidney Webb), had published a White Paper which proposed restrictions on Jewish immigration into Palestine so severe as to amount virtually to a stoppage. That White Paper evoked a hail of protest, not only from Jews but from many other quarters as well, and it became clear that a member of the Government standing in Whitechapel would probably be defeated.

The best chance of winning, it was thought, was to have another TGWU candidate in order to mobilise a good turnout of the Wapping dockers to offset the potentially lost Jewish vote. Bevin refused to stand himself, and instead put up a man named Hall, a member of his Executive who had the advantages of being local (Wapping) and of having spent many years organising the stevedores and tally-clerks in the up-river docks.

Bevin was desperately keen that Hall should win and he therefore embarked on a damage-limitation exercise amongst the Whitechapel Jews. He had meetings with *Poale Zion* and other local organisations and told them about representations he had made to the Party to get the Passfield White Paper modified. It wasn't difficult for him to do that because similar strong representations were coming in from many trade unions and constituency parties all over the country.

In the end the Government backed down, but in the meanwhile both the unfortunate Hall and, to a lesser extent, Bevin himself were peppered with a lot of flak from the Whitechapel Jews, much to Ernie's anger. Hall won the by-election, but with a majority reduced from 9000 to 1000, which presaged the defeat he was to suffer in the following year's general election, and Ernie's bitter resentment overflowed.

I have the feeling that when he became Foreign Secretary and found papers across his desk about some rebellious Jews in Palestine defying the Mandatory Authority, he started his consideration of them from a flashback to Whitechapel in 1930 and 1931. The effect of that, as Kenneth Morgan tells us, was that 'without doubt, he was emotionally prejudiced against the Jews, as Foreign Office advisers of his at the time have admitted to the present writer'. That emotional prejudice was evidenced by the pejorative and often vulgar language of many of Bevin's references to Jews: Morgan charitably calls them 'examples of elephantine *gaucherie*'.

We criticised the policies of the Government in other areas besides foreign affairs; there were also Northern Ireland, and conscription, and economic planning. For a year after the general election we gave voice to those criticisms only internally rather than publicly, at meetings of the Parliamentary Party and in private representations to Ministers. But by mid-1946 we realised sadly that those procedures were getting us nowhere, and that, however reluctantly, we would have to go public if we wanted our views to be heard and considered. The way we chose to do that was to put down a critical amendment on the Address for the King's Speech inaugurating the 1946–47 Session. Dick Crossman drafted the amendment, fifty-seven members signed it: its appearance and the debate on it dramatically opened the division between the socialists and the pragmatists in the Labour Party which has persisted ever since.

# Chapter 8

LOOKING back at 1946 from this distance it seems quite remarkable that the 1945 hope and expectation of a great leap towards a socialist Britain should have faded so fast that it took only a year to throw up a rebel group. It's difficult to recapture now the deep disappointment and disillusion which afflicted many of the new young Members as we saw our Government moving rapidly away from the Party's socialist philosophy and principles and settling comfortably, as to the manner born, into the welcoming arms of the capitalist Establishment, and as we saw some of our Ministers taking the easy option of continuing what they had been thinking and doing as members of the Churchill Coalition Government.

The most pungently evocative account of the descent from 1945 is to be found, as is often the case in political literature, in a work of satire. The *New Statesman* of those days regularly carried satirical verses by an author writing under the pen-name Sagittarius. (I never got to know the identity behind that *nom de plume*, but I was told the archer-poet was a woman.) The poems were little gems of delicate irony, flashing wit, acute percipience and ingenious rhyming. Sagittarius wrote a slim volume called *Let Cowards Flinch*, deliciously illustrated by Vicky, in which the events of the time are described in terms of the French Revolution, with our leaders as the original revolutionaries in 1945 and our Keep Left group as the Jacobins of a second revolutionary surge.

This is how Sagittarius saw our Ministers taking up their new offices:

101

'Appointed as the Coalition's heirs,
They grasped the helm and cleared the decks for action,
State-strategists, not hidebound doctrinaires
Devoted to political abstraction!
The Red Flag was no oriflamme of theirs,
A mere red herring of the fallen faction,
And England knew, while Labour's Mandate lasted,
The Union Jack would flutter at the masthead . . .
The State machine grinds on in well-worn grooves
Along the wonted middle course progressing;
The Red Flag hangs above the Whitehall camp,
But folded like a Foreign Office gamp.'

On conscription, Sagittarius described the Government and the Tory Opposition in complete harmony

'demanding
Compulsory enlistment in the Forces,
Establishments defensively expanding
To limits of the national resources;
In totting up the military quota
The Parties do not differ one iota.'

That may now read like the black-and-white oversimplification and exaggeration which are the satirist's licence, but in fact it's a faithful account of what was happening, and it was no wonder that some socialists in the Party felt they could no longer take it without open protest. It was that feeling that led us to put down the Crossman amendment and to demand a debate on it.

Mind you, we weren't hurling thunderbolts of condemnation at our leaders, much less rolling out the tumbrils to cart them off to Tyburn Gate. Our amendment, modest and moderate, was couched in terms of sweet reason: like Bottom the weaver we roared as gently as any sucking dove. Our text avoided such terms as criticising or deploring, much less condemning – it mostly expressed the hope that the Government would 'so review and recast its conduct of international affairs as to . . . provide a democratic and socialist alternative to an otherwise inevitable conflict between American Capitalism and Soviet Communism'.

You wouldn't think, would you, that this was calculated to shock-horror any member of a democratic socialist party. Moreover, Crossman, in moving the amendment, and those who spoke in support of him were at pains to pay tribute to the achievements of the Government, to recognise the difficulties it faced, and to balance criticisms of United States policy with an attack on the ideology of one-party communism and on some of the policies of the Soviet Union. (That didn't protect the 57 signatories of the amendment, who included some Members a long way from the Left, from being dubbed communists by the Tories, the press and some of our own colleagues, including, in private, Attlee himself.) But we got little thanks for our moderation: both Attlee and Bevin were furious with us almost to the point of hysteria. Sagittarius put it well:

'The rupture of the old *esprit de corps*
The nonplussed Cabinet finds most abhorrent,
Particularly as these rash nonentities
Presume to wear their own cast-off identities.'

Bevin missed the debate because he was in the United States at the time, and some of his supporters argued that the House ought not to be debating foreign affairs while the Foreign Secretary was away – an inane proposition which, carried to its logical conclusion and applied to all Ministers, would reduce Parliament to silence for much of its time and on a lot of its concerns.

It is significant that in the whole of that debate the most fulsome and enthusiastic praise of Bevin was expressed not by anyone on his own side of the House but by the official spokesman for the day of the Conservative Opposition, a character named Captain Crookshank. (He was a man I was always a bit sorry for: he was permanently frustrated, and therefore crabbed and acidulated, because he was continuously on the fringe of the Tory First XI but never quite made it beyond the substitutes' bench.) Crookshank described our amendment as 'a stab in the back' of the Foreign Secretary: a year later, at the 1947 Labour Party Conference, Ernie blasted off into a tabloid-level demagogic attack on the authors of the amendment and got a great cheer out of many of the delegates when he complained that while he was abroad we had stabbed him in the back: as I listened to that I wondered if those delegates would have cheered so loudly if they had known that the voice was the voice of Ernie but the words were the words of one of the most extreme of Tory reactionaries.

All the authors of that amendment, none more than I, were taken aback by this extremely disproportionate hot-under-the-collar reaction of our leaders to a genuine protest which was motivated honestly and helpfully and was expressed in terms not merely respectful but actually deferential. It taught me a sharp lesson about the nature of political power and its effect on those who wield it. It was my first experience of a phenomenon which many times over the next forty years I was to see acted out by different leading players – the metamorphosis, the pantomime role-change, which induces a democratic politician, as soon as he reaches the pinnacle of power, to feel himself to be a king or even a godhead, so that any expression of dissent from his ukase becomes a combination of *lèse-majesté* and blasphemy, and therefore puts the heretic/traitor (i.e. the man who dares to think things out for himself) in danger of excommunication and the headsman's axe. The corruption which, in Acton's dictum, is the product of power is the erosion of tolerance: the power-wielder assumes that he's omniscient and infallible, and therefore ought not to have to put up with people who develop views different from his own.

Of course this corruption of political leaders-in-power is not confined to leaders of the Labour Party – aside from the Stalins and the other unelected dictators, one has only to think of Otto von Bismarck, Adolf Hitler, Juan Perón, Richard Nixon, Indira Gandhi, Habib Bourguiba, Felipe González, David Owen and Margaret Thatcher. But it always feels worse in the Labour Party than in any other because we pride ourselves on our democratic structure, which should ensure the accountability of our leaders to those who elected them. Yet every leader of our Party since 1945, starting with Attlee, was intolerant of dissent, and almost every leader since Attlee has, to a greater or lesser extent but mostly greater, sought to abstract policy-making and decision-making power from the bodies elected to wield it – the Annual Conference and the National Executive Committee – and abrogate it to himself and a close circle of his cronies, who are sometimes a few members of his Cabinet or Shadow Cabinet and sometimes the faceless courtiers in his private-office kitchen-cabinet. It is this process of centralisation of power, and the resistance to it put up by the Party's rank-and-file, which has been the *casus belli* of the struggles over the Party's constitution, and particularly of the eventually successful campaign to have the Leader elected by the whole Party and not merely by the (nearly always docile) Parliamentary Party.

Like Ernest Bevin, but for a different reason, I missed the debate on the King's Speech because I was abroad. I was in Austria, on my first overseas assignment as a management consultant. After the

*Anschluss* of 1938 the Germans built an industrial complex at Linz to serve some of the needs of Greater Germany: it consisted of a steel works, called the Hermann Goeringwerke, and beside it a *Stickstoff-werke* which produced nitrogenous fertiliser from the waste coke-oven and blast-furnace gases of the steel factory. Both these plants had very large output-capacities which were readily absorbable by the Third Reich but much beyond the needs of little Austria, which could neither produce nor afford to acquire the massive quantities of fuel which the plants consumed. The problem of what to do with the surplus capacity was passed to one of the leading Austrian banks, who invited a couple of economists and a couple of industrial planners, including me, to look at the problem, separately, *in situ* and advise on it. Eventually the rundown was accomplished successfully, and the Hermann Goeringwerke became VOEST (United Austrian Iron and Steel) and developed an important new technology in steelmaking which was taken up all over the world.

I think I did a reasonably good job in the week I was there, but I remember it also for two somewhat untoward experiences.

The first was a brush with the armed forces of the United States, no less. Austria, like Germany, was divided into four zones controlled respectively by Britain, France, the United States and the Soviet Union, with central Vienna administered by each of them in turn on a weekly rota (and you can imagine what a ripe collection of assorted cock-ups was produced by that idiotic arrangement). Linz was in the American Zone, but to get to it from Vienna I had to be driven through the Soviet Zone. The frontier posts between the two were at either end of a bridge in a small town called Enns. On the Soviet side a soldier who looked as though he was just out of school took a quick flick through our papers and waved us on. On the American side a large and surly GI went through the papers slowly and clumsily and ordered us to go into the delousing station. I walked over to have a look at this health-protecting institution. It was a wooden hut, indescribably filthy, with an inch depth of chemical sludge all over the floor, and it stank abominably. Inside the hut a raggedly-dressed, bored civilian wielded a none-too-clean spray-gun filled with DDT. I watched him as he inserted the nozzle of this unsavoury implement between a victim's Adam's apple and his collar, and then pressed the plunger vigorously. I turned to the large and surly GI and told him that short of picking me up bodily (and I am a 200-pounder) there was no way he was going to get me into that Augean stable. After some mutually uncomplimentary exchanges, in which I commanded a much wider and more colourful vocabulary of ruderies than my opponent, he picked up a telephone, and that produced a fresh-faced young officer. 'Look,' I said to this lad, 'you know as well as I do that a delousing operation that doesn't include the subject's hair is absolutely useless, so I suppose the purpose of this charade is merely to humiliate the local citizenry and put them in their place.'

He didn't argue but instead opted for the quiet life. He made a show of looking through my papers, and waved me on. I thought he was finding it difficult to suppress a smile.

My other contretemps arose from a simple error which made me a millionaire for the week I was in Vienna. In preparing for the trip I had to go along to the Control Commission Section at the Foreign Office who were very kindly arranging my transport and accommodation, and giving me some briefing and some introductions. (The transport was a hideously uncomfortable ride in a roughly converted Lancaster bomber, and the accommodation was in the Hotel Sacher, which was reserved for British officers, but they wangled me into it by the fiction of giving me some notional army rank, which wasn't bad considering that my real military career had been confined to the Home Guard in which, by dint of three years of dedicated service and blind obedience to my superiors, I rose to the rank of private.) At the end of my interview at the Control Commission Section they told me that Vienna was the hottest hotbed of black-marketeering in the whole of Europe, and so there were strict limits on what a visitor could take in. They handed me a duplicated slip of paper with the list of what was permitted: it began with a few ounces each of tea and coffee and butter and tinned meat and tinned fish, and ended with 80 cigarettes. When I got home I handed this list to Mary and asked her to collect the stuff and pack it for me. (In all my hundreds of trips Mary packed for me: she always sent me off with a bag looking like a bride's trousseau, and it always came back looking as if a cow had chewed and regurgitated it.)

When I got to the Sacher Hotel and unpacked I saw that my bag contained not 80 but 800 cigarettes: Mary had just misread the figure. I flopped into a chair and sat staring like a zombie at those four 200-cigarette packs. If my bag had been opened at the airport, I suppose I would have got three years in the slammer plus a fine the size of Fort Knox. I had been warned that in Austria cigarettes were the primary currency and mere money was a poor second: one cigarette was a large tip, five would buy the favours of a lady of the sidewalks, and for my 800 I could possibly have acquired a controlling interest in the State Opera House and got a couple of lesser Hapsburg palaces thrown in to make up the weight. Those blasted cigarettes were a source of worry and embarrassment to me all the week. I gave a lot of them away in dribs and drabs, but I still found myself with far too many on the eve of my return. After dinner that evening I went out for a walk, saw a cheerful-looking bar with a lot of British soldiers in it, walked in, and was immediately greeted by four of my constituents serving in the Royal Berkshire Regiment who recognised me. We had a few rounds, and then a couple of the lads walked back with me, and on the dark pavement outside the tradesmen's entrance of the Sacher Hotel I gratefully offloaded my remaining contraband into their eagerly welcoming hands.

When I got back to England and Westminster I found that our small group's little revolt on the Amendment to the Address had made waves, and deep ones, right through the Party membership all round the country. That didn't surprise us, because in all the trips which most of us had made to the constituencies to speak at meetings or day-schools or seminars, we had found the local activists as worried as we were about the Government's downward slide from the peaks of its socialist promise to the flatlands of conformity and conventional respectability. We felt that we owed a duty to our supporters in the Party to continue the argument and to broaden it. I tried to persuade my friends that we ought to form ourselves into an organised group, meeting regularly to discuss current events and future policy and to publish papers which, supplementing the pieces which some of us contributed to *Tribune* and other papers, would spread our ideas amongst the activists in the Constituency Parties and trade unions and keep us in touch with them. But this attempt of mine failed: at that stage many in our little circle reacted strongly against anything that smacked of organised activity, and it was only at the second attempt, some months later, that I managed to get my proposal accepted, and then only partially and hesitantly.

[*Digression*. The outstanding unrecognised and unrecorded feature of the Left versus the Right struggle within the Labour Party – and I've seen the same phenomenon in other democratic socialist parties as well – is that the Right is always much better organised than the democratic (as distinct from the trotskyist) Left. This fact is contrary to popular belief, because, whilst right-wing organisations are indulgently shielded from the arc-light of publicity, people fall for the lurid pictures drawn by many of the pundits in the newspapers and the other media who forever see the Left as no more than a conspiratorial cabal, meeting hugger-mugger in dark, dank dungeons and conspiring, for their own ambition, to overthrow and supplant the Party leadership.

Dick Crossman's diary entry for 24 March 1955 records a truth-stranger-than-fiction conversation he had with Hugh Gaitskell in the run-up to Gaitskell's abortive hate-powered attempt to get Aneurin Bevan expelled from the Labour Party. Dick records that during this conversation Gaitskell made 'a long speech about Bevanism. "Bevanism", he said, "is and only is a conspiracy to seize the leadership for Aneurin Bevan. It is a conspiracy because it has three essentials of conspiracy, a leader in Bevan, an organisation run by Mikardo and a newspaper run by Foot." I laughed and said, "You really believe in this talk about the Bevanite organisation of Mikardo?" Gaitskell said, "Certainly. It's widespread in the constituencies."'

Of course this nightmare of Gaitskell's, this picture he had of me sitting on a high stool in front of a giant console pressing buttons to manipulate my puppets in six hundred Constituency Labour Parties, didn't have the least shred of truth in it. I didn't have any Bevanite agent or organiser, or even contact, in a single constituency, not even in my own bailiwick in Reading. The very idea was so impracticable-fanciful that only a paranoiac could have entertained it and become obsessed by it.

The principal reason why the people of the democratic Left are so difficult to organise is that they are in general ideas-men rather than organisation-men, policy-formers rather than power-brokers, so they're better at talking than doing, better at debating than recruiting. Most of them are happy to go to a meeting to discuss a policy paper but shrink from a meeting with an agenda of points for action: they think that sort of thing is redolent of 'fixers' like Herbert Morrison and Hugh Dalton and Morgan Phillips and Arthur Deakin and Walter Citrine and Sara Barker and Tom O'Brien and Bill Rodgers. Of all the people I've worked with, none reacted against inner-Party organisation more than Aneurin Bevan. He loved to let his mind wander round wide horizons, and he did that with a breadth of imagination, an originality of analysis and a fertility of prescription far beyond the capacity of anyone else I've ever known. But he had no patience for the nitty-gritty of who should do what when – indeed, as others have written (though I believe I was the first to use the phrase) he was a reluctant

Bevanite. He generally tried to avoid, or at least to postpone, making a decision between two possible courses of action, and consequently he reacted strongly whenever he thought someone was trying to press him into making such a decision. To anyone who knew him and worked with him the idea of Bevan as a power-hungry conspirator was a belly-laugh.

Another problem in left-wing groups is that they consist of nonconformists with deep convictions who sometimes over-react against any of their friends who don't go along with them all the way. So you get divisions of principle, on top of the inevitable personality clashes. There are some differences of outlook between the ambitious and the unambitious, between the full-time politicians and the part-timers, between the wholehoggers and the tacticians, between the few who are willing to work and the rest who are willing to let them.

The divisions we had in the Keep Left Group between 1947 and 1951 were of no great significance, but the Bevanites after 1951, under the strain of being constantly harassed and beleaguered not merely by the Tories but even more viciously by our own Party machine, developed some serious internal strains. Nye became, with good cause, suspicious of both Crossman and Wilson. Crossman, in turn, developed an intellectual-superiority contempt for most of his colleagues: what can you make of a man so big-headed that he could write, as Dick did in his diary, 'I have never felt such a strong sense of personal superiority as I have had this week, looking at Mr Gaitskell or even poor, soft Nye' (31 October 1958)?

Of course it may be that the same internal strains and fissions exist in groups of the Right. I've no means of knowing whether they do or not, though there may be some conclusions to be drawn from the way in which the SDP Gang of Four, in the course of only a few rancorous days, was dramatically reduced to a Gang of One.

Another problem faced by groups of the Left – and this time it is one which certainly doesn't affect groups of the Right -- is the danger of destructive infiltration by trotskyists of one stripe or another. In 1958 a few of us took over a small and moribund society called Victory for Socialism and set about building it into a nationwide organisation. It was a mistake, and after a year or two we cut out of it because many of the branches had been taken over by the trotskyists, and we had no means of stopping them.]

As I was saying before that digression, in the early months of the 1946–1947 session my friends and I felt that we had to spell out in great detail the analysis of international problems and policies which we had made in the debate on the Address, and to add to it a similar analysis of internal problems and policies, and then publish it. We took the task seriously: even before the Keep Left Group was established formally, a few of us had a number of meetings to work out what we should write. Though these meetings were not very regular and were only loosely structured, the discussions, often based on a background note or a position paper which one of us had written, were serious, constructive and deep. By the time of the Easter recess we had clarified our ideas and had assembled enough material for a long pamphlet. On the morning of Good Friday Michael Foot and I, accompanied by Rose Cohen, who was Dick Crossman's secretary, and Jo Richardson, who was mine, descended on Dick and Zita at their cottage in the hills above High Wycombe. Almost without pausing for breath, Michael and Dick and I got down to work: we divided up the synopsis, and as soon as one of us had produced a slab of text we all went through it together, amending or expanding or cutting or even redrafting, until we thought we'd got it all right. With only short intervals for food and drink (Zita was the ministering angel) and exercise we worked through the rest of Friday, all day Saturday and Sunday, nonstop right through Sunday night and on until we completed *Keep Left* at Monday tea-time. The three of us wrote, dictated, and wrote and dictated again; and Rose and Jo, miraculously tireless, clattered out of their typewriters first drafts, redrafts and final drafts (what a blessing a word-processor or a computer would have been!). It all went very smoothly and happily: I can recall only one serious argument during the whole weekend – an argument between Dick and me over one sentence, not concerning content but concerning word-order, about which I tend to be fussy – or, as Dick put it, over-pedantic.

*Keep Left* was widely and avidly read in the constituencies and the trade unions. It provided not a ray but a whole beam of hope for the socialist activists in the Party who had begun to despair of ever seeing the sort of restructuring of our society which the electoral victory of 1945 had led them to expect. It showed them that there was a viable alternative to middle-ground conformity, and that there were people capable of working out that alternative and effectively arguing the case for it. The pamphlet knitted together the Keep Left Group and spurred its members to greatly increased activity. Our second pamphlet, *Keeping Left*, though it lacked something of the verve and passion of its predecessor, kept up the momentum of debate throughout the Movement. That debate illumined for the rank-and-file of the Party the basic differences between its two elements, the social democrats and the democratic socialists, and therefore helped them, when the really sharp clash was precipitated by the three ministerial resignations in 1951, to understand clearly what it was about.

I shall come to 1951 and the birth of the Bevanites in the next chapter; but I break off for a while from inner-Party affairs to write about two quite different areas of activity which I got myself involved in during that period. Each of them represented problems to which I sought to apply my own central principles of scientific management which, as I mentioned earlier, are: start with a blank sheet of paper, define on it precisely the objectives you want to achieve, and then construct instruments and evolve methods specifically and individually tailored to the achievement of those objectives. (It may sound a bit pompous, but in practice it really does work.)

The first of these two new concerns of mine related to the running of a parliamentary election campaign, notably in a marginal constituency like my own. I began teasing my brain on this subject immediately after my victory in 1945, because I could see that the victory was a hollow one. Though my majority looked good I had polled a minority of the votes cast: I had beaten my Conservative opponent by less than the number of votes cast for the Liberal candidate. I estimated (correctly, for it was obvious) that in future elections the Liberal vote would decline, and that more of the Liberal defectors would vote Tory than Labour, and so I would always have to sweat and struggle to hold the seat. That induced me to ask myself whether the practices which were used at that time in all elections, including my own in 1945, were the ones most likely to achieve a second win.

I didn't have to work hard to answer that question, because the answer was self-evident. We all carried out the same procedures whether we were fighting a safe Tory seat that we couldn't win with or without intense organisation or a safe Labour seat that we couldn't lose with or without intense organisation or a marginal seat which could be won with intense organisation and lost without it.

In a safe Tory seat there's no point in mounting a difficult and expensive campaign, and running one's workers into the ground, in order to lose by only 15,000 instead of 16,000; in a safe Labour seat there's no point in doing so in order to win by 16,000 instead of only 15,000; it is only a marginal seat, where that thousand votes more or less is the difference between winning and losing, which justifies the massive organisational effort that is required for a detailed elector-by-elector campaign.

To put it another way, if I were fighting a safe Tory seat I would distribute a single and cheap election address and not much else, get some publicity for the Party's policies, and lead my workers to the nearest marginal seat where our door-knocking might make the difference between No Change and Labour Gain; if I were fighting a safe Labour seat I would run a cheap campaign, draw on my large electoral support to collect funds for the Constituency Party and recruit members into it, and again lead my workers to the nearest marginal seat; if I am fighting a marginal seat I set out to identify and list accurately all the electors who, if they vote at all, will vote Labour and then set up a field organisation which will tackle them on a one-to-one basis to get them to the poll.

Instead of that selective, discriminatory strategy, the general practice in our election campaigns is that we have, from one type of constituency to another, three radically different tasks, and yet we use the same methods and do the same things in every one of them. It is axiomatic that this can't possibly be right.

The other great misconception which afflicts many candidates and their agents is the assumption that the major purpose of the election campaign is to talk to people who were intending to vote for another Party and persuade them to change their minds and vote for us instead. Of course it is a fact that many electors switch their votes (or abstentions) from one general election to the next, but almost all that switching takes place not in the four weeks of the election campaign but in the four years or so between elections. Most of the bit of switching that does take place during the campaign results from national media presentation and not from the local efforts of each candidate and his workers. Yet a great deal of the money and effort which we expend in our campaigns goes into trying to convert opponents (or waverers). There are all those little schoolroom meetings (fewer now than we used to have, but still quite a lot) addressed by the candidate and some supporting speakers: they cost money to hire the hall and publicise the meeting, and manpower to run it, and they're attended only by a few dozen of one's own supporters who would be doing more good out in the streets canvassing their neighbours. Yet we go to all this sweat in the belief that some Tory or Liberal will wander into the meeting and hear a speech from the candidate or Councillor

Bloggs or Ian Mikardo and be smitten like Saul on the road to Damascus with a blinding light and an instant conversion to the gospel of socialism. It doesn't happen.

Similarly we spend a lot of money printing leaflets and wear out a lot of shoe-leather putting them through every letterbox in the constituency; but half of them serve only to help our opponents by reminding anti-Labour voters that there's an election on. We do it out of the delusion that one of those anti-Labour voters will pick up one of our leaflets off his doormat, read it and at once realise the lifelong error of his ways, becoming an instant convert to our cause and candidature. It just doesn't happen.

I got together a group of the bright young activists in the Reading Party and put these ideas to them. I presented the argument in this way: suppose I am fighting a seat which I lost at the last election by 900 votes. In order to win it this time I need to do one of two things: either persuade 500 people who voted Conservative last time to vote Labour this time, or alternatively identify a thousand of the (probably) four to five thousand people who would have voted Labour last time if they had voted at all but in fact didn't go to the poll and persuade them to vote this time. It's obvious that the second is much the easier of these two tasks. The inescapable conclusion to be drawn is that the objective of the election campaign is not to convert Conservative voters but to identify Labour voters and get them to the polling station. All the campaign mechanisms should be devised for, and directed to, that task and no other.

When I first met Kim Mackay, I discovered that he had been thinking independently along the same lines. We pooled our ideas and fleshed in some details. Over the years, with the help of David (then Councillor, later MP and now Lord) Stoddart and Clive Jenkins and a burly rough-diamond Reading bus-driver named Don Courtneidge, we added many original refinements of method and mechanisms which would be interesting and comprehensible only to the *cognoscenti*. Thus was evolved what has come to be called the Reading system, parts of which (in some constituencies updated by computerisation) are now used all over the country, and not only in the Labour Party.

That other field in which I broke some new ground in that period was an extension of my work as a management consultant. After the election I carried on with my consultancy practice, though only to the limited extent that was possible within the amount of time (not very much) that I was prepared to spare from my constituency, from the House and from the Party. Pursuing two careers at once was a heavy burden, but I was determined, with a growing family, not to be forever totally dependent on a parliamentary salary which could disappear at the next general election (and which in fact did disappear in the election of 1959).

But that wasn't the only reason for continuing my industrial work. I soon realised that the first-hand experience I was getting in the management offices and on the shop floors in a number of different industries would enable me to talk with more authority than most other MPs about the real basis – that is, the productive basis – of the economy. In the 1950–51 debates in which the Keep Left Group opposed the Government's huge increase, in response to American pressure, in the rearmament programme, I carried some knowledgeable authority for my assertion that we didn't have the resources – in particular the machine-tool capacity – to carry it out.

It wasn't until much later that I learned that Nye Bevan, while still in the Cabinet, was arguing the same case, and I heard him argue it in his resignation speech and subsequently. The Government, putting obeisance to Washington before any other consideration, blundered on blindly into these unfulfillable commitments, which of course were never fulfilled. After Churchill became Prime Minister in 1951 he admitted, in his first speech on defence, that Nye had been right all along.

My bit of extra-parliamentary earnings provided not only a measure of financial security but also a modicum of political independence. In those days the whips weren't at all delicate in the pressures, sometimes even threatening pressures, that they sought to exert, sometimes successfully, to keep backbenchers in line, and a man who had given up his vocation to come into Parliament and who might not easily get it back if he left Parliament was more vulnerable and more susceptible to those pressures than one who retained a sheet-anchor outside.

I had first-hand experience to illustrate this fact. On one occasion Clem Attlee took exception to something I'd said in a speech in my constituency and the following day I was summoned to his room like a first-former summoned to his headmaster's study for six of the best. When I arrived I found Attlee flanked by Will Whiteley, the chief whip, and Frank Bowles, who by then had become chairman of the Parliamentary Party and who was almost wriggling with embarrassment. From their point of view the meeting wasn't a great success. To begin with I made it clear that I was taking a close record of the proceedings, and when Whiteley asked me, 'What for?' I answered, 'For posterity – which could be next century or next week'. Later in the interview he hinted that Members who kicked over the traces might find their parliamentary careers somewhat curtailed. I told him that was a disaster I could survive, and that I could serve the cause of socialism as well outside Parliament as in it. Finally, when the Prime Minister had had his say, I reminded the three of them that the Parliamentary Party could call a Member to account only for what he said and did in Parliament, and that, like every other member of the Party, I was answerable for what I said and did outside Parliament only to the National Executive and not to them. So saying, I bade them a warm fraternal good-afternoon and walked out. I'm not sure I'd have been capable of that cheeky defiance if I hadn't had an established persona, and an established income, outside politics.

There was another occasion, much later, which produced an interface between my political and professional careers. It was just before my return to the House in 1964 after my five years out of it. Patrick Gordon Walker, in anticipation of becoming Foreign Minister in the Labour Government which we all expected to be elected that year, was doing a bit of globe-trotting, and in the course of it he spent three days in Israel and was shown round by Eppi Evron, who was on home leave from the Israeli Embassy in London. Gordon Walker was about as far to the right as you can get in the Labour Party without toppling over the edge – his banishment of Seretse Khama was an act of blatant racism, and he always contemptuously pooh-poohed the notion that a Labour Government should pay any attention whatever to the decisions of Annual Conference. He told Evron that he and some of his friends were worried about my impending return to the House because I would organise the Left members – and there would be more of them in the new Parliament – perhaps causing trouble for the new Government. (He obviously expected that Government to move rightwards.) He asked Eppi whether he thought it might be possible to buy me off with a job on the Steel Board or in civil aviation, and added sadly that it wasn't likely because he and his friends had heard that I was making a fortune in business. (I wasn't actually, or anything like it, but I was quite happy for them to think I was.)

From that flash-forward I come back to the late 1940s. In the course of my consultancy work with companies in a number of different industries I became interested in the export drive, and I soon got to know that the one market in which British exporters were furthest behind their competitors from other countries was the Soviet bloc. Though all the countries in that bloc were in an economic mess, largely because they had been overrun and blasted and stripped by the Nazis, I recognised that they were a market of great potential as a group of underdeveloped countries in Europe which were clearly going to develop and expand their economies much faster than the underdeveloped countries in the other continents of the world.

I did a bit of research, both in Britain and Eastern Europe, analysing why our exporters were making much less impact than other western countries in this market. Some of the reasons were silly: Britons always assumed that buyers in other countries would be willing to abandon their own languages and do business in English; and many British businessmen were convinced by bogey tales in the tabloids that if they went on a business visit to Eastern Europe all sorts of horrendous things could happen to them – whereas in fact a Briton visiting Moscow who obeys the law of the land and fits in with its customs and doesn't do anything he wouldn't want his mother or his wife to know about was never in any more danger than a similarly law-abiding, well-behaved and circumspect Russian visiting London.

Aside from the silly reasons there was one of real substance: the failure of British business, except for a few large companies, to understand how different were the structure and practices of a centrally-controlled economy from those of the open economies which they knew and understood. They didn't realise that it was a waste of time using in the Soviet Union, Czechoslovakia or East Germany the marketing techniques which they used in France, Italy or Canada.

I spent a lot of patient hours in boardrooms and export sales departments explaining what five-year plans were, and how they were broken down into sub-plans, and how they were translated into lists of requirements, and what were the relative priorities of sourcing those requirements from home suppliers and from suppliers in the rest of the rouble bloc and, as a last resort, from hard-currency suppliers, and how purchasing decisions were made, and what criteria were applied in making them.

It took a while to sink in; but eventually I acted in the markets of communist countries for a number of the best British manufacturers, both public corporations and private-sector companies, and for a trade development council in one of our colonies. Jo Richardson quickly graduated out of being my secretary and became my co-director: she proved to be a better organiser than I am, and much more skilful at handling difficult situations and difficult people. It wasn't an easy job: it involved much bone-aching travel, and demanded a lot of ingenuity and a lot of patience, but it was full of interest and challenge, and in the course of it we made a lot of friends and had a lot of fun. We carried on till 1977 when we wound up the company and went our several ways – I to my proper place as the Eternal Back-bencher, and Jo to well-deserved recognition on the Party Executive and in the Shadow Cabinet, and pre-eminently as the first-ever prospec-. tive Minister for Women.

Notwithstanding all this pioneering work in electoral organisation and East-West trade, my first commitment in that period was to the establishment and organisation of the Keep Left Group. It has become received wisdom among some of the historians and biographers (I suspect each of them accepted it from what others had written) that the Group slid into relative inactivity after 1948, but I can be more authoritative than they on this subject because I have access, and they hadn't, to the minutes of the Group's meetings and its other papers, all of which (Keep Left Group, then Bevanites and then Tribune Group) have providentially been preserved by Jo Richardson, who was the secretary of all three groups over three decades. But that story deserves a chapter to itself.

# Chapter 9

THE KEEP LEFT GROUP was much smaller than its successors, the Bevanites and the Tribune Group, but it was close-knit, dedicated and very hard-working. We met frequently and regularly, sometimes in the House, sometimes in Tom Horabin's flat in Victoria or Dick Crossman's house in Vincent Square, sometimes in a modest little Cypriot restaurant in Soho. Once we stayed on in Margate for the weekend at the end of Annual Conference, and we spent another weekend – a truly delightful one – in a fairy-tale mansion called Buscot Park, which belonged to Gavin Faringdon and which he subsequently donated to the National Trust. A few years later the Bevanites also spent two weekends in conference there, and later still Gavin hosted a high-level think-tank at which I presented a paper, and Mary and I played after-dinner bridge with Sir (as he then was) Solly Zuckerman and another boffin. We then slept in a seven-foot-wide fourposter and we had a jumbo-size bathroom lined with nineteenth-century pictorial tiles illustrating the love-life of Catherine the Great which could now be shown on television only with the permission of Mrs Whitehouse and after the kids have gone to bed.

Unlike its successors, the Keep Left Group was concerned with the long term rather than the immediate. The agendas of the later Bevanite and the Tribune Group meetings were and are dominated by the week's business in the House and other current or imminent issues, but in Keep Left the greater part of our discussions was about the basic philosophy of the Party and the sort of broad economic and social order we should be seeking to create. Between 1947 and 1950 we concentrated on the production of a wide-ranging programme for the next Labour government: we worked hard at it, writing and circulating papers, some of them long and detailed, on different policy areas, and discussing and amending them. We had as our advisers three of the top socialist economists, Tommy (later Lord) Balogh, David Worswick and Dudley Seers – in that field our resources were better than those available to the Party leadership. We kept up our activity (and this certainly did not happen in our successor groups) right through the parliamentary recesses: I was the Group's secretary at that time (and until I was elected to the NEC, when Jo Richardson succeeded me), and in the recesses the members of the Group kept my mailbag and my telephone and my duplicating machine at full stretch.

Re-reading some of those many papers forty years later fills me with admiration for how serious of purpose we were, and how industrious and how far-seeing. John Freeman and I separately wrote about the aircraft manufacturing industry; Dick Acland, Dick Crossman and Tom Williams went, separately, to have a look at the British Zone of Germany and combined to write some conclusions on it which Tommy Balogh supplemented in a paper called 'Germany: an Experiment in Decontrol'; David Worswick wrote a mini-thesis on 'The State and Private Enterprise'; I did an analysis of the National Assistance Board scales which showed that inflation rates for national assistance recipients were higher than for anyone else because poor people spend a higher proportion of their income on necessities that rise in price faster than the average of other goods (later, when Geordie Buchanan became Chairman of the National Assistance Board, he asked me to come and explain all this to him and his officials, and I did, and he took the point and introduced a separate inflation index based on the spending-pattern of national assistance recipients); Dick Crossman wrote an options-paper asking 'English-speaking or European Union?' which contained the prescient sentence 'We cannot risk the Commonwealth for the sake of European unity'; Tommy Balogh explained the Schumann Plan; Stephen Swingler produced a list of 'Ten things to do now, and ten things to do next' as a summary of a projected pamphlet setting out a programme for Labour for 1950–55. In fact the Group never produced a pamphlet in that form, but I included much of the fruits of our discussions in a pamphlet, *The Second Five Years*, which I wrote for the research series of the Fabian Society. Amongst the policies advocated in it are eight measures which have been adopted, at one time or another, as Labour Party policy but which today, forty years after the pamphlet was published, including fourteen years in which Labour was in power, have still not been legislated.

The Group was radically changed, as was almost everything else in and around the Labour Party, when Aneurin Bevan, Harold Wilson and John Freeman resigned from the Government in 1951. Overnight we were transformed, not by ourselves but by the media, from the Keep Left Group to the Bevanites. The three ex-Ministers joined the group, and so did a number of other Members, bringing with them a substantial accretion of political expertise, practical experience and intellectual riches. In 1951 there were thirty-two of us, and by the following year that number had risen to forty-seven MPs and two peers.

We were a pretty talented company. Those forty-nine people included five ex-Ministers, two future Leaders of the Party, fourteen future Ministers, nine current or future members of the Party Executive and nine who were to become peers out of merit, not patronage. We had among us six distinguished writers, and nine members who were in the front rank of parliamentary orators and debaters.

Notwithstanding the shock-wave turbulence caused by the ministerial resignations, we continued through 1951 and most of 1952 the same sort of work we had been doing before – researching, writing and discussing policy papers. The Group was now big enough to set up separate committees for some of the main policy areas, and that increased our output. Some of the outstanding papers were: Barbara Castle (with acknowledgements to Ted Castle, Ellis Smith and Jo Richardson) on the reasons for the resignations; the indefatigable Dick Acland on living without dollar aid, on the purposes of the Colombo plan, and on colonial trade and marketing boards; Dudley Seers on marketing board policy; Tommy Balogh's paper and updating note on the Soviet situation; Dick Crossman's analysis of the problems which would be created by German rearmament; Fenner Brockway's reports on the Sudan and Uganda, which he had visited, and on his talk with Pandit Nehru about the American efforts to keep China out of the United Nations; and my own paper on industrial relations. Altogether we produced, and discussed at length, more than seventy papers.

Quite soon after the resignations we decided that we must project to the Party members throughout the country, and others as well, the reasoning behind our wide-ranging dissent from the policies and actions of the Party leadership. We arranged to publish a number of Tribune pamphlets. The first, *One Way Only*, sold 100,000 copies: it had an introduction by Nye, and he also contributed to it, to quote Michael Foot's biography of him, 'the enlargement of vision which gave it its element of surprise and its virtue'.

The pamphlet argued that the current problems of Britain and the world could best be tackled within the framework of socialist principles; but it also examined the myth that the Soviet Union was waiting eagerly for the moment when it would launch its military machine (whose strength was, as it still is, greatly exaggerated by vested interests on our side) westwards across Europe in order to take the whole continent in thrall, and that only the Bomb protected all of us living anywhere between the North Cape and Gibraltar and between the Bosphorus and the Atlantic from becoming helpless helots of a Soviet colonial system which one of the West's nuttier leaders was later to call the Evil Empire. To anyone who has seriously probed the minds of the leaders and thinkers in Moscow, this myth can be only an object of ridicule – not because the Soviet Government, any more than others, is at all finicky about how it pursues its national interests (in many ways its nationalistic attitudes and policies are not different from those of the Tsars), but for two hard practical reasons: (i) the Russians saw how the Nazis were finally broken not by the effort and cost of conquering territory but by the effort and cost of retaining it and by the effort and cost of holding down hostile populations; and (ii) they knew that they didn't have anything like enough actual or potential resources to sustain a successful invasion of the West. (Some twenty years later I chaired a Labour Party study group on defence, which included not only politicians but also high-level strategic experts. After two and a half years of meticulous research and analysis we produced a report called *Sense about Defence* in which we reached conclusions on the lack of Soviet will and capacity for an invasion of the West which fully supported the argument in *One Way Only*. It also established and measured the inverse correlation between a nation's defence expenditure and its economic health, that is, that the countries which spend the lowest proportion of their gross national product on arms have the highest productivity and the best export performance, and those which spend the highest proportion of their gross national product on arms have the lowest productivity and the worst export performance.)

121

We followed up *One Way Only* with *Going Our Way?*, and continued with a regular outflow of pamphlets, some of them, like the first two, expounding the general Bevanite case, and others dealing with specific aspects of policy. Geoffrey Bing's *John Bull's Other Ireland* was by far the best-seller of them all, with sales much bigger than even those of *One Way Only*, many of them in the Republic of Ireland; Woodrow Wyatt contributed a carefully observant study of Israel in *The Jews at Home*; and I wrote a somewhat lighthearted but nevertheless meaningful critique, called *It's a Mug's Game*, of the report of a Royal Commission on Betting and Gaming: if everybody had read it and accepted its argument, the proprietors of William Hill, Ladbroke's, Coral, Mecca *et al.* would now be queueing at the job centres.

*Going our Way?* contained a passage which brought down on our heads the raging wrath – nay, the jovian thunderbolts – of the right-wing trade-union leaders, especially the Big Three (I used to call them the Trinity), who were Arthur Deakin of the Transport and General, Will Lawther of the Mineworkers and Tom Williamson of the General and Municipal.

In spite of their common purpose and their political alliance these were three very different men. Deakin was the poor man's Ernest Bevin, with the same tendency to gut reactions, the same ruthlessness in crushing opposition, but without the least scintilla of Bevin's intelligence or skills. (At one Conference I made a reference to him which he didn't like, and he reacted in two ways: first by entrusting one of his – no, his union's – officers to investigate my professional and private life to see if he could dig up any dirt, and then by refusing to vote against a Tory councillor in his ward because the Labour candidate was my brother Norman.)

Will Lawther was another bull-at-a-gate. I always reckoned that his extreme rightwingism was an overcompensation for the foibles of his youth, when he was on the edge of, if not actually within, the communists. (It's noteworthy that many communists who become ex-communists move to the right very fast: my Israeli friend, Eppi Evron, whom I mentioned a little while back, and who knew Denis Healey well, believed that when Denis was making one of his bullying attacks on the Left he was subconsciously living down his early devotion to communism.)

Tom Williamson was a very different type from the other two. He was a quiet and somewhat negative man, whose political attitudes derived not from passion but from Pavlov-dog subservience to the Party leaders. He had all the appearance and manner not of a crusader but of an *apparatchik*: I could easily envisage him as the local commissar running the *Agitprop* office of District Five in Moscow.

These three had decided between themselves some time earlier that they wanted Hugh Gaitskell to succeed Attlee as leader of the Labour Party. A somewhat incongruous alliance developed between these horny-handed sons of toil and the delicately-nurtured political aristos of the Hampstead Set who surrounded Gaitskell.

Not surprisingly the anti-Labour newspapers gave powerful support to this alliance by running a continuous campaign of vilification of Nye Bevan. It is the most heartfelt permanent wish of these Tory pundits that the Labour Party should fail and be swept away, but that doesn't stop them from telling us, brazenly, what's good for our Party and whom we should choose to lead it. They are to be trusted as far as you would trust the medicine prescribed by a doctor for a patient he's seeking to kill. They're always ready to disparage any leader of the Labour Party – except when he is attacking and disciplining the Party's left wing, and then they make a hero of him.

It is, of course, limpidly clear why the Fleet Street-Wapping mafia should engage in this machiavellian exercise against the Labour Party, and it's not at all surprising that all the anti-Labour readers of their papers should revel in it. But what I've never managed to understand is why some members of the Labour Party fall for it and swallow it whole. In many of the meetings of Party members I've addressed over the years I've heard one or two of them criticise Stafford Cripps or Nye Bevan or Jack Jones or Hugh Scanlon or Michael Foot or Tony Benn or Ron Todd in terms of a 'loony-left' quotation from the *Daily Mail* or the *Daily Express* or the *Sun*, and have wondered why a man should take a sword from his enemy's hand to slay his brother. Members of a democratic and progressive party should never forget that often the heresy of one generation becomes the orthodoxy of the next.

Through 1951 both the parties to the Trinity-Hampstead compact became increasingly worried by the meteoric advance of Bevanism amongst the Party membership throughout the country. The sails of that advance were filled by two breezes: one was our widely-read pamphlets, and the other our widely-attended Tribune brains trusts.

Those brains-trust meetings were a runaway success, drawing much bigger audiences than any of the Party's leaders could command. We tried one as a fringe meeting at a Party Conference without the least idea of its being more than a one-off. That meeting went so well that we were flooded with requests for similar meetings from constituency parties and other Labour organisations all over the country. Within a very short time the venture had taken off spectacularly and we were topping the charts.

The formula was of course plagiarised from the original BBC Brains Trust: one questionmaster and four question-answerers. I was generally the questionmaster, and for each of our teams of four we could draw on a pool of top-level and varied talents. The most regular participants included six (Dick Acland, Dick Crossman, Jennie Lee, Stephen Swingler, Tom Williams, Harold Wilson) who were natural teachers; three (Geoffrey Bing, Leslie Hale, Julius Silverman) who were skilled advocates; six (Fenner Brockway, Barbara Castle, Tom Driberg, Michael Foot, Bill Mallalieu, Konni Zilliacus) who had the gift of words not merely to educate and convince but also to inspire; and five (John Baird, Hugh Delargy, Gavin Faringdon, Will Griffiths, Marcus Lipton) who had a very different but valuable gift, the capacity to clarify an argument with a folk tale or a homely example or a flash of wit. But the star of the show whenever he appeared, the one who always brought the house down, was Harold Davies. It wasn't for what he said – he never finished any sentence he started, he often lost the thread of his argument, his quotations were generally inaccurate – but no audience could resist his ever-twinkling eye, his infectious laugh and the rippling torrent of his colourful phraseology that carried an echo of his homeland in the Welsh valleys.

People flocked to hear us: every hall we appeared in, even the largest, was full to overflowing. I particularly remember one Friday evening when we had a date in Worthing, scarcely the most fertile soil for the seeds of socialism. It was high summer and the sun was still bright and hot – a natural evening for the sea-front rather than an indoor meeting – but we still had over nine hundred in our audience. And I remember, too, turning up with some of my team at the Co-operative Hall in Oldham one Sunday afternoon and finding a crowd milling round on the pavement, and people offering money for any spare tickets like it was Wembley Stadium on Cup Final day.

That meeting in Oldham turned out to be the apotheosis of Harold Davies as our all-time undisputed star. Some of us had done a meeting on the previous evening in Pudsey, and we stayed overnight in Leeds. In the morning Leslie Hale, Will Griffiths and I set off to drive over the Pennines, and we stopped on the way for an elongated and largely liquid lunch, so that when we arrived in Leslie's constituency in

Awaiting the General Election, 1945,
with Mary and daughters Ruth (*right*) and Judy.

Mikardo there, a *Tallien* contumacious,
Denounces Labour's truce with Capital,

From *Let Cowards Flinch* by Sagittarius, illustrated by Vicky (1947).

May Day Rally in Reading, 1952.
*Left to right:* Harold Wilson, me, Bill Davidson, Bert Oram,
Bryn Roberts and Harry Grierson.

Outside the House of Commons, 1987.

With Natan (Anatoly) Scharansky, 1987.

Launching an anti-racist campaign, 1987.

Oldham we were a bit out of training. There we were joined by two colleagues who were in much better shape: Harold, who had come from lecturing at a weekend school in Wortley Hall, and Tom Williams, who had come from lay-preaching in North Lancashire. The hall was crowded: we entered the platform to a great cheer, and Leslie's eyelids dropped shut as soon as his bottom hit his chair. After the introductions I turned to Harold for the first answer to the first question, and he let loose a lovely verbal torrent culminating in a Lloyd-George-type peroration leading up to 'And I end by quoting a solemn thought of Lowell Thomas,' and he did. There was a roar of applause, which woke Leslie Hale: he opened one eye and said, 'I have nothing to add to Harold's answer to that question, except to quote correctly the couplet from Lowell Thomas which he quoted incorrectly,' and he did, and reshut the eye.

Half an hour later Harold was off again, and this time his storming peroration ended with a quotation from St Mark. When the applause had died down, the ever-gentle ever-diffident Tom Williams said quietly, 'I hope I may be forgiven for pointing out that the passage which Harold has just quoted from St Mark is in fact verses 28 and 29 of the sixth chapter of the gospel according to St Matthew.' The audience loved it.

But of course there was much more to the brains-trust meetings than those occasional flashes of light relief. What brought people flocking to us was the opportunity to hear a political case spelt out clearly and unequivocally, on its merits and without stereotyping innuendoes at the expense of those who took a different view from ours, by contrast with the regular practice of the Right of evading debate with us by just writing us off, as in Gaitskell's notorious Stalybridge speech (which I believe lost us the 1955 general election), as a bunch of crypto-communists. Our audiences were intrigued when, as happened quite often, members of our panel would disagree with one another and argue out their differences on the platform, so pungently as to provoke thought but so equably as to encourage comradely tolerance. Above all, they queued and paid to get in to hear us because they believed what we believed and they got from us the evidence to confirm and reinforce that belief.

This surge of popular support for the Bevanites inflicted sleepless nights on the members of the Trinity-Hampstead axis. The big trade-union bosses were well aware that many of the people who thronged our meetings were their own members doing some thinking for themselves instead of obediently following the line laid down for them by their general secretaries, and they rightly saw this deviation as a threat to, or at least a questioning of, their personal authority. At one meeting of the National Executive, at the height of the attempted excommunication of Bevan and his followers, one of the Lesser Brethren of the Trinity, Harry Douglass of the Steelworkers, proposed that the NEC should formally prohibit the continuation of the Tribune Brains Trusts. In the short discussion on this monstrous proposal I produced and read out aloud the text of a report which might appear in the following morning's newspapers if a ban were imposed: it was headlined 'Tribune Brains Trusts Banned – Labour Leaders Condemn Public Meetings as a Grave Threat to Democracy'. A few of the people round the table laughed, some a little nervously; one or two (but not Mr Douglass) had the grace to look a bit shamefaced; and we proceeded to the next unpleasant item on the agenda.

The other manifestation of the growing popularity of Bevanism was the success of our candidates in the annual election of the Party's National Executive Committee.

Of the then twenty-seven (now twenty-nine) seats in that Committee, only seven were elected by the Conference delegates of the Constituency Labour Parties (CLP); of the rest twelve were actually elected and six more virtually elected by the trade union delegates. The only electoral sector in which the Left could hope to win seats was the CLP sector, and since the trade union leaders had a permanent built-in two-thirds majority on the Executive there was no reason for them to fear that their political power-base would be threatened by our winning some, or even all, of the seven seats in the constituency section. But there was more to it than simple arithmetic: the seven constituency places were the prestige sector because they provided NEC seats for the Ministers and ex-Ministers who constituted the leadership of the Parliamentary Party and who were the Party's household names.

For some years the Right had resented the fact that Aneurin regularly topped the poll in the constituency section, and their resentment overflowed in a torrent of rage when Barbara Castle and I were elected in that section in place of two of the Old Guard.

In my own election I took the place of Emmanuel Shinwell, who had been an NEC member for many years. Immediately that result was announced to Conference, Manny walked out of the hall and up the path to the Grand Hotel, collected his wife Flora and his baggage, and caught the next train to London. Until then Flora and my Mary

126

had been regular Conference companions, but from that moment Flora never spoke to Mary again. Manny, by contrast, resumed some sort of diplomatic relations with me not long after; but more than thirty years had to pass before, at a party at Toynbee Hall in Aldgate to celebrate his hundredth birthday by putting up a plaque on the site of his Spitalfields birthplace, he was ready to tell me that I was fully restored to a place in his good books.

On the very evening of the day that Barbara and I won our NEC seats, the Trinity convened a meeting in a Scarborough hotel to discuss how to deal with the nuisance of these upstart Bevanites. Nothing was further from their minds than the idea of dealing with us by entering into a debate about the merits of the policies we were advocating: they were concerned not to controvert our views but to suppress them, not to use argument to defeat us but to use disciplinary measures to silence us.

During the following twelve months they stoked their anger into an ever hotter blaze, and at the next Conference, Morecambe 1952, it burst out into a shattering explosion. Deakin set the tone by telling the constituency delegates that what they thought and said didn't matter because he paid the piper and would call the tune. Will Lawther's message to those constituency delegates was equally comradely but even more succinct: 'Shut yer gob,' he shouted at them. To cap it all, Harold Wilson and Dick Crossman were elected to the NEC, knocking off two of the most powerful figures of the Party hierarchy, Herbert Morrison and Hugh Dalton. The Bevanites now held six of the seven constituency seats: the only surviving representative of the Old Guard was Jim Griffiths, a kindly well-meaning former Welsh miner who obscured his indecision and ineffectiveness in a cloud of generalised moral-uplift rhetoric: someone once said of him, cruelly but with some justification, that he spoke not just with his hand on his heart but with both hands on both hearts.

Hugh Gaitskell and his friends, and not least Hugh Dalton, believed that the Wilson-Crossman defeat of Morrison-Dalton was the result of a secret campaign around the Constituency Parties which I had engineered, alone and unaided. In fact I hadn't done anything of the sort, not because I wouldn't have liked to, but because I didn't have anything like the time and resources which such a campaign would have demanded.

Hugh Dalton was a strange mixture – on the one hand a man of great talent and on the other a large stentorian-voiced Barnum-type showman: I don't remember who it was who once said, 'I walked into the room, and there was Hugh Dalton, his eyes blazing with insincerity.' Even before the 1952 trauma he actively disliked me, perhaps because he saw me as the diametric opposite of the Old Etonian that he was, perhaps because I wasn't, and didn't want to be, one of the coterie of young men whom he gathered around him to sit at his feet and hang on his words of wisdom and in return receive the benison of his patronage. His defeat at Morecambe turned his dislike of me into the most intense hatred, to the extent that ever afterwards he referred to me in gutter language that he never used about anyone else.

[*Digression*. There are two nonpolitical sidelights which are the only things that happened in that agonising Morecambe week that I can look back on at all pleasurably. My brother Sidney has reminded me – I had forgotten – that one evening between the end of Conference and dinner, in the billiard room in the basement of the Conference hotel, we played a doubles frame of snooker, he and Nye Bevan against Michael Foot and me. His recollection is that Nye was the best player of the four, but only the best of a very bad bunch.

The other sidelight is that it was at Morecambe that I began my career as an amateur bookmaker on political events. During the initial weekend and the run-up to the NEC election there was intense discussion amongst the delegates, and not least amongst the MPs, about how those elections would work out. I was in a drinking circle at a bar on the Saturday evening, and someone said he thought the Bevanites would win all seven of the constituency seats. I offered to bet him ten bob that he was wrong, and some of the others began to offer bets, and then the barman, a highly interested eavesdropper, leaned over towards me and said, 'Why don't you make a book on it?' On impulse I picked up the price-list which was on the bar, and on the back of it I wrote what in the bookies' trade is called the tissue, that is the opening list of prices (so called because it was originally written on tissue-paper), and immediately booked half-a-dozen bets, and took many more over the rest of the weekend.

Thereafter I regularly made a book on all sorts of elections – parliamentary general and by-elections, NEC, party leaders (both Labour and Tory), Shadow Cabinet, United States Presidents, the Common Market referendum, and other political happenings. My clientèle was made up of a score or two of MPs of all parties, parliamentary journalists and personal friends: I kept the stakes low, totted up at each

128

Party Conference my winnings since the previous one (you can't win much when there's no facility for laying off), and put the proceeds into the collection at the *Tribune* conference rally. Over the years they varied from a few pounds to a record £74: the exception was the year of the election of President Kennedy, when I failed to balance the book, and lost some money, and my contribution to the *Tribune* collection had to be made from the proceeds of honest toil.]

The acid bitterness of Morecambe spilled over into the proceedings of the Party Executive. It so happened that in those years we had on the Executive a number of people who were dedicated haters in the gold-medal class. All of them except one were women – Alice Horan, Jean Mann, Alice Bacon, Bessie Braddock and the undisputed world heavyweight champion hater Edith Summerskill. The only male fit to take the ring with those amazons was Jim Matthews, an NUGMW official: it was he who persuaded the Executive to reinterpret the buggins'-turn rule for choosing the Party chairman in such a way as to keep me out of the chair when my turn came. But in due course 'the whirligig of time brings in his revenges': when, some years later, my turn came round a second time I became the only member of the Party who has chaired three successive conferences, and I felt a wee twinge of conscience for the agony which poor Jim Matthews would have suffered from this dénouement. Hugh Gaitskell often looked and sounded like a hater, particularly of Nye Bevan, but I always felt that his hatred was not pristine but was second-hand, that he was egged into it by some of the people round him – 'his lunatic advisers', as Dick Crossman called them. One of those acolytes, Tony Crosland, still hadn't cooled off more than ten years later: the Board of Trade, in the period when he was its President, was setting up advisory bodies on exporting to Eastern Europe, his officials put up a list of proposed members, and my name was on it. Tony instantly and unhesitatingly struck it out: even on a functional body of business experts, he told his Minister of State, he wasn't going to have any bloody left-wingers.

During that period – virtually the whole of the 1950s – the morning of the fourth Wednesday of every month, when the Party NEC met, provided us Bevanites with a short cine-trailer of the horrors of Hades. The Right used their majority as a cudgel to beat us over the head, a cudgel studded with spikes of venom. They were never interested in arguing with us, only in voting us down: in every discussion one of them would move at the earliest practicable moment that the question be now put, and the monolithic majority would faithfully raise their hands. That's why NEC meetings were much shorter then than they have been since.

Tom Driberg used to come from those meetings washed out like a dish-rag: it's their *vulgarity*, he used to say in italics, which is the one thing I can't stand. Dick Crossman records that at the end of one particularly vile session, 'Nye and I went across to the House to have lunch, with our entrails acid with anger. These meetings do really turn your stomach.' I didn't myself get as worked up as that, perhaps because I was more phlegmatic or less sensitive than some of my comrades, or perhaps because I estimated – correctly, as it turned out – that what we were going through was a phase that would pass, and therefore I could feel philosophic about it.

What we didn't know at the time was that our leaders were using the National Agent's Department in Transport House and the Regional Organisers out in the country to compile MI5-type dossiers on us, and on some of our supporters in the constituencies, as a basis for taking disciplinary action against us, including expulsions, whenever they would feel ready for it. The department of the Party machine whose function was to organise a lot of members into the Party was being diverted, instead, to organising a few members *out* of the Party.

It was by the sheerest accident that I discovered this le Carré-type apparatus of espionage. At the beginning of every general election campaign the National Executive and its standing committees go into suspense to make way for the election organisation, but some fall-back arrangement has to be made to provide NEC endorsement of any candidates who may be adopted at the last minute. At the beginning of the 1955 campaign it was known that there were likely to be such candidates, and the Executive chose three of its members, of whom I was one, to act on its behalf in respect of endorsements.

We three met, together with Sara Barker, the National Agent, to look at some late-selected candidates. Sara immediately proposed that we should reject Konni Zilliacus, who had been selected for Manchester Gorton, and Ernie Roberts, who had been selected for Stockport South. I asked why. For reply Sara began leafing through two files which she had on the table in front of her, and read some passages from them, most of them consisting of criticisms which Konni and Ernie had made of some of the policies and actions of certain of our leaders.

I reached across the table and said to Sara, 'Give me those files,

I want to have a look at them.'

'Oh no,' she said, 'you can't do that – they're private.'

I exploded. 'Don't be daft,' I said vehemently. 'Those files are not your personal property, they're the property of the Party.' And I grabbed them and went through them.

They were an eye-opener. No MI5, no Special Branch, no George Smiley could have compiled more comprehensive dossiers. Not just press-cuttings, photographs and document-references but also notes by watchers and eavesdroppers, and all sorts of tittle-tattle. I'm convinced that there was some input into them from government sources and from at least a couple of Labour Attachés at the United States Embassy who were close to some of our trade-union leaders, notably Sam Watson.

I turned to my two colleagues and said: 'I move that the candidatures of Zilliacus and Roberts be endorsed. I must tell you that if I am voted down I shall walk out of here and announce publicly that I am resigning from the Executive as a protest against my friends, and doubtless myself as well, being spied on as though we were criminals, and that will make a great story to start our election campaign.' My motion was carried unanimously.

Sara Barker never forgave me. Konni won at Gorton, but Ernie lost at Stockport South and had to wait a long time to get into the House. Some years later Ron Hayward became National Agent, and the first thing he did on taking office was to tip out all Sara's secret-service dossiers and make a bonfire of them.

But they were all still in place, and being steadily added to, in the years after Morecambe when Hugh Gaitskell and his friends worked towards throwing Nye and some of his supporters out of the Party.

The crucial NEC meeting at which Gaitskell brought on the executioner's block and raised his axe above Nye's neck was in March 1955. How I almost missed that meeting but finally came to be present at it and to cast what proved to be a crucial vote is an involved story with a little element of romance in it.

In the early part of March 1955 I went to Pakistan on an assignment for one of my client companies which proved to be more complex and therefore more time-taking than either they or I had anticipated. I wasn't particularly worried about the delay, because I had cleared my diary for a couple of weeks, and was even prepared if need be to miss the NEC meeting due on the 23rd because it didn't appear that anything important or specially interesting was likely to come

131

up for discussion. So I went unhurriedly about my business in Karachi, and filled in the leisure interests with watching some good cricket, experimenting pleasurably among the variegated riches of Asian cuisine, looking up my trade-union brothers in the British Overseas Airways spares-and-service base on Karachi airport, and spending a couple of moderately profitable days at the races.

It was only after I left London that Gaitskell started the process which was planned to culminate in a motion to expel Bevan at the March NEC. If all this had been happening at the present time I'd have heard it in Karachi almost as soon as in London, through International STD or the newspapers or the BBC World Service; but thirty-odd years ago long-distance communication wasn't that easy or reliable: the London newspapers turned up late or not at all, the local paper, *Dawn*, wasn't highly informative, and both radio reception and the telephone were unpredictably intermittent and inaudible. If it were not for a totally nonpolitical decision made halfway between Britain and Pakistan I'd have gone on sitting in blissful ignorance in Karachi while my friend Nye was hounded out of the Party in my absence.

The totally nonpolitical decision which got me to leave Karachi quickly was made by my elder daughter, Ruth: she decided, just on impulse, to get married the following week. She had emigrated to Israel a year or two earlier, and was a member of a *kibbutz* called Gaash which had been founded by socialist immigrants from Argentina and Brazil. On Thursday 17 March I got back to my hotel in Karachi to find a cable from Mary: 'Ruth getting married next Tuesday,' she wrote. 'Judy [our other daughter] and I flying out tomorrow: get there as soon as you can.'

It wasn't easy. The only route to Tel Aviv was via Cairo and Nicosia. I had to go to our consulate in Karachi to get a second passport, because I wouldn't get into Egypt on a passport with Israeli stamps in it. My smallpox certificate had run out of time, and I had to find a doctor who would not only give me a vaccination but also (for an appropriate consideration) antedate it so that it would appear to be valid on my arrival in Cairo.

I got through the obstacle-course successfully, and arrived at Israel's international airport on the Sunday afternoon, to be met by Ruth and Arie, her husband-to-be, and another couple of Gaash members called Joseph and Naima who were joining Ruth and Arie in a double wedding.

132

'We've all just come from the registry,' Ruth said. 'We went there to bring forward the wedding from Tuesday to tomorrow.'

'Why?' I asked. 'What's the rush?'

Ruth was surprised by the question: she didn't know how out of touch I was. 'The rush,' she said, all in one breath, 'is because there's a meeting of your Party NEC on Wednesday morning, and there's going to be a motion to expel Nye, and there's been some counting of heads, and it looks a close-run thing, and so you've got to be there, so I've booked a flight for you on Tuesday, and so we'll be married tomorrow.'

And so they were, the four of them, in a garden in the cool of the evening after the *kibbutzniks* had finished their day's work, under the boughs of an orange tree instead of the traditional canopy, and with the redolence of blossom to bless them; and we all went back to the *kibbutz* dining hall, and sang and danced into the small hours, and got high on orange juice and happiness.

When I walked into the board room in Transport House on the Wednesday morning, my friends welcomed me in gratified surprise: the heads had been counted on the assumption that I would be absent, and one more on our side was an uncovenanted bonus. I had another and very different welcome as well: Edith Summerskill, who was in the chair, fixed on me a baleful stare like she was Medusa the Gorgon and I would be instantly turned into stone.

Attlee's amendment which killed off the expulsion motion was carried by fourteen votes to thirteen. If I hadn't got back in time the vote would have been tied, and of course Edith would have used her casting vote for the expulsion. So Ruth's prescience and the change of her wedding-day were fully vindicated.

Edith couldn't contain the venom of her defeat. When, in a discussion of a different subject later in the meeting, I put up my hand she couldn't bear to let my name cross her lips and called me to speak as 'the man over there in the brown suit'. That evoked the only laughter of the morning, and it relieved the tension for a moment or two. From that day on I unfailingly wore a brown suit to every meeting that Edith was to chair.

# Chapter 10

NOT LEAST among the pleasures and advantages of being a Member of Parliament is the enhanced opportunity it provides for meaningful and enlightening contacts with people from other lands. I was never one of those Members who seize every opportunity of 'swanning' travel for its own sightseeing sake: I never sought to get into the established circle of regular globetrotters under the auspices of the Interparliamentary Union and the Commonwealth Parliamentary Association and travel scholarships and sponsored lecture-tours. I was never prepared to face the brassy artificiality of riding in aeroplanes and living in hotels unless there was some political point and purpose in the trip or some political education to be got out of it. Even when I was a member of the Trade and Industry Select Committee in the 1979 Parliament and of the Foreign Affairs Select Committee in the 1983 Parliament, I opted out of some trips which I thought didn't promise enough serious content to justify the time, effort and discomfort they demanded.

But over the years, choosing carefully which invitations to accept and which to decline, I had some trips abroad in which I made important contacts and a few lasting friends, and had some interesting and instructive experiences. One of them provided the sharpest moment of drama of my whole life, a flash of revelation which still lives with me vividly.

It was September 1954. The Polish Committee for Friendship with Foreign Countries – that was the standard instrument used by all the communist countries as a front organisation for their foreign ministries – invited a group of Labour parliamentarians to make a working visit to Poland. The group was a very mixed one: it was led jointly by two peers, Viscount Stansgate and Lord Silkin, and included George Brown, Roy Mason, Hugh Delargy, Desmond Donnelly and me.

Before we set off we had a session at the Polish Embassy to arrange our programme. It consisted of things we were all to do together – talks with Ministers and party leaders (not always the same people) and trade-union leaders; Auschwitz; the Ghetto Memorial; co-operative and private farms; Chopin's birthplace; the miraculously reconstructed Old City of Warsaw; a few factories. In addition each of us was asked whether he had any special aspect of Polish life he'd like to look at: ex-miner Roy Mason wanted to see a coal-mine and talk to the miners; Hugh Delargy, more in hope than expectation, asked to meet Cardinal Wyszynski, who was in prison (and of course Hugh's hope went unfulfilled); and I said I'd like to meet what was left of the Jewish community. I also arranged to slip away from the delegation for twenty-four hours because I had a commitment in Budapest to put the finishing touches to an export contract I'd been negotiating for one of my client companies.

We arrived in Warsaw on a Saturday evening, to be greeted at the airport by our Polish hosts and by the British Ambassador and one of his officers. The Ambassador, Sir Andrew Noble, was an archetypal Edwardian diplomat ('How come,' I asked, 'he doesn't sport a monocle?'). He told us in a confidential whisper that he had arranged for us all to go to the Embassy on Monday morning so he could brief us on what was really happening in Poland before our hosts could get at us and brainwash us. On the Saturday evening Hugh Delargy and I went for a walk into the town centre, and quite near our hotel we came across a large church with the doors wide open and the sounds of an organ and of prayer coming out of them. We walked in and stood at the back, behind the last pews. I was amazed to see groups of two or three young men, dressed in their weekend best and groomed for a night out, coming into the church, dropping down on their knees, crossing themselves and saying a prayer before they walked out towards their Saturday evening's quest for a few beers and some fun and a girl. Hugh said, presciently, 'If you look at that you can see why the communists in this country are always going to be hard put to counteract the influence of the church.'

We spent the Sunday in the country, listening to music in the garden of Chopin's birthplace, meeting some highly private-enterprise farmers and visiting a writers' and artists' colony. The next morning the cars duly picked us up and we were taken to the Embassy for our briefing.

The briefing was almost completely empty. The Ambassador treated us to a long monologue whose character was polemic rather than instructive. His main theme was that the acute shortages of some consumer goods, which we ourselves had noticed in the forty hours we had been there, wasn't the result of overriding economic conditions or of mismanagement but was created deliberately by the Government (that was exactly what the Housewives' League had said about our postwar Labour Government). When one of us asked what the Polish Government could hope to gain by unnecessarily depriving people of some basic necessities, he flapped around like a bird with a broken wing, and I noticed a couple of his officers shuffling uncomfortably in their chairs. 'The worst thing,' he said, 'is razor blades. We all get nagged to death by our Polish servants for a few razor blades.' It was obviously a refrain he liked the sound of, because twice he did a *da capo* and so we heard it three times in all.

We left the Embassy in warm sunshine. We had no commitment till the afternoon, so Hugh Delargy and I decided to walk the two or three kilometres back to our incongruously-named Bristol Orbis Hotel while the others went by car. We'd gone only a few strides when Hugh remarked that he couldn't understand the bit about the shortage of razor blades because on the counter of the kiosk in the foyer of our hotel there was a tray full of packets of razor blades and presumably anybody could walk in and buy them.

As we wandered along the wide boulevard we came to a row of shops, and one of them was called Apoteka, which of course is a pharmacist in a lot of languages (including our own 'apothecary'). We went in and found that the chemist spoke German, and we asked him if he had any razor blades. Yes, he said, but only three brands – one made in Poland, one imported from the Soviet Union and the third imported from Israel.

We bought a packet of the Israeli blades and went on our way. A bit further on there was a timber kiosk on a street corner selling newspapers and magazines and cigarettes and sweets and odds and ends, including the same three brands of razor blades, so this time we bought a packet of the Polish blades. By the time we got to our hotel we had acquired six packets of razor blades, two of each of the three kinds, so we made a parcel of them addressed to His Excellency the Ambassador with a note to thank him for his briefing, and

136

to express the hope that this little present would help to defend him against the strident importunings of his Polish servants. We saw him only once more, on the eve of our return to London when he threw a farewell party for us: it said a lot about him that almost all the guests were people from other western embassies and fewer than half a dozen of them were Poles. He forgot to thank us for our present (maybe one of his deputies had kept it from him): my abiding memory of that party is of Hugh Delargy, who had been educated in a Catholic seminary in France, conversing animatedly with a Polish bishop in the only language they had in common, which was Latin. I listened in for a while, but my own Latin was too rusty to keep up with them.

That trip wasn't an altogether pleasant experience – somehow the delegation didn't jell. Most of the time George Brown was in a filthy temper, perhaps because he'd been horribly airsick through the whole of our flight from London or maybe merely because he was George Brown. He made an ass of himself, and didn't endear himself to his colleagues, by telling our Polish hosts that he and Roy Mason were the only two proletarians in the delegation and all the rest of us were middle-class types who couldn't be of interest to them.

I was relieved and happy to get away from all that for my quick trip to Hungary, so much so that I deliberately missed my return flight and had a couple of extra days in Budapest, seeing a superb open-air *Swan Lake* and quaffing a lot of *Soproni Kekfrankos* (which I reckon to be one of Europe's great wines, much superior to the better known *Egri Bikaver* or Bull's Blood) and making a pig of myself over the paprika fish soup in Matthew's Cellar. When I finally got back to Warsaw I was met at the airport by one of our guide/interpreter/minders, a woman whom none of us liked because she was totally unsmiling and rigidly stalinist: we suspected she was a secret-police informer assigned to write a daily report on us. She told me that the rest of the delegation were in Cracow and would be back that afternoon, and that arrangements had been made for me to spend the morning with representatives of the Jewish community.

She took me first to the synagogue to meet the Chief Rabbi and the elders of the congregation, and then on to a meeting with the leaders of the Jewish lay organisation, which was pivoted on a Yiddish-language publishing-house. (The very much larger Catholic lay organisation, Pax, was similarly based on their publishing-house.) I was met at the door of their community house, an impressive multistorey building, by the eighteen members of their central committee who conducted me on a tour of the premises: they spoke in Polish and I in English and the stalinist minder did the interpreting. In the basement I saw a substantial library and some very valuable archive material. The publishing centre produced a four-times-a-week newspaper, which was no more than an abbreviated Yiddish translation of the official Party organ *Trybunu Ludu*, plus a few original works in prose and verse, some very good translations from English, French, German and Russian literature, and some anti-American propaganda pamphlets which were obviously self-defeating because they were too abjectly crude to impress even the most credulous reader. Then I was taken to the upper floors of the building to be shown a truly splendid and moving exhibition marking the tenth anniversary of the Ghetto Uprising, with exhibits arranged round the walls of seven rooms. We went through six of them, and I was fascinated by what I saw, and then the chairman said time was getting short and we'd miss the seventh room and go downstairs for a talk.

We sat round the boardroom table, the chairman at the end, the interpreter next to him and I next to her. There was a rapid two-way question-and-answer session. I asked them why they had reversed at the last minute an intention to send a delegation, for the first time, to the World Jewish Congress. Was it because of any political restriction? They said no, it was only because of technical reasons. They told me that very large numbers of their community had, with government permission, emigrated to Israel, but many of them were now sending letters desperately wanting to come back.

I was in the middle of putting a supplementary question when a man sitting opposite me said to his neighbour in a stage-whisper in Yiddish, 'This Englishman is by no means a gullible fool.' I stopped in mid-sentence, leaned across to him, and asked in a loud voice, also in Yiddish, 'And what made you think this Englishman would be a gullible fool?'

The effect of this intervention was electric. A great roar of laughter broke out all around the table and suddenly it was cut off in a moment into a deep and eloquent silence as tense as anything in any dramatic work from Aristophanes to Shakespeare: they were overwhelmed by the sudden realisation that we had a means of direct communication without going through the interpreter, whom they obviously trusted no more than I did. They were like caged birds suddenly finding the door of the cage open, so that they could stretch their wings and fly out into the fresh air and sunshine.

138

The rest of the meeting was conducted in Yiddish, with the interpreter red-faced from frustration because she was the only person in the room who didn't know what was going on.

We went back over some of our earlier exchanges but with very much of a difference. The 'technical reasons' for their withdrawal from the convention of the World Jewish Congress was that the passports issued as exit permits to the members of the delegation had been withdrawn at the last minute. It was true that many of the Polish Jews who had emigrated to Israel were asking to come back, but that was only because their wives and children weren't being allowed out to join them.

I got back to the hotel, downed a couple of shots of Zubrovka (the superb Polish vodka with a sprig of bison grass in each bottle), had a bite of lunch and looked forward to a siesta. But I didn't get it because I had phone calls during the afternoon from three of those committee members who wanted to talk to me privately, but not at the hotel. So I went out and met them on a street corner. Then we took a walk along the river bank, and this time I got a briefing which really was a briefing.

One of the three took me back to the community house to see the seventh room of the Ghetto Uprising exhibition which we had missed in the morning, and I understood why we had missed it. It was dominated by a blown-up mural captioned 'the fascist Chaim Weizmann presenting a *Sefer Torah* (a ritual Hebrew scroll of the Pentateuch) to the fascist Harry Truman.'

I never expected to see any of those men again, but in 1986 I went to Oxford to hear a lecture in Yiddish by the distinguished Jewish historian S.S. Levenberg, and in the audience there was a member of that committee who greeted me, after thirty-two years, like a long-lost brother.

My first visit to South-east Asia was also as a member of a Labour Party delegation, this time invited by the government set up in Hanoi after the decisive Vietnamese victory at Dien Bien Phu in 1954 and the consequent expulsion of the French colonial government. The delegation consisted of five MPs – Lena (later Lady) Jeger, John Baird, Harold (later Lord) Davies, Bill Warbey and me – with Betty Boothroyd (later to become an MP and a deputy Speaker) as the delegation's secretary.

We flew to Peking via Moscow, and from there we had a thirty-six-hour train journey to Hanoi, changing to a narrower-gauge railway on the China-Vietnam border. We whiled away the journey in different ways: the two girls chatting and writing up some notes; Bill Warbey, the solemn old owl, earnestly reading a lot of tracts we'd been given in Peking; and the more frivolous Baird, Davies and Mikardo playing a three-handed variant of cribbage for rapidly escalating stakes. By the time we reached Hanoi I had an IOU from John for a little over three million pounds and one from Harold for over four million, and when we got back to London they were commuted into a pint of bitter each.

When we got to Hanoi we were told that the only hotel left in the city was occupied by the officers of the Tripartite Commission (India, Canada, Poland), and so we were housed in two lakeside villas which had belonged to the French Governor-General and his deputy. That wasn't as nice as it sounds because lakeside is where the mosquitoes are at their most prolific; but at least we had the consolation that the spacious cellars bulged with a priceless stock of superb French wines and brandies. (There was no Scotch, but Betty Boothroyd filled that gap by beaming her very attractive smile on a couple of young Canadian officers.)

We went to the May Day march, which began at seven in the morning so that it could be got through before the heat of the day made marching virtually impossible. But no amount of heat was going to stop the football-match that followed the march: the opposing teams were the postal workers of Hanoi and the port workers of Haiphong, playing in bare feet on grassless baked earth. I dripped with perspiration just watching them.

There was something fresh to see, something fresh to learn, something fresh to think about in almost every hour of our travels through Vietnam; but the most precious couple of hours were those we spent early one morning with Ho Chi Minh in his garden. He was an enthusiastic and expert gardener, and when he showed us round he gave us a mini-lecture on each of the rarer varieties he was growing. Then we sat down to breakfast on a lawn between his flaming flower-beds, and he beguiled us with an account of the time he had spent in London as a youth, working as a commis-waiter in a West End hotel, an account reminiscent of George Orwell's *Down and Out in Paris and London*. Then he went on to describe for us, with crowd-scenes as vivid as in a David Lean film, the herculean effort by which his people had defeated the French, hiding from the bombers by day and crossing mountains by night, dragging heavy arms and ammunition on bicycles up and down the steep slopes. (Ere long they were to outdo that feat of defeating a Great Power by defeating a Superpower.)

I was also a member of the first British parliamentary delegation to China, this time an all-Party delegation. On our way out we stopped overnight in Moscow, and over dinner we decided not to elect a leader, but instead that each of us would be the leader for a day at a time, rotating in alphabetical order.

That was before the days of jet-engined aircraft, in that part of the world at any rate, and we flew from Moscow in a little Ilyushin 14, managing three hours or so in the air between landings at Sverdlovsk, Omsk, Tomsk, Krasnoyarsk, Irkutsk, Ulan Bator and Peking. I particularly remember the stop at Ulan Bator, the capital of Mongolia. As we were coming in to land we looked out of the window and saw that the airport was an oasis in a sand desert. As far as we could see, it consisted only of two Portakabin-type buildings with a couple of parked trucks and a few tethered pack-animals with nothing else in sight. Leslie Hale said, 'This is Shangri-la, the ultimate perfect hideout, the place to get away from it all, especially if the police are after you.'

The Ilyushin taxied to a stop, and we were guided to the second of the two white shacks. There were three wooden steps up to the door, and on the top one stood a little brown man. He started when he saw me and said, 'Hello Mik, what are *you* doing here?' Before I could answer, Leslie said, 'Let that be a lesson to you, Mik: no hiding-place for you, so you'd better keep on the right side of the law.' (The little man remembered me from a few years back when he was the chairman of a meeting I'd addressed of one of the student societies at the London School of Economics. He was now the Burmese ambassador in Moscow, going back on home leave by a leisurely roundabout route.)

On the day we got to Peking the lot of the buggins-turn leadership fell on Bob Mathew, a Tory MP from the West Country whom I hadn't known before the trip and who turned out to be a most pleasantly clubbable companion. We were greeted on the tarmac by a receiving-party with flowers and a formal speech of welcome. Bob, as our leader, replied to it less formally but with more charm.

Early the following morning the man who seemed to be the organising secretary of our host committee arrived at our hotel, with an assistant, for a meeting with us to discuss our programme. He naturally turned first to Bob Mathew as the leader of our delegation, only to be told that Bob had ceased to be the leader and I had taken his place. The two Chinese, though courteously hiding their feelings, were obviously surprised by this development: I suppose they assumed that during the night there had been a left-wing *putsch* in our delegation's politburo which had deposed the Conservative leader and installed a socialist in his place. But the next morning, when they were again taken aback on discovering that I too had been deposed and replaced by a fresh upstart colonel, we took pity on them and told them about our rotating leadership arrangement. This time they found it more difficult to hide their feelings: they clearly thought we were exhibiting the decline and fall of a people fatally enfeebled by creeping democracy.

That trip was full of exciting new experiences, of new sights and sounds and smells, of new ideas and revelations of a different people with a different culture and perceptions and a different mode of life and thought.

Our hosts threw a farewell party for us on the eve of our return, and Chou En-lai turned up at it and talked, at varying length, to each of us in turn. In my conversation with him I asked him what was his Government's thinking about Taiwan. He replied, 'We Chinese are a patient people. We shall wait, and eventually the Taiwanese will come back to us of their own free will.' Then, after a moment's thought, he added, 'Perhaps someone else will open the gate for them.' At the time I wasn't at all sure what he meant by that somewhat cryptic addendum. In later years I often wondered whether he was already foreseeing, that far back, the scenario now being played out in which Hong Kong is reabsorbed into China light-handedly and benevolently and with a substantial element of self-rule in order to tempt the Taiwanese to follow the same path.

Some of my most rewarding international contacts were made at the meetings of the East–West Round Table. This was a modest, unpretentious, informal grouping set up in the most glacial period of the Cold War by two or three dozen people who wanted no part of that Cold War and were seeking a meeting of minds to end it. On the eastern side the two moving spirits were Oskar Lange, a Polish professor of econometrics, and the renowned Russian novelist Ilya Ehrenburg, a larger-than-life septuagenarian who seemed to have been given, or had taken, a dispensation which allowed him, even in that highly un-*glasnost* time, to speak his mind even when, as often, his mind wasn't the mind of the Central Committee of his Party. On the western side there were members from a number of countries, particularly Britain, France and Italy, and one lonely United States Congressman: the most active British members were two men supremely well-informed on all the complexities and nuances of international politics, John Mendelson and Konni Zilliacus.

We met in Paris and Moscow and London, and talked for days about how we could try to influence our respective governments away from mutual hate-propaganda, away from nit-picking Pavlov-dog confrontation, and towards détente and disarmament. We had no illusions: we knew we were just one of the little battalions that God is not on the side of, and we didn't expect the Oval Office or the Kremlin or Downing Street to tremble at our words; but we still thought we ought to try and see if there was an alternative to ice-bound rigidity that might one day be explored by the Powers. And at least we had a not inconsiderable reward for our efforts in that we all learned a good deal from one another.

In all political conferences the greatest value is derived not from the formal proceedings during the day but from letting the back hair down over a drink or two in the evening, and that was very much the case with our East–West Round Table. I recall in particular one evening when a dozen or so of us sat in a circle in the café of the Metropole Hotel in Moscow exchanging both profundities and witticisms rapid-fire in seven languages, most of us coping with two or three but Zilli fluently at home in all seven.

There was another memorable evening too, this time in Paris. After a long and somewhat wearing all-day Saturday session, our American colleague Charlie Porter proposed that some of us should spend the evening exploring the famed pleasures of Montparnasse; but instead Paolo Vittorelli and I persuaded Ilya Ehrenburg, a noted gourmet who was more at home in Paris than in Moscow, to take us out for a dinner to imprint on the memory. He did, and indeed it was a memorable meal – three courses, each in a different restaurant with taxi-rides between: *quiche Lorraine* and *gewürztraminer* in Alsace en Paris, *caneton à l'orange* and Lafitte in the Restaurant Voltaire, and goat-cheese with *Marc de Bourgogne* in a tiny bistro off Montmartre. Throughout this odyssey Ilya talked nonstop, and Paolo and I got an open, vivid account of what was really going on in the Soviet Union that we couldn't have got in any other way.

Ilya supplemented these thoughts on Soviet life when, a few months later, Mary and I went to visit him and his wife in their *dacha* in

143

the Chechov country an hour or so from Moscow. It was a very fine timber house which they'd had as a gift from their comrades in Sweden, and it was set in a radiant split-level garden which the two of them, unaided, developed and tended with a lot of effort and expertise.

Ilya forecast, as we sat in his garden, that the next decade or two would produce radical changes in the political and social life of the USSR. What is going to produce these changes, he said, is our enormous expansion of higher education, with ever-rising standards. The most immediate result of that programme is – though it may seem paradoxical – shortages of some everyday consumer articles, and the poor quality of them when you can get them: 'I've been waiting five months,' he said wistfully, 'for a new watering-can, and I had to bring back a garden fork from Holland because I can't buy a decent one here. That's because the million scientists and engineers we are turning out of the universities and polytechnics each year all want to go into hi-tech, since each of them knows he's not going to become a Hero of Soviet Science by designing a better garden fork or a Hero of Soviet Labour by accelerating production of watering-cans.'

But the important long-term effect, he said, of this explosion in higher education will be the erosion of the monolithic power of the Party. If you teach youngsters to make a fresh and sceptically enquiring approach to the state-of-the-art wisdoms in solid-state physics or biochemistry they're likely to apply the same treatment to Marxism-Leninism, and if you encourage them not to accept as gospel everything their teachers tell them, they're not going to accept as gospel everything their political commissars tell them. Today one can see that prophecy of Ilya's coming to pass, though perhaps more slowly than he expected.

I had another revealing venture into Eastern Europe when the UK branch of the Inter-Parliamentary Union were sending a delegation to Romania and asked me to lead it because at the time I was the only member of our Parliament who knew that country at all well. It was a period when Romania was a subject of considerable interest to western politicians because it seemed to be deviating, at least partially, from the directives laid down by Moscow for the whole of the Soviet bloc. President Ceauşescu, helped by the fact that his country was the only oil producer in the bloc apart from the USSR, had embarked on his 'opening to the West', notably to West Germany and Israel, and had achieved a certain measure of independence within the Warsaw Pact and Comecon. It was a point which our delegation pursued closely, and we were particularly struck by the sharp contrast between this liberal external policy and their internal régime, which was by far the most rigid police-state of all the East European countries.

Some years later, during my period as chairman of the Labour Party's International Committee, I developed a close friendship with one of the veteran members of the Romanian Communist Party's polit-buro, and over lunch one day I took advantage of that friendship to ask outright how the régime's heavy-handed internal discipline could be reconciled with the relative liberality and flexibility of its general policies. 'How is it,' I asked, 'that if I sit in a pavement-café in East Germany or Bulgaria reading a Penguin or a Pelican paperback I will often be approached by local people, mostly students wanting to prac-tise their English or ask about student life in Britain, but in Bucharest nobody talks to a westerner without looking over his shoulder first to see who may be listening? Why do you have to keep such a close and suspicious watch on all your citizens?' The answer surprised me, not for what it said but because a high-ranking official would say it so frankly to a westerner: 'Oh, the authorities in East Berlin or Sofia have got it easy: they need to look out for subversion only from the West. We've got a two-way problem.'

Another frank exchange sticks in my memory: it took place in Cairo, during a two-day stop-off on a flight back from Asia, a few months after King Farouk had been overthrown and expelled. General Neguib invited me to call on him at the Abdin Palace for a talk. When I got there and was ushered in, I found him accompanied by Colonel Nasser and a young air-force officer named Hakim Amir. Neguib was a cuddly old teddy-bear of a man, not very bright, and in our two-hour talk he waddled along behind while the other two dashed on ahead and made the running. The lower right-hand pocket of his tunic was full of black Burmese cheroots which he crushed and used as pipe tobacco: he offered me a fill, and I took it, and regretted it.

Our conversation ranged wide. The two of them saw very clearly all the complexities and the attendant dangers of power-politics in the Middle East – the competition between the USA and the USSR for both influence and bases; the equivocal roles being played, with more pretension than power, by Britain and France; the danger inher-ent in Syria's long-term ambition to re-create Greater Syria by absorb-ing Lebanon and Palestine and Jordan; the threat of Islamic fundamentalism, then a cloud no bigger than a man's hand but begin-ning to spread, and its spin-off in the Sunni-Shia rivalry; the split in the Ba'ath Party; the rival claims of Israelis and Palestinians. They asked me why I was a Zionist, and followed that up with some probing but not hostile questioning.

In all that they said there was a substratum of a hostility towards the British that derived not from political but from social origins, from the still-remembered resentment at being treated by our colonial nabobs, both civil and military (and perhaps more by their memsahibs), as lesser breeds without the law, as objects at best of paternalistic condescension, at worst of contempt. I've head that sound echoed, manifold, in the Indian subcontinent, in Malaysia, in Ghana and Nigeria, even in Hong Kong.

A week after I got back I gave my monthly report-back to my constituents in the Labour Hall in Reading. I told them about my talk in the Abdin Palace, and offered them a prophecy, which was that within a year Neguib would be ousted by Nasser, and within three years after that Nasser would in turn be ousted by Hakim Amir. The first of those tips proved to be a winner, but not the second – but that was only because Nasser foresaw the danger and dismissed his young colleague and rival, and put him under house arrest. (Any professional tipster will tell you that he'd be well satisfied with an average of one winner per two forecasts.)

In 1968 an antiwar group in the United States invited some Tribunite MPs to go over there to talk to them, and to Congressmen, the Secretary of State and the media, about the British Government's support for the American invasion of Vietnam, and about our opposition to that support. It was a team of close friends who made the trip – Stan Orme, Norman Atkinson, Russ and Anne Kerr, John Mendelson and I – and we had quite a hectic time in the States. We met Dean Rusk, the Secretary of State, whose thinking was so deeply embedded in the anticommunist groove that he was incapable of taking in any fresh idea: I suspect that he wouldn't at all welcome the Gorbachev of *glasnost* and *perestroika* and the destruction of missiles because he would much prefer a Soviet leader whom he could hate unreservedly. We had a long working breakfast with about forty Senators and Congressmen with whom we had a lively exchange, partly confrontational but mostly co-operative, which was thoroughly enjoyed by both sides. After that there were so many demands for us that we split into pairs, each covering a different city. Stan Orme and I went to Philadelphia, and during our twenty-four hours there we heard from a young draft-dodger (a distant cousin of mine) a sharper and more effective demolition of United States policy than we had got from any of the politicos.

Of all my trips abroad there is one which I cherish most because it was the one which most directly, immediately and significantly affected the course of events. There aren't many occasions when back-benchers get the opportunity of precipitating policy changes, and when one of these opportunities crops up it's welcomed as a red-letter day because it's like chancing on one of the widely-separated oases in a long desert march. (The only time I ever succeeded singlehandedly in changing a course of action was during one of the debates on steel nationalisation: I thought the Government were overpaying for the assets of the industry, and by threatening a vote which could have resulted in their being defeated I got the Minister to change the method of calculating compensation and thereby reduced its total by £80 million.)

In the 1984–85 parliamentary session the Foreign Affairs Committee of the House, of which I was a member, carried out a close examination of relations between Great Britain and the Soviet Union. It followed Mikhail Gorbachev's visit to London in December 1984. That was before he was elected to the top office (though he was already universally recognised as the general-secretary-in-waiting), so he came in his capacity as chairman of, and leader of a delegation from, the Foreign Affairs Commission of the Supreme Soviet. The niceties of diplomatic protocol demanded that the delegation's hosts should be their British opposite number, which of course was our Foreign Affairs Committee, so our chairman, Sir Anthony Kershaw, did the honours.

It was arranged that in the course of our enquiry we should spend a week in Moscow. In order to avoid a clash with the Soviet celebration of the fortieth anniversary of the World War II victory we fixed a date a bit later than we had planned, and eventually got to Moscow early in July 1985.

By that time Mikhail Gorbachev had succeeded to the throne and had launched the good ship *Glasnost-perestroika*. In our planning of the visit we asked ourselves whether that new policy would result in our getting some frank uninhibited back-hair-down reactions from the people we were going to talk to instead of the standard, pre-fixed, defensive, party-line rhetoric (I called it The Gramophone Record, though I suppose I ought now to update that term to the CD) which we had all suffered from in the past. In the plane on the way over I said to our chairman that we'd have the answer to that question within the first hour of our first meeting, and if it then seemed that all we were getting was The Treatment it would be immediately clear

147

that our week's work was going to be a waste of time.

Our first engagement was an all-day meeting with the Soviet Foreign Affairs Commission. When we arrived at the Kremlin the auspices were bad, because the man who greeted us, and who was to chair our meeting, was the veteran Boris Ponomareev. I'd first met him ten years or so earlier when he acted as host to a Labour Party delegation led by the deputy leader of the Party, Ted Short (later Lord Glenamara), and when Ponomareev brought the return delegation to London a couple of years later I was the host as chairman of the Labour Party's International Committee. So I knew a bit about Comrade Boris, and in particular I knew that since the death of the ideologue Suslov he was the last surviving unreconstructed stalinist troglodyte in the top echelons of the USSR Communist Party.

The two delegations faced each other across a long table. After the routine preliminary pleasantries Comrade Ponomareev suggested that he should make an opening statement to get the discussion going. He then dropped on the table a typescript an inch thick, which had obviously been put out as a press release, and spent the next eighty minutes reading it. There wasn't a single word in that elongated screed that deviated by so much as a hairsbreadth from the rigid Party line: it was a long-playing – no, a two-disc – version of The Gramophone Record. In order to hammer home his points Mr Ponomareev was prepared not merely to trespass on the time of the meeting but even to encroach upon eternity.

Tony Kershaw, as one could have expected of him, had the good sense not to respond in kind. Just a couple of sentences, and then we tackled in turn the various policy items on our agenda. Here, too, there was very little give from the other side of the table, and by the time the day's discussion ended and we went off to take a press conference in the British Embassy we were all pretty pessimistic about our chances of getting anything worth while out of our week of studies in Moscow.

Sparring with the journalists at our press conference, plus the hospitality of the Embassy, put some ichor back into our veins and some spring into our step. That day was my seventy-seventh birthday, and one of the embassy wives had baked for me a birthday cake which not only was rich to the taste but also, we decided, required a lot of washing down with morale-uplifting liquors.

We came down to earth again, and with a bump, the following morning when our interpreter read to us the report in *Pravda* of the previous day's meeting. Almost the whole of it was taken up by Mr Ponomareev's speech in full, covering a substantial acreage of *Pravda*'s space, and at the end our chairman was quoted in a single sentence. As that report had been put out to the press before the meeting took place it didn't quote what Tony Kershaw had said but what they anticipated he would say, which was something quite different.

But within the next twenty-four hours there was a radical change in the Russians' attitude towards us. The total eclipse of the sun passed over, and the light and warmth again beamed down on us. We received a request from the Foreign Affairs Commission to alter our programme so as to provide for another full meeting with them at the end of our stay, and they made proposals for the structuring of that meeting which showed that they were expecting it to be a real exchange of views and not just another set of statements of preordained and immutable positions. And as the week wore on we found that almost all the Soviet Ministers and officials we met were more and more forthcoming with every day that passed. It was obvious that somebody on high, receiving a report of our first day's meeting, had decided that we were serious people who ought to be treated seriously and listened to carefully, and had made that view known around the government apparatus and its ancillaries. And when we had that second meeting with the Foreign Affairs Commission it was very different from the first – more sophisticated, more thoughtful, more exploratory, more constructive, more bridge-building. (Not long after that meeting Mr Ponomareev was put out to grass.)

After the publication of the Committee's report on our enquiry into UK–USSR relations we had the satisfaction of seeing some practical results flowing from the work we had done. There is evidence that the report was studied and appreciated by the foreign ministries of both countries, that they accepted many of its recommendations, and that it stimulated them into seeking, and achieving, greatly improved relations with one another. It was a little candle lighting up one corner of a dark world.

# Chapter 11

WHEN the Parliamentary Labour Party passed a resolution instructing the Bevanite Group to fall on its sword and expire gracefully we obeyed that order, but with the unspoken rider that no motion passed by the Parliamentary Party, and no standing order it might adopt, could prevent one of its members asking a few friends round for a meal and a drink whenever he felt like it, especially as that was a regular practice of the Hampstead Set (I suppose that's where Roy Jenkins first developed his taste for the more *recherché* clarets). So a few of us forgathered every Tuesday lunchtime at Dick Crossman's house in Vincent Square, where we ate sandwiches and Dick butled some unfussy but decent wine. We went dutch on it and contributed six shillings and sixpence *per capita*.

Those lunch-parties were attended by the six Bevanite members of the NEC – Nye, Barbara Castle, Dick, Tom Driberg, Harold Wilson and me – plus the four members of the Group who (in addition to Dick) were our political journalists – John Freeman, Michael Foot, Jennie Lee and Bill Mallalieu – plus Tommy Balogh, a man it was always good to have around.

I found these little gatherings addictive: except when I was abroad I never missed a single one of them. The level and sophistication of discussion, of political analysis and synthesis, tempered with wit and enriched by relaxed good fellowship, were much above anything I experienced before or since. It's no exaggeration to say that I felt a bit like an acolyte sitting at the feet of sages.

But there was another factor, quite apart from the discussions, which made these meetings riveting for me. I sat back and watched and listened, and drew my own conclusions about the subtle interplay, the delicate rapier-fencing, between some of these strong, sure-of-themselves characters, and about the underlying differences of purpose between these broadly like-minded colleagues which were bound to set up, even in this tight little group, tensions which were eventually to erode our solidarity and set friend against friend.

To begin with, and for a long time, that solidarity held firm, and our common beliefs and purpose easily overrode any differences of view – which were seldom on policy, generally on tactics. That cohesion was not surprising: we were the beleaguered rump of an army which had been dispersed by a stronger and more ruthless force, and we knew only too well that unless we fell obediently into line with the Party leadership it was ready to jump in with another attack which would eliminate us altogether. But acquiescence was not a price we were prepared to pay: we continued resolutely to fight our corner on the National Executive and in the Parliamentary Party; we produced motions and amendments; we made our no-punches-pulled critique of the leadership's policies, and put forward our alternatives to them, in pamphlets and memoranda and articles in *Tribune* and the *New Statesman* and anywhere else that would take them; we raised our voice, and to great effect, in the House and in large numbers of well-attended meetings all round the country. We knew we were risking a lethal bombardment from the big guns, and so we stuck close together in our dugout.

Those later internal differences within our group that I was talking about stemmed from the interaction between three very strong and very different characters – Nye, Dick Crossman and Harold Wilson. The trouble with Nye was that he wasn't a team-player: that was a defect which often worried me and occasionally irritated me, though sometimes I wondered whether it was too much to expect a man of his incomparable political genius, of his stature head and shoulders above the rest of us and of everyone around him, to have the patience, the restraint, the self-abnegation that teamwork demands. Some of the others in the group were less ready than I to make those comradely allowances: Crossman and Wilson, in particular, were often critical of some of Nye's actions which they considered (sometimes justifiably) to be tactically wrong, and they became very angry with him when, as happened occasionally, he went off on a spur-of-the-moment new line or made a fresh commitment without consulting us and then

151

expected us to give him unquestioning support in what he had said or done. That resentment may have been intensified by their realising, as we all did, that with all his faults, and however reluctant a Bevanite he was, Nye was the only one amongst us who was totally indispensable to our common effort, and that, in spite of our considerable array of talent, without him we wouldn't be a force to be taken seriously.

In sharp contrast, neither Dick nor Harold ever suffered the perils of spontaneity, or ever made a move without first thinking it out very carefully: in their separate ways they were operators, wire-pullers, bargainers, persuaders, dealers, manoeuvrers, fixers. I found it ironical that they were precisely the left-wing equivalents of the two men they had knocked off the NEC, Morrison and Dalton.

The difference between Dick and Harold was that they engaged in all these esoteric activities with very different intents. Dick entered into these machinations because he was amused by them and enjoyed them as a challenge, particularly as he was very good at this kind of operation and knew it: political power-broking was for him the breath of life. He loved setting up confidential talks over little lunches or dinners: even in the period of our roughest confrontations with Hugh Gaitskell, Dick consorted regularly with him (at one time he thought he had a chance of detaching Hugh from the most implacable extremists in his coterie, notably Roy Jenkins and Douglas Jay), and also with some Tories, notably Bob Boothby and Alec Spearman. Not one of the rest of us could possibly have done that.

Dick, as I have said, enjoyed the game for its own sake, and revelled in his ability to dribble round opponents. He was always ready, if he couldn't get in a shot, to pass the ball to a colleague, and if that didn't result in a goal he was prepared to wait for the next breakaway and the next opportunity. But Harold Wilson was quite different: he had eyes for nothing but the goal, and his goal was to become Leader of the Party and then Prime Minister; every thought and action, every word he said or wrote, every contact he made was all directed singlemindedly to that end.

As for the rest, Jennie had sacrificed most of her own potentially important political role in order to help her man to fulfil his even more important one: she exerted herself to protect him from his critics, and sometimes from himself, though (as I shall show) she didn't hesitate to differ from him when she thought he was wrong. It was only very much later that she achieved her own fulfilment as a highly esteemed Minister for the Arts and the very successful organiser of the Open University.

The pellucidly honest Michael Foot and Bill Mallalieu, though always conscious of the practical tactics which our vulnerable situation forced us into, never deviated from their principles. Nor did Tom Driberg and John Freeman, though these two were always a bit less involved in the hurly-burly than the rest of us. Barbara had already begun to hitch her wagon to Wilson's star, though her commitment to him was not complete till several years later.

I always had the feeling, though I was never courageous enough to face it and bring it into the open, that sooner or later the strains in our group between the principled and the pragmatists were bound to drive a wedge between them. That eventually came about in April 1954, following a decision by the United States Government to set up a regional military bloc in South-east Asia. Anthony Eden gave full backing to this proposal, and the Shadow Cabinet agreed to support Eden. Attlee stated this position at question time in the House, and there followed a tense scene in which Nye went to the dispatch box and openly dissociated himself from the statement which Attlee had made from the same dispatch box only a few moments earlier. The next day, without consulting anybody, Nye resigned from the Shadow Cabinet.

Under the standing orders of the Parliamentary Labour Party the vacancy in the Shadow Cabinet created by the resignation would be offered to the highest unsuccessful candidate in the last Shadow Cabinet election, and in this case that was Harold Wilson. In my innocence I took it for granted that Harold couldn't possibly distance himself openly from Nye by taking that place, particularly as he had strongly supported Nye on the issue of policy in South-east Asia which had led to the resignation. I went along to that week's lunch meeting in Vincent Square assuming that that matter wouldn't occupy more than a minute of our time and that we'd then get on with the other things we had to discuss.

Not so. It soon became apparent that Harold had quickly decided to take the vacancy: he had had a talk about it with Dick, though with no-one else, not by way of consulting him but merely to enlist him as an intermediary to break the news to Nye and to arrange for the three of them to meet.

Because we were in a short parliamentary recess, a few days were to elapse before Harold's decision was announced, and so we were able to discuss the position again at another of our lunches. I think Harold was banking on getting support from those members of the group, of whom I was one, who thought that Nye had made a mistake in resigning, and who particularly resented his having rushed into it without consulting his friends and allies. (I was to recall that resentment twenty-seven years later when Tony Benn aroused equal resentment by making a middle-of-the-night announcement of his challenge for the Party's deputy leadership without consulting his Tribune Group colleagues. In his case, unlike Nye's, this error was the beginning of the end of his chance of ever gaining either of the two top positions in the Party.)

That second discussion extended our lunch meeting, for the first and only time, well into the afternoon. Dick alone supported Harold's decision: the rest of us, however critical we were of Nye's resignation and of the manner of it, believed – and we were proved to be right – that Harold's action would inflict serious damage not only on Nye but on the Left as a whole. But the decision was Harold's, and he made it by himself and for himself.

It wouldn't have been at all surprising if this overt, sharp and hurtful division had prevented our continuing to function as a group in the way we had functioned before. But in fact that didn't happen. We got through the crisis as one gets through it in an attack of pneumonia: there is a zenith moment of danger when life hangs precariously in the balance, and if the patient survives that moment he makes an untroubled return to normalcy. Except that Nye never fully recovered his trust in Crossman ('too clever by half'), each of the two sides in the Wilson-acceptance argument showed an understanding tolerance of the other: we accepted that each of us had acted in what he believed, rightly or mistakenly, was in the best interest of all of us and of the Party as a whole. We resumed our discussions with the same seriousness of purpose, the same depth of thought and the same wit that had always made our meetings a highly enjoyable blend of intellectual challenge, good fellowship and sophisticated fun.

The wounds of that internal skirmish healed the more quickly because we were called upon to re-form our battle-lines and our squares to face, once again, the external enemy. It was not long before we had to deploy all our strength and ingenuity, both on the NEC and in the Parliamentary Party, against the attempt to expel Nye from the Party, and after that in support of his candidature when he stood for election as Leader of the Party.

That election has for me an abiding, poignant memory of one of the three candidates – not of my friend Aneurin Bevan but of my longtime opponent Herbert Morrison. Herbert seized upon Attlee's retirement as an opportunity to avenge and reverse his disappointment of 1945 and make his bid for the office which he had craved for so long. Nobody but he thought he had the ghost of a chance of beating Gaitskell, and perhaps he himself didn't expect to win, but I'm sure he was expecting to poll a good vote from the Right and the Centre. He reckoned he could count on votes of people on the right who thought Gaitskell too extreme, and of trade unionists who would vote for the proletarian against the middle-class intellectual, and from centrists who were alienated by Gaitskell's ill-starred attempt to expel Nye, and from the many friends who had fought side by side with him over the years, amongst them many who owed a great deal to him, including their seats and their 1945–51 front-bench positions.

The declaration of the poll took place at a meeting of the Parliamentary Labour Party in the large Committee Room 14. (That room always strikes me as sombre and forbidding: it would make a good courtroom for a trial of war criminals.) The chief scrutineer stood up on the platform and slowly and solemnly read out the ballot result: Gaitskell 157, Bevan 70, Morrison 40. That figure of 40 hit Herbert like the dash of a sjambok across his face. His whole body crumbled – the shoulders rounded, the head bowed – and then he stood up and walked, a bit unsteadily, to the door, with not a single one of his friends saying a word or even offering a gesture to him. I said to George Wigg, who was sitting next to me, 'Poor devil, what an awful way to finish,' and George replied, 'Yes. Come on, let's buy the old blighter a drink.' We walked out of the room and saw Herbert in the corridor looking like a man whose house, whose whole world, had fallen in on him and crushed him. I said, 'Never mind, Herbert, you can take it: that's the occupational hazard of our trade.' That produced a wan smile from him. 'Come on,' said George, 'we're all going to have a drink.' We each took him by an arm and guided him into the lift and down to the Harcourt floor and along to the Strangers' Bar (I don't think Herbert had ever been in there before), and sat him down with a drink. He was shattered not by being defeated but by that very low vote, which showed that he had been coldly deserted by many whose support he had expected and indeed been promised.

George and I did what we could to comfort and console him. In an appallingly trite, pedestrian phrase I said, 'It's the way of our world,' and added, 'We've always got to remember that old geezer Seneca in ancient times who reminded us that more people gaze upon the rising sun than gaze upon it when it sets.' When we broke up Herbert was at least a bit more cheerful and his step a bit lighter.

In addition to removing Morrison from the arena, the leadership election established that Nye was bound to become, and before very long, an important and influential member of the Party leadership. Gradually a working relationship developed between him and Gaitskell: they were incompatibles, and of course it wasn't a love-match but a *mariage de convenance* – yet I've known many a husband and wife who didn't like each other very much, and slept in separate rooms, but nevertheless managed to operate an effective and successful business partnership.

Nye and Hugh differed not only in their political outlooks (in some policy areas they were further than poles apart), and not only in that one of them wasn't ambitious and the other was, and not only in that one was always thinking ahead into the next century and the other never cast his eyes much beyond the next general election, but also in their temperaments. It wasn't, as a lot of people thought, that Nye was an emotional man and Hugh a desiccated calculating machine: Hugh's tight-lipped ascetic countenance, his correct but icy manner and his carefully controlled speech were misleading because he, too, was often the subject of strong emotions. The essential difference of temperament was that Hugh arrived at his conclusions through a slow process of cerebral evolution, cautiously testing them at each stage as he went along, whilst Nye's instincts and inspiration enabled him quickly to transmute facts into a conclusion whilst everyone else was struggling some way behind. On the occasions when they were in harmony because they were handling an issue they agreed on, they were a formidable combination.

One such occasion, and a notable one, was when they led the Opposition's campaign against the Eden Government's violation of international law and treaties, its wanton choice of invasion rather than negotiation, in its harebrained Suez aggression in 1956. Michael Foot wrote of this campaign that 'the speeches of Gaitskell and Bevan throughout the crisis – the combination of Gaitskell's relentless, passionate marshalling of the whole legal and moral case against the Government's expedition to Suez and Bevan's sardonic and reflective commentary upon it – complemented one another and constituted together the most brilliant display of opposition in recent parliamentary history.'

That's a correct assessment of their joint performance as the debates between Opposition and Government developed, but they didn't get it completely right at the beginning, and they got it right later only as the result of one of those off-chance accidents that so often influence, or even change, the course of events.

The crisis was sparked off when Colonel Nasser, angered by the withdrawal of United States aid to build the Aswan dam, nationalised the Suez Canal Company. In common with almost all other members of the Labour Party, and in direct contrast with the Government and all its supporters, Nye defended Nasser's right to nationalise the Canal Company, but he was sharply critical of the way it was done and of many other elements in Nasser's policies and actions, which blunted his attack on Eden. He wrote an article in this vein for the 3 August issue of *Tribune*, and when it arrived at the *Tribune* office it caused some embarrassment because it was out of line with a much stronger uncompromising leading article which had been written in the office. Two or three telephone-calls produced a comradely solution of the difficulty, which was that the leading article appeared on page 1 and Nye's piece on page 5. (Some Tories noticed the disparity between the two, and made a bit of play out of it.)

Between the day those articles were written and the day they appeared there was a debate on Suez in the House of Commons. Gaitskell led for the Opposition. He put forward some well-argued criticisms of parts of Eden's speech, but the criticisms were a long way short of total and unreserved opposition: the reservations were in some respects similar to Nye's on page 5. (Morrison also spoke in that debate, from the back benches: predictably and characteristically he was more Edenesque than Eden, and won warm approval from the Tory benches.)

Millions of words have been written about the political impact in Britain of the Suez adventure, but they don't include any account of the off-chance accident which shunted Nye, and hence Gaitskell, on to the right track. It was on the Saturday evening, two days after the debate and a day after the *Tribune* articles appeared, that John Mackie gave a dinner party, arranged some weeks earlier, at his farm on the Essex-Hertfordshire border. (On two occasions the farm provided the arena for the annual cricket-match between *Tribune* and the *New Statesman*. I played in the first of them, and made a good score because the cartoonist Vicky, who didn't know the difference between lbw and ICI, was one of the umpires, and he wasn't going to give me out come what may.)

John (later Lord John-Mackie) was one of Nye's closest friends:

he is a big braw Scot, a large-scale farmer and the possessor of a warm heart and an infectious chuckle.

When the guests had all arrived John took us on a guided tour of the farm, and then we dawdled over drinks and then we had dinner (Mary whispered to me, 'This is the best beef you've ever eaten, or ever will') and the talk turned inevitably to Suez. It soon developed into a skirmish, and from there into a battle, in which Nye stood virtually alone against the rest of us, like Horatius on the bridge in ancient Rome singlehandedly defying the Tuscan hordes. (John alone raised a lance in his defence, but only halfheartedly, and less from conviction than from a good host's consideration for his favourite guest.) The others let me have the first go at Nye because I had, and still have, the reputation (not altogether undeserved) of knowing more than most people about the byzantine twists and turns of Middle East politics, and then Jennie came in strongly on my side, but the centurion who wielded the sharpest and fastest blade was Leslie Hale, always a clear thinker and a powerful advocate. Nye, of course, however outnumbered, stood his ground and fought back vigorously and skilfully ('Nasser's a thug,' he said, 'and he needs to be taught a lesson'): he was (to change the metaphor) nimble in his footwork and crisp in his punching, floating like a butterfly and stinging like a bee, as Mohammed Ali did in his heyday. Leslie and John and I agreed afterwards that this was vintage Nye at his best, and that we had never heard a more brilliant performance.

One of the great things about Nye was that, however hard he opposed you in an argument, he would go away and retrace the argument in his mind and ask himself seriously whether there wasn't some validity in what his opponent had said; sometimes that would result in his rethinking his attitude and accepting that opponent's view in place of his own. Three days after our dinner-party he was arguing the very case we had put to him, even using some of Leslie Hale's phraseology, and Gaitskell followed him. From that point Labour's anti-Suez campaign, 'Law, not War', took on a stronger impetus and a sharper edge.

And that brings me naturally to his greatest and most dramatic U-turn, from supporting to opposing unilateral nuclear disarmament, in the two days from Wednesday to Friday of the week before the Labour Party Conference of 1957.

On the Saturday morning Nye and Jennie asked Mary and me to join them for coffee on the balcony of their room overlooking the sea. (We were in the old Bedford Hotel, antique and slightly shabby but homely and welcoming. Some time later it burned down and was replaced by one of those smart modern off-putting accommodation factories, those luxury barracks, which are taking the place of good hotels.) We chatted over our coffee about anything and everything except the Bomb, and then Nye said, 'Come on, boyo, let's leave these girls and go for a walk and talk.'

We went down to the lower promenade where our walking and talking were less likely to be interrupted by strolling delegates, and past the fish stalls all the way to the Palace Pier and back. Of course I was as shocked – no, shattered – as all the other unilateralists by Nye's defection from our cause, and dreaded the declaration which he was to make a few days later. But on that walk I didn't argue with him or make any attempt to get him back: I knew that the decision he had reached, after two days and nights of agonising, was absolutely firm. Instead I got him to talk about what might flow from that decision, what effects it might have on the Party, on Great Britain and – if he ever got into a position of power – on the world.

I knew that for a long time he had been thinking about how to end the Cold War, about how to replace confrontation and nuclear overkill with détente and disarmament. He had established, over the years, a notable rapport with like-minded statesmen in other countries, among them Pandit Nehru, President Tito, Pierre Mendès-France, Pietro Nenni and Yigal Allon, and he believed that if he ever got to be Prime Minister or Foreign Secretary of Great Britain he could put together an anti-Cold War axis strong enough to divert the two superpowers from their collision course. That belief had been reinforced by two men who had talked to him at length in the previous two weeks – two very different men, Nikita Khrushchev and Sam Watson. Sam and Nye were politically far apart, but they were bound by the affinity which in the last resort binds every miner to every other miner: moreover, Sam was as appreciative of Nye's worth as any of Nye's own friends and associates, and he was the one man of the Right who could get close enough to Nye to influence him. What Sam had said to him, had begged him to believe, was that the world needed Nye to become Foreign Secretary of Great Britain, and that this couldn't possibly come about unless Nye turned his back on unilateralism.

We got back from that walk with lungs expanded and minds cleared. I still wept for what he was going to do, but I understood better why he was doing it. And I had the selfish afterthought that I was a lucky man in that I was never going to suffer the torture of having to make such a heartrending decision.

The reverse suffered by the Labour Party unilateralists at the Party Conference was one factor that contributed to the formation and rapid growth of the Campaign for Nuclear Disarmament. I threw myself into it from the moment when Michael Foot took me to one of the early exploratory meetings at John Collins's house in Amen Court, by St Paul's Cathedral. I spoke at many meetings, rallies, demonstrations; but I made my principal contribution as an unskilled labourer in the team servicing the Aldermaston marches.

When Peggy Duff organised the marches she had to get together teams to do the mundane and thankless work of erecting and clearing mobile loos, disposing of litter and garbage, and feeding and watering the thousands when they stopped for a break. She found a CND-er named Harrington who was a professional caterer, and he supplied the expertise we needed, notably in buying the supplies and in whistling up field-kitchens and other equipment and teaching the helpers how to use them. As Harrington's deputy Peggy wanted a very good organiser; her choice lighted on Jo Richardson, and a happy choice it turned out to be. Peggy told her to get as her assistant a big man strong enough to hump the heavy stuff and not very bright so's he would do as he was told and not stop to ask questions which no-one had the time to answer. The two of them decided that the job specification was tailor-made for Ian Mikardo, and I assumed the role of First Dogsbody, first of about half a dozen. We set up our snack-bar at the starting point before the marchers arrived, and as soon as they set out we loaded up the van, which was supplied and driven by a gem of a lad whose only name appeared to be Jimpy. In went the provender and the boilers and the trestle tables which were our serving counters, and off we drove to the next stop, unloaded, humped a lot of water to the boilers and fired them up, put out the tables and the food and drinks, and awaited the arrival of the hungry and thirsty marchers. It all went very well. There was only one point on which the born rebel Mikardo defied authority: one of our fast-selling items was Lyons' Individual Fruit Pies, which Peggy said we ought to sell at sevenpence each; but I reckoned we wouldn't have the time to give five pennies' change out of a shilling and insisted on selling them at sixpence. To this day I often run into a comrade, anywhere in the country, who recalls that I sold him/her a cup of tea and a sausage-roll and a fruit pie at a roadside halt or on a village green somewhere in Berkshire or Buckinghamshire.

From the beginning CND had amongst its members and supporters a substantial number of Labour MPs, including almost all the Bevan-ites: that number grew steadily, so that when a parliamentary branch of Labour CND was set up after the 1959 general election (I was its treasurer) its members were more than half the Parliamentary Labour Party. Nye's speech at the 1957 Conference inevitably created a gap between Nye and some, though by no means all, of these CND supporters, and at the same time it established the Gaitskell-Bevan axis as the leadership of the Party. The partnership between them was built on shifting sands and was always fragile. Hugh, though he increasingly recognised Nye's worth and became increasingly dependent on him, never changed his opinion of him. Equally Nye continued to believe that Gaitskell was too inflexible and brittle to ever make a full and successful leader of the Party. They just strung along together, like a married couple who had grown to hate one another but stayed uncomfortably together for the sake of the children. The partnership was in fact not really a partnership but a co-existence, an agreement to live and let live. It continued that way up to the 1959 general election, and it is fascinating to speculate on how it would have developed if we had won that election and formed a Labour government with Gaitskell as Prime Minister and Bevan as Deputy Prime Minister and Foreign Secretary.

I had a greater regard for Hugh Gaitskell than most of my friends and associates. Some of them were surprised, and told me so, when in an article I wrote for *Tribune* in September 1958 I paid a tribute to him. 'Hugh Gaitskell,' I wrote, 'brings to his job as Party leader many qualities which I respect and admire, and sometimes envy. He has a highly penetrative and astute mind, he is (within some limits) interested in other people's opinions, he is always on the *qui vive*, he is selflessly dedicated to his job and he is one of the hardest workers I have ever met. These qualities make him a much better leader than his predecessor.' But I went on from there to assert that he was lacking in political judgement, and so he was. In particular he made, during the period of his leadership of the Party, three gross errors of judge-ment. The first of them had been his unsuccessful and demeaning attempt to expel Nye Bevan from the Party. The second was the gross error which he made during the 1959 election campaign (briefly men-tioned in Chapter 6) in his dubious-sounding and counterproductive pledge, made with consulting any of his colleagues, that under a Labour Government 'there will be no increase in the standard rate or other rates of income tax'. David Butler and Richard Rose, in *The British General Election of 1959*, wrote succinctly that with this pledge Gaitskell 'played into his opponents' hands', and they recorded that as a result 'all the opinion polls indicate that about ten days before the vote the tide which had been flowing so strongly to Labour was checked and then reversed'. That was a judgement which my own election team could confirm from our experience on the doorsteps of Reading.

Gaitskell's third great error of judgement arose from his panicky reaction to that 1959 election defeat. I suppose it was natural that he should seek to find some reason for that defeat other than his own bungled tactics: the reason he found was that the Party was too socialist, and that it was bound into that socialism by clause 4 of its constitution, and that therefore clause 4 must go. This concept alienated not merely and predictably the Left but also many in the Centre and on the Right, including the trade-union leaders who had provided the shoulders on which he had climbed to power: even they could see that this thesis of Gaitskell's was born not of logic but of obsession. The boomeranging tax pledge and the poll defeat had him already rocking unsteadily on his feet, and the hostility he aroused over clause 4 sent him reeling and hanging on the ropes. When we met at Blackpool for the weekend substitute for the Annual Conference (which had been cancelled because of the election) it was doubtful whether he could hang on until he was saved by the bell. His keynote speech to the Conference, sharply in contrast with a superb socialist-oriented chairman's opening address by Barbara Castle, worsened his situation. Though Conference applauded his speech, it soon began to express some sharp criticisms of him.

Nevertheless he *was* saved from a knockout, by Aneurin Bevan. In Nye's own speech, the last he ever made, which Michael Foot ranks as one of his best, he distanced himself from Gaitskell's analysis, notably in this passage: 'You cannot really go before a country with a programme and tell the country that you thought the programme was good for the country and, immediately the country rejected it, say you would like to alter it. It won't work.' (That truth, even if fairly obvious, points to a course of wisdom as applicable after the 1987 election as it was after 1959.)

But after that statement of faith Nye turned, as he always did in the last resort, to salving the Party's wounds and bridging its breaches.

While noting the differences between Barbara's approach and Hugh's and his own, he concentrated on the areas of common ground in their speeches. That diverted the wrath of Conference from Gaitskell. To go back to my boxing metaphor, Nye tended the bruised Gaitskell in his corner at the end of the round, and got him fit to stand up and face the next one. As always it was Vicky who, with inspired perception and a few bold strokes of his pen, produced a stark straight-between-the-eyes picture of what was happening, in terms which nobody could fail to understand. One of his cartoons showed Gaitskell throwing himself off the top of Blackpool Tower, and being prevented from falling by Nye, and shouting 'Help! Help! He's saving me!', and another, at the end of the two-day Conference, was a before-and-after picture, first Gaitskell and Bevan riding into Blackpool on a tandem bicycle with Hugh on the front saddle and Nye behind, and in the second frame leaving Blackpool with Nye in front and Hugh behind.

When I saw that second cartoon my mind clicked back a year to my *Tribune* article which I quoted a few pages back. What I had written towards the end of it seemed, after Blackpool, to be a prophecy which was now being fulfilled: it was that Gaitskell's reaction to socialist principles 'over the next few months may well decide whether his partnership with Aneurin Bevan . . . can be maintained; and, in combination with the result of the General Election it may well decide whether he can retain the leadership of the party'.

It was my view then, though very much a minority view, and it is still my view that if Nye had not been stricken down a few weeks after Blackpool, Gaitskell would *not* have been able to retain the leadership of the Party. The contrast between Gaitskell's inept performances over the previous three months and Nye's cool, confident mastery of the situation was too glaring to be missed by even the right-wing majority in the Parliamentary Labour Party, and I'm convinced that if Nye had been available in 1960 and had been willing to offer himself as Party Leader they would have elected him. Their reaction to his illness and death, like that of the whole nation, is a pointer in that direction.

It had been arranged that soon after Blackpool the half-dozen people who were responsible for running *Tribune* would meet to discuss what the paper should be saying, and how it should be run, in the following year. Howard Samuel, a director and generous patron of the paper, hosted a lunch for this meeting in a private room at the Café Royal.

Nye ate only a tiny piece of steamed fish because, he said, there was something wrong with his stomach; he was going straight from the lunch to a medical check and would probably have to undergo an operation quite soon.

I saw him only once more, not long before his death. Jennie asked me to come over to their farm at Asheridge to have a talk with him. My French niece, Marilyn, a pretty and lively ten-year-old, had come over from Paris to spend her annual holiday with us, as she always did, and I took her with me because she would love to see the farm animals. Nye had got up from his bed for an hour or two, and he sat with us, a shadow of himself, in the big typically-farmhouse living-room. Marilyn was wearing a bright tartan skirt, and Nye asked her if she could dance a Scottish dance. In her attractive Gallic accent she said she could, and she did. Nye's eyes and his countenance lit up for a few moments as he watched this vivacious little creature stepping a graceful circle to a self-accompanying tune. He was savouring a morsel of the life which he knew, only too well, he was about to leave.

# Chapter 12

THE TAIL end of the 1950s, which I've been writing about, was a bad time for me personally. In 1958 Mary and I each had a major illness – Mary a massive heart attack and a persistent lung infection, and I a rare and dangerous glandular failure – and we were in hospital simultaneously, Mary in Guy's and I in St Mary's, for four months. We wrote to each other every day, lying to disguise how seriously ill we were.

When I got back into action at the beginning of 1959 I had a lot of leeway to make up. In the previous couple of years the Reading Labour Party had slipped from its earlier high level, and my long absence hastened the decline. The Reading Conservatives had adopted a keen young candidate, Peter Emery, who was working hard in the constituency, and I knew very well that the odds against my retaining my seat at the next election were lengthening rapidly.

In fact I did lose my seat in the 1959 election, and salt was rubbed into my wounds when, at the two-day Conference a few weeks later, I also lost my seat on the Party Executive. (The candidate who narrowly beat me was Tony Benn, who thus came on to the NEC for the first time, and I won the place back from him a year later.)

When I had got over the withdrawal symptoms I decided that I wouldn't go after any by-elections but use the next five years to recharge my batteries and my bank balance, and just look out for an opportunity of getting selected for the next general election in a seat somewhat safer than Reading. How I won such a selection is a story worth telling for two reasons: (i) it's an outstanding example of a phenomenon

165

I've mentioned before, which is that the most momentous events in a man's life are generally the product of chance accidents; and (ii) it demonstrates how inadequate and defective are the methods by which parliamentary candidates are selected.

The first invitation I had to participate in the selection of a candidate was at Tottenham, and I accepted even though I knew I was merely making up the numbers since that was an AEU-sponsored seat and the AEU had put up an estimable young candidate, Norman Atkinson, who was virtually certain to be selected. (He was, won the seat, and made a notable contribution to the work and performance of the Party in Parliament.)

The next invitation I had to a candidate selection was from Poplar, when the sitting Member, Charles Key, announced that he wasn't going to fight the next election. I viewed this invitation with no enthusiasm whatever. After Tottenham I had decided not to contest any other selection where I had no chance of winning, because every failed attempt at a candidature creates some discredit which lessens one's chance of success in the next attempt in another constituency. And I was sure I had no chance in Poplar, because it had always chosen a local man – it was a seat sponsored by the Transport and General Workers' Union and its management committee had a very strong TGWU representation through delegates from the union's many branches in the area, most of them covering stevedores and tally-clerks in the West India and Millwall docks.

I also knew that there were already two strong candidates in the field, both of whom fitted admirably into every element of those conditions: Bill Guy, the Constituency Party's agent, the son of a former MP in the constituency and a longstanding member of Poplar Borough Council; and John Branagan, treasurer of the Constituency Party and its representative on the London County Council (LCC), as it then was. John had another advantage running for him: the Poplar party had a substantial proportion of Roman Catholics, mostly descendants of Irish immigrants, amongst its members and on its management committee, and John is a leading lay Catholic and a knight of one of the Catholic orders.

So when I was telephoned by a man I didn't know, who introduced himself as Bill O'Dell and asked whether I would let my name go forward, I replied with a quick and very firm No. But Bill wouldn't take it just like that, and said he was coming to see me. He did, and he hadn't talked for five minutes before I realised that this was a formidable high-quality man who had to be listened to. In the years to come, till he was struck down early by cancer just like Nye, I learned to love this man for his big heart and his socialist dedication, and to respect him for an outstanding talent which, if his lot had fallen in pleasanter places, could have raised him to who knows what eminence.

Bill said he understood my hesitation, but the picture wasn't as simple or as black as it appeared. He thought (rightly as it turned out) that Bill Guy would be disqualified from standing by the rule which debarred a professional constituency agent from becoming the candidate in that constituency for two years after the end of his agency appointment; and he added that there was a growing number of members in the Poplar party who were fed up with its performance and would welcome having as their representative an ideas man who could lift the Constituency Party out of the conventional run-of-the-mill ways into which it had sunk since the great days of George Lansbury and the Poplar revolt. He had a few friends, he said, who were ready to put up a fight, and he reckoned he could weld them into a winning team. Would I come to his house one evening and meet them?

It was an invitation I couldn't refuse. When I got to his house a few days later Bill introduced me to his friends, some six or seven of them. With one exception they were all middle-aged men; without exception they were all working-class types: Bill was a hospital chef, Jack Tucker was a railwayman, and almost all the rest were dockers. They told me a lot about Poplar and about the Poplar Labour Party which, they said, didn't give a thought to any political event that took place outside the borough boundaries, particularly as many of the management committee were aldermen or councillors and their only political activity was directed to holding on to their seats (they held all the Council's 72) and deciding what the Council should do. (Within the next couple of years I was to witness two priceless examples of this parish-pump parochialism: the first was at a meeting of the management committee when the two delegates of the Youth Section, newly formed on my initiative, put forward a resolution on Vietnam, and one of the older worthies asked, 'This 'ere Vietnam they're talking about, is it this side of Bow Bridge or the other side, and if it's the other side what's it got to do with us?'; and the second was in 1965 when Poplar was forcibly merged with two neighbouring boroughs to form the London Borough of Tower Hamlets and some of those older worthies showed more hostility to their new Labour colleagues and comrades from Bethnal Green and Stepney than they had ever shown to any Tories.)

After this introduction Bill handed round copies of a list of members of the management committee; and his wife, Lil, a natural working-class aristocrat if ever there was one, handed round bottles of beer. They started going through their lists, name by name, marking each name as certain supporter (only a handful), probable, possible, doubtful, unlikely, or certain opponent. They then totted them up, and the conclusion was that to win we should need all the supporters, all the probables, all the possibles and over half the doubtfuls. It didn't look at all promising. Bill, who was a small but regular punter on the horses, reckoned that on the form book our entry was 100–7 against, but he added that over the years he'd backed quite a few quadrupeds at 100–7 which had turned out to be winners, and he was ready to back this one as well. Their enthusiasm infected me, and I agreed to have a go.

I didn't at all share Bill's optimism and I wondered gravely whether it was wise of me to enter this apparently unequal, perhaps hopeless, contest. Those doubts were heavily reinforced over the next two or three weeks during which a lot of my friends, one after another, and some of the Party's organisers, who knew the score better than anyone else, urged me to pull out in order to avoid the humiliation of a crushing defeat which would damage my reputation and severely reduce my chance of being selected in another constituency.

Bill's little group met regularly over the next two or three weeks, and he arranged to get the team together in his house for their final meeting on the Sunday evening before the selection conference. As it happened I had an engagement to lecture earlier that day to a weekend school which the Transport and General Workers' Union had arranged for some of their officers at a country house in Sussex. Mary came with me, and when we got there Jack Jones was in the middle of a talk which on the agenda preceded mine. After my lecture Jack took me aside because he wanted to talk to me about the selection in Poplar. He knew what my friends had been doing, and I told him about the meeting I was going to that evening.

Jack very strongly urged me, indeed begged me, to pull out. He said I was bound to be beaten out of sight, and by a much lighter man, and that would do me immense harm, perhaps irreparable harm. I said it was very difficult to pull out at this late stage. He replied 'Bite the bullet. Go to that meeting and thank your friends for all their support, and tell them you're sorry to let them down but you've got strong reasons for pulling out.'

On the drive back to London Mary and I talked the thing through and decided that it was quite impossible to ignore such a good friend and wellwisher, and one who was closely in touch with his many members in Poplar and therefore knew all about the balance of forces there. So I decided that when we got to Bill O'Dell's I'd break the news to them, as unhurtfully as I could, that they had lost me as a candidate.

We got to Bill's a bit late, and when we walked in and sat down he was in the middle of going round his team (by then substantially bigger than the original group) and getting each of them to report on the result of the contacts he had made. I was absolutely staggered to hear of the skilful, detailed organisation they had set up, and of the thought, effort and dedication that every single one of them had put into it. Suddenly Mary leaned over and whispered in my ear, 'Win or lose, you can't let these comrades down': that was a piece of husband-and-wife telepathy, because a split second earlier I had come to exactly the same conclusion.

And so, the following Thursday evening to the Bromley Public Hall for the selection conference.

The off-chance accident which upset the form-book and brought the outsider home at the head of the field was that a few weeks earlier there had been published the report of the latest enquiry, chaired by Viscount Rochdale, into the port transport industry.

John Branagan and I were the two main contestants at the selection conference, but a third – Ted Bishop, a solid but colourless Party stalwart who later became MP for Newark and a junior Minister, and later still a peer – was put in to make up the number. I was the first to face the delegates: after I'd said my little piece there were questions. The first two or three were hostile and mainly personal, and then one of the dockers' delegates got up and asked me (maybe spontaneously and maybe prompted by my friend Bill) what I thought of the Rochdale report. I gave a quick summary of it, especially those parts which impacted on the up-river docks (by far the largest source of employment in the constituency), and that answer clearly made an impression on a number of delegates. One or two more questions, and then another delegate came back to the Rochdale report and asked me to say a bit more about it and about how it might affect their jobs. So in a minute or two I told them that they would have to prepare for, and face, a situation in which containerisation and roll-on-roll-off would demand ships of deeper draught which would need to berth in or near the estuary instead of the upper river, and that's where the jobs would go to.

I was selected by a substantial majority on the first ballot, and over celebratory drinks in a nearby pub I was told that similar questions had been put to the other two nominees and neither of them had read the Rochdale report. I'm convinced that if that report had been published a couple of weeks later, after the selection conference, I would never have become MP for Poplar.

(Ever since my selection in Reading twenty years earlier I had always argued – and I argued it again later in a pamphlet, *Labour: Party or Puppet?*, which I wrote in partnership with Frank Allaun and Jim Sillars – that the process by which parliamentary candidates are selected in the Labour Party – and doubtless in others as well – is too short, too casual and too superficial to ensure that most times the best nominee will be chosen: indeed it is a process which inevitably advantages not the most worthy but the most articulate – hence the high proportion of winners who are professional articulators, such as lecturers, public-relations operators, teachers and lawyers. In my case it advantaged the most articulate and the luckiest. In recent years there has been some improvement in the practice; but it is still broadly true that no institution and no company would choose even a junior official or executive by means of an examination as depthless as we use in choosing an MP, in many cases an MP who will be there for the next thirty years or more.)

After that selection I felt I had an obligation to make myself an expert on the port transport industry, and I did – so much so that when, three years later, the Labour Party set up a study group on the port transport industry I was chosen to chair it. I had a formidable team: two trade union leaders, Jack Jones and Andy Cunningham, who knew the industry well; two fellow-MPs, Peter Shore and Tam Dalyell (that was my first acquaintance with him, and it ripened into a firm friendship); an industrial executive, Michael Montague (later to become a tourist board supremo); and an economist, John Hughes. We produced our report in March 1965, and I take some pride in the quality of it. We exposed the ills of the industry by delving with a scalpel deep into its intestines, and we recommended a total restructuring of it under public ownership and with a system of decentralisation and of workers' participation in management much wider than has ever been envisaged for any other industry.

The 1966 Cabinet accepted that report – George Brown fought hard for it against the resistance of some timid Ministers – and decided to legislate it. But they didn't produce the Ports Bill till the last session of that Parliament, and the Bill when it came was something of a disappointment because it fell a long way short of implementing the study group's proposals in full. With some colleagues I tried to get the Bill stiffened up, and made a bit of a nuisance of myself over it: in spite of that the Minister, Fred Mulley, offered me the chairmanship of the National Ports Authority when it was set up ( I suspect I was the second choice after Jack Jones, who was the obvious first choice). The offer was intriguingly attractive, but I declined it because I knew two or three people who could do the job better than I. I recommended one of them, and he was offered the post and accepted it; but it never materialised because the 1970 election was called before the Bill completed its passage. (But my recommendation wasn't in vain, because the subject of it later became chairman of one of the other nationalised industries.) If that reorganisation of the ports had ever been carried out, the industry would have been in much better shape to cope with the radical changes, and especially the lowered demand for labour, which resulted from falling traffic and new technology, with more still to come when the Channel Tunnel gets going.

Back in 1962, on becoming the candidate for Poplar my first task was to get to know the Poplar Labour Party. I found it radically different from, and appallingly inferior to, the well-informed, politically conscious, sophisticated, highly organised, hardworking Party I had behind me during my nearly twenty years in Reading. The Poplar Party had the advantages of quite a lot of money, acquired by running bingo evenings, and a main-road office, but it had a far smaller actual than nominal membership, no agent, no youth section, no electoral organisation and little political awareness. I set to work to remedy these defects, and some of the local worthies were less than enthusiastic about my efforts. They preferred their settled, undemanding life-style: after all, they said, there can't be much wrong with us if we win every single seat on the Borough Council. I agreed that that achievement gave them every right to pin a few victory medals on their own chests, but argued that that wasn't the alpha and omega of what the Labour Party was about. It was some years before a new wave of younger, more with-it members began to oust the Old Guard and turn the Party into a meaningful political institution.

As I began nursing the constituency I discovered that the East End

171

community had become, since I had last been involved in it, a very different mixture of ethnic groups. Where I had seen, in Brick Lane and Whitechapel, posters in Yiddish there were now posters in Bengali; where there had been kosher butchers there were now halal butchers; there were fewer synagogues but some newly-founded mosques (the synagogue in which I was married is now a Sikh temple); and the odour of cholent wafting out of restaurants had given way to the olfactory delights of vindaloo. The Protestant *Église Neuve*, which the Huguenots founded in Brick Lane in 1743, and which a century and a half later became a synagogue, was now a mosque. Exploring the East End these days is like working an archaeological dig in the Middle East, finding the relics of a different people in each successive stratum that one uncovers.

By the time of my East End rebirth in 1962 the area had become a melting-pot with an even wider variety of ingredients than New York, the product of a dozen or so different immigrant waves spread over more than three centuries. There were a small number of Jews who, after centuries of exile, came over from Holland in 1660 with another restored exile, the prince who became King Charles II. Then, after Louis XIV's revocation of the Edict of Nantes in 1685, a large number of persecuted Protestants, the Huguenots, fled from France, and some of them settled in Spitalfields and built lovely houses (a few are still carefully preserved) with silk-weaving lofts in the top storey: the ward adjacent to Spitalfields is still called Weavers' Ward. In the nineteenth century there were two immigrations from Ireland, the first in the Hungry Forties, and a later one when Irish labourers were brought over to build, and then to man, the up-river docks. Then came the large immigration of Jews from Eastern Europe that I wrote about in chapter 1. Throughout all this period there were lesser additives to the mixture from two sources: one was a small number of political refugees from various countries, and the other consisted of seamen disembarking in the port and choosing to stay on – it was they who were the origins of the Limehouse Chinatown and of the substantial Somali colony. Next came the Afro-Caribbeans who in the 1960s were recruited for jobs that Britons weren't taking, notably in London Transport's campaign to import conductors and drivers from the West Indies. After that came many tens of thousands of people from all the countries of the Indian subcontinent, with Bangladeshis as the largest contingent, and finally some Vietnamese boat-people. (During the whole of 1982 I kept a note of all the constituents who came to my advice sessions: they included West Indians from all the main islands and Guyana, Nigerians, Ghanaians, Sierra Leonians, Kenyans, Tanzanians, Somalis, Ugandans, Greeks and Greek Cypriots, Turks and Turkish Cypriots, Irish, Jews, Pakistanis, Sikhs, Indians, Bangladeshis, Hong Kong Chinese and Vietnamese.)

From the moment I took up my candidature I knew that this melting-pot was going to face me with some special problems, and that was a challenge I was happy to tackle, particularly because I would be reversing, and in a way compensating for, the role of one of my predecessors, the first parliamentary representative of the anti-immigrant racists. He was Captain Colomb, MP for Bow and Bromley (part of the Poplar constituency), who as far back as 1887 demanded severe limits on immigration and thus blazed the trail for the following-on East End Tories who campaigned for restrictions on immigration which they eventually won in the Aliens Act, the forerunner of the racist anti-immigration legislation and regulations of our time.

I discovered a new racism which ran wider and deeper than I had expected. It was a rerun, with a minor change in wording, of the racism of half a century earlier. 'Some of my best friends are Jews, *but* ...' had become 'I'm not prejudiced against blacks, *but*....' The local Conservatives, to their credit, had abandoned the racist attitudes of their predecessors, but racial prejudice was, and still is, exploited by two groups – the fascist organisations (the National Front and its breakaways) and the local Liberal Focus Team, a coven of populist poujadists who disgrace the traditions of Liberalism and shamingly embarrass the leaders of the Liberal Party.

It was the degraded areas, blighted by unemployment and poverty and run-down housing, which, as always, provided the most fertile ground for the seeds of racism, but there was also another area where those seeds sprouted and flourished, and that was the docks. At the turn of the century the dockers had a slogan, 'No Jew in Wapping', and in my own time I never saw a black face in any of the docks in my constituency or on any tug or barge or lighter. To the dockers, keeping out the 'foreigners' was a part of their operation of a closed shop which excluded everybody who wasn't of their ilk – in the case of watermen everybody who wasn't of their own families. When Enoch Powell made his rivers-of-blood speech it was a group of dockers, accompanied by some of their brothers the Smithfield meat-porters, who marched on the House of Commons in support of him.

In the 1964 General Election campaign it was obvious from the start that I was going to win by a large majority. So at our first campaign meeting I proposed that we should run only a skeleton organisation in Poplar and divert most of our troops to a nearby marginal constituency.

'There aren't any marginal constituencies near here,' I was told.

'Oh yes there are,' said I. 'There's a couple within fifteen minutes of here in Lewisham, just beyond the other end of our Blackwall tunnel.'

'What!' shouted one of the councillors, aghast, almost trembling with horror, 'you expect us to go *other side of the river*?'

General applause. I gave in.

When I got back into the House after the election I soon linked up with all my old buddies. There were also a lot of new MPs whom I had known well as left-wing rank-and-file activists: a few of them had been members of what the Bevanites used to call the Second Eleven, a group of actual and potential parliamentary candidates whom the First Eleven met periodically and whom we briefed and supported. Soon there was a spontaneous demand to re-form a left-wing pressure group in the Parliamentary Labour Party: we foresaw the danger that the new Labour Government, with its very small majority, might be tempted to follow the same path as its predecessor and waver in its commitment to some of the policies on which we were elected.

But we felt we'd better tread carefully. The pontifical excommunication which had brought the Bevanite Group to its end was still in place, and we had no guarantee that the cudgel of Party discipline would not be wielded again. So, taking a leaf out of the organisational book of the revolutionaries, we began by operating a cell. Eight of us met hush-hush in my company's office in Palace Chambers across the road from the House (it would have been truer to art, if not to life, if instead of sitting in comfortable chairs in a well-lit office we were sitting on upturned crates in a cellar lit only by a candle stuck in the neck of an empty beer bottle), and each of us had his list of seven to ten Members for whom he was the contact. But after a while the widening gap between what the Government was doing and what we thought it should be doing convinced us that we needed a more effective instrument to co-ordinate and articulate our views, and so we began to meet in the House, quite openly, as a group. We called ourselves the Tribune Group: I would have preferred a different name, but on that I was in a minority of one. We wrote to the Chief Whip, John Silkin, telling him what we were up to, and inviting him to come to one or more of our meetings and see for himself. He accepted that invitation, and after an interval he came along and sat in with us. In later years he joined the Group and made a notable contribution to its work.

In our Group, as in the Party outside parliament and in the trade unions, disillusion with the Government grew apace. We worked hard and fought hard to get the Government to change some of its policies, and if they didn't we would oppose them. But in the last resort our opposition was constricted by the straightjacket that we always had to stop short of a vote that would bring down the Government and let in a Tory administration that would be far worse.

Our quarrel with the Government straddled a wide range of issues: immigration; Rhodesia; the Parliament Bill, which, with others, we succeeded in aborting; the Government's support for American savagery in Vietnam; Wilson's forked-tongue equivocation over the Common Market; economic policy; and industrial relations policy. Like our predecessors in the Keep Left Group we had three economists to advise us – Henry Collins, Richard Pryke and Sean Gervasi; and we produced some detailed analyses of the Chancellor's policy and some detailed remedies for its defects. We summed them up in our *Tribune Manifesto* of July 1967, and again in our statement, *A New Economic Strategy*, in January 1968 (this one had the supporting signatures of a number of trade union leaders) in which we 'condemned the Government's acceptance of classical Tory deflationary measures as a method of solving our economic problems'. That wasn't too strong a description of what was happening: the Chancellor's policy was all the panicky way back to Philip Snowden and the disastrous Ramsay MacDonald Government of 1929.

Our fierce opposition to the Government's industrial relations policy – it was no exaggeration to call some aspects of it simply an anti-trade-union policy – led us into an alliance with a number of trade-union leaders of the type who refused to be overawed and mesmerised by Number Ten or suborned by the beer and sandwiches which the Prime Minister served to trade-union leaders, and only to them. (I never discovered what he laid on when he entertained the chiefs of the CBI.) We began to have periodic meetings with these trade-union leaders, sometimes over dinner in St Stephen's Tavern or some other nearby pub: amongst them were such formidable warriors as Frank Cousins, Terry Parry, Clive Jenkins, George Doughty, Cyril Cooper, Alex Kitson, Lawrence Daly, George Elvin, Jack Jones, Alan Sapper, Hugh

Scanlon and Bob Wright. We and they worked together to co-ordinate views and project them to the rank-and-file of the Movement and to the annual Party conference.

In that way we mobilised a powerful opposition to the Prices and Incomes Bill and to Barbara Castle's White Paper restricting the rights and powers of the trade unions – a forerunner of the worse that was to come when Thatcherism descended upon us.

The Tribune Group's opposition to the prices and incomes policy was directed not at all to the principle on which the policy was based but only to the selective and discriminatory way in which the Government was proposing to implement it. I had myself argued in a paper I had written for the Group, and in subsequent discussion of it, that as socialists we were committed to a planned economy and that one couldn't have an effectively planned economy if the wages sector within it were unplanned. But, I added, there's another side to that medal, which is that you can't logically expect workers to accept a planned wages sector in an economy in which every other sector is totally unplanned.

I went on to show that the so-called prices and incomes policy wasn't in fact a policy for prices and incomes – it was merely a policy for restricting increases in wages at the lower end of the scale. It was completely out of balance: price-restraint was voluntary, which meant that there wouldn't be much of it, and what there was would be token and temporary, as against the income side where the controls were statutory and enforced with all the full penalties of the law. And even within the income sector there was a major imbalance: unearned incomes, even the largest, were untouched by any semblance of restriction, and in earned incomes there was no restriction on professional earnings or managerial salaries: it was only the workers on the shop floor and in the offices, that is those in the lowest wage-brackets, who were to suffer limitations on increases in their pay-packets. The document which Barbara had called (at the suggestion of her husband, Ted) *In Place of Strife* was instead a provocation to strife -- and that strife was repeated when another Labour government made precisely the same mistake between 1977 and 1979.

In the standing Committee on the Prices and Incomes Bill 1968 I gave Barbara, as her diary acidly records, a torrid time, especially in all-night sittings. (The only supporter I had on the Committee was Ted Fletcher.) The government whip on the Bill was Walter Harrison (later he became deputy chief whip), a man who prided himself on his incomparable deviousness and who fancied himself as a wheeler-dealer above the highest standards of a Levantine bazaar. He set out loyally to act as a shielded between Barbara and me. He would come to me in the small hours and whisper, untruthfully, that Barbara wanted to talk to me privately, and then he went to Barbara and whispered, equally untruthfully, that I wanted to talk to her privately. He told me, very confidentially, that Barbara couldn't stand late nights, which I didn't think was true, and then he told Barbara that she could beat me by keeping the Committee sitting late because I couldn't stand late nights, which is certainly not true because I'm a bird that sings best in the night, and throughout the years I've made some of my best and liveliest speeches (and some of the longest) in the witching hours.

When the Committee stage was completed Barbara, in accordance with what had become standard practice, threw a party for the members of the Committee to celebrate the completion of that stage of the Bill. When I received my invitation to the party I replied to it in an open letter which said that I couldn't come to the party because I had nothing to wear as my last suit of sackcloth-and-ashes was at the cleaner's, so she and her friends would have to celebrate without me and I hoped they'd all have a filthy hangover next morning. It was a long time before Barbara forgave me for that, and even longer before I received absolution from her husband, Ted, who was even more ambitious for Barbara than she was for herself, which was more than somewhat.

The other main involvement I had in that 1966–70 Parliament was in an all-Party activity. I was asked to chair the Select Committee on Nationalised Industries: I accepted with some diffidence because I had never sat on a select committee and wondered whether as chairman I would find myself out of my depth. But I soon slotted in, and I think I can fairly say that I helped the Committee to improve its performance in both quantity and quality. With enthusiastic support from the Committee I introduced or extended some innovations, in sharing out the Committee's work more fairly amongst the members, in recruiting specialist advisers, in looking at some of the industries' problems *in situ* instead of in a committee room in Westminster, in opening some of the Committee's sittings to press and public, and in drafting myself some sections of what are called the chairman's draft reports – so called euphemistically since in general practice they are written not by the chairman but by the clerks to the Committee.

During my three years of chairmanship the Committee carried out some important investigations and produced some weighty reports. It is quite remarkable that although those reports made some highly controversial recommendations I got them through the Committee without contested votes: there was only one occasion in the whole of the three years when a dissenting amendment was moved (by Nicholas Ridley), and it failed for want of a seconder.

There were three of our investigations which gave me particular satisfaction. One was into the Post Office, in which we took a close look at the advantages and disadvantages of hiving off telecommunications into a separate corporation from the mail. We came to the conclusion that the balance of the argument favoured keeping them together, but in the light of hindsight I'm not sure that was right.

In the course of that investigation I achieved a tasty political victory which, however, turned to ashes in my mouth. It had long been a demand of the Labour Party that the Post Office should have power to manufacture some of the equipment which it used, particularly in order to escape from the domination of a tightly-knit group of manufacturers of telephone equipment who comfortably carved up the market between them. Prima facie it was to be expected that this encroachment into publicly-owned manufacturing would be strongly resisted by Conservatives, but I managed to get the Tories on my Committee to accept it as a recommendation in the report. The other thing that was to be expected, and confidently, was that a Labour Postmaster-General would seize on this recommendation with a whoop of joy and implement it as quickly as he could. Not so: the Postmaster-General at the time, John Stonehouse, turned it down flat, and repeated the rejection when a deputation of the Party NEC called on him to ask him to reconsider that decision. (Since I do not subscribe to the common cliché on how one should speak of the dead – the one which Harold Laski amended to read *de mortuis nil nisi bunkum* – I am free to say that, quite apart from his strange performance in this matter, John Stonehouse was the Minister of my acquaintance whose talents fell furthest short of his reputation.)

The Committee also decided to have a look at the Bank of England, which no-one had cast an eye on, not even the most casual of eyes, since it was nationalised more than twenty years earlier. The Chancellor of the Exchequer, Jim Callaghan, was rendered speechless with horror by this proposal: the idea of a group of questioning MPs crossing the sacred portals of the Bank caused him to react like a High Priest at the sight of the innermost sanctum, the Holy of Holies, being invaded by a group of malodorous swineherds.

I had a meeting with him and told him that the Committee derived its authority from the House and not from the Government and that he had no right or power to impose a veto on any part of our programme of work. In the middle of my argument with him there was a Government reshuffle, and Jim was replaced as Chancellor by Roy Jenkins. Roy took the same view as his predecessor (in fact, as I discovered later, they were both parroting the view of the Governor of the Bank), and so I proposed to the members of the Committee, and they agreed, that we should join together in a bit of arm-twisting: we began using a procedural device to block after-ten-pm business, and we clogged up the works, and we went on doing it till Jenkins (or rather Sir Leslie O'Brien, who was the Governor) gave way.

Our report on the Bank of England was less informative than the others we produced because we found ourselves blocked at almost every turn by the steel cocoon of secrecy that is wrapped round all the Bank's important operations. But we penetrated far enough to discover that the purposes for which the Bank had been nationalised had not been at all fulfilled – indeed there had been a role-reversal. The nationalisation Act made the Bank the instrument through which the Treasury would control the City, but that wasn't happening – instead, the Bank was acting as the mouthpiece of the City influencing the Treasury. A small but revealing piece of evidence in that direction was that the Governor knew how much the Chancellor was paid, but the Chancellor had no idea how much the Governor was paid.

The longest and weightiest and most original of our reports was the first report of the 1967–68 Session, which came to be widely studied and discussed by civil servants and academics and everyone else interested in the machinery of government. It analysed in detail the relations between a public corporation, its sponsoring Minister and the Treasury, and in the course of that analysis it threw the final shovelful of earth on the coffin of the Morrisonian concept of the autonomous public corporation as the best instrument for running a publicly-owned industry or service. Under that concept the sponsoring minister would lay down broad sectoral policy (e.g. for the fuel-and-power sector or the transport sector) and would then leave the board of each corporation to manage its industry within that sectoral policy and with no intervention by the Minister in its day-to-day operations. The role reversal which we discovered was that in practice the Ministers did *not* make sectoral policy (which instead tended to grow like Topsy) but they *did* intervene, and extensively, in day-to-day management, and their interventions were not always beneficial.

There are a few lines in that report which I hugely enjoyed writing. It is the only example in all select committee reports of the use of a passage of comic verse to illustrate a serious political/organisational point. We were very critical of the long-drawn-out, painful process by which the investment plan of a public corporation obtained government approval. The corporation submitted its plan to the sponsoring Ministry, and the civil servants of that Ministry entered into a long argument about it with the corporation, as a result of which it might be amended but eventually, after not inconsiderable delay, was agreed. But that wasn't the end of the concatenation: the next link was that the civil servants of the sponsoring Ministry submitted the so-far-agreed plan to the civil servants of the public affairs unit in the Treasury, who entered into a long argument about it with them (but not with the corporation, who had the right to talk to the monkey but not to the organ-grinder). As a graphic illustration of this process we quoted A. A. Milne:

> 'The King asked
> The Queen, and
> The Queen asked
> the Dairymaid:
> "Can we have some butter for
> The Royal slice of bread?"
> The Queen asked
> The Dairymaid,
> The Dairymaid
> Said, "Certainly,
> I'll go and tell
> The cow
> now
> Before she goes to bed."'

A bit frivolous maybe, but spot on.

# Chapter 13

IN THE 1970 general election campaign in my constituency I discovered in the first three days of canvassing that there was a significant swing against Labour compared with the 1966 result. It wouldn't be enough to endanger my own seat – I won with a still large, though reduced, majority – but it was clearly enough to destroy our majority in the House.

What I heard on the doorsteps was not that a lot of people who had voted Labour in 1966 were going to vote Tory or Liberal in 1970, but that a lot of people who had voted Labour in 1966 were, in 1970, not going to vote at all. We were about to suffer defeat not from floating voters but from floating abstainers.

To me this was not a new phenomenon. All my experience as an election canvasser, from my baptism as a youngster, had convinced me that the floating voter is only the second, not the first, cause of electoral swings: the first cause is differential abstentions. To put it simply, Labour wins at any election at which it can get to the poll a higher percentage of those who, if they are going to vote at all, will vote Labour – a higher percentage than the Conservatives get of those who, if they vote at all, will vote Conservative – and ditto the other way round.

After the election I went through our polling-day records and made a list of a random sample of 120 electors who had voted for me in 1966 but not in 1970, and I called on 116 of them (I could never catch the other four at home). Of these 116, three had voted Conservative and two Liberal, and the other 111 hadn't voted at all. With some minor variations they all gave the same reason for not voting: in broad terms it was that they couldn't see much, if any, difference between what the Labour Government had done in the last four years and what a Conservative Government would have done in the same circumstances. The fact that I had been one of the group of Labour MPs who had fought hard for more radical and un-Conservative policies influenced the attitude of some of my electors in my favour, but not many of them, and not all that much.

[*Digression:* It is this factor of differential abstentions which undermines the reliability and accuracy of public-opinion polls on how people intend to vote. We know that in practice a fifth to a quarter of all electors don't go to the poll in a general election, and rather more than that in a parliamentary by-election, and very many more than that in a local authority election, but the percentage poll in a public-opinion poll is nearly 100 per cent, since of all the people who are asked, 'If there were a general election tomorrow, how would you vote?' there are very few (only Plymouth Brethren and Jehovah's Witnesses and a handful of others) who are honest enough to reply, 'If there were a general election tomorrow, I wouldn't vote at all.' What this amounts to is that in this type of poll the pollster asks one question and the interviewee answers *a different question*: the question which is asked is 'If there were an election tomorrow, how would you vote?', and the question which the interviewee answers is, 'If there were an election tomorrow, how would you vote if you voted at all?'

The polling organisations certainly understand that this is what happens and that the gap between the two questions fractures the accuracy of the results they publish and therefore damages their credibility. They try various means of narrowing this credibility gap: the most direct and obvious of them is to ask some such follow-up question as 'How likely are you to vote?'; but that's a question which many people don't answer honestly, since few people will ever give an answer to any question which they think may lower their esteem in the eyes of the questioner, and so the figures obtained from this type of follow-up are the least reliable of all. That's one of the reasons why competing polls published within a few days of each other often produce between them a conclusion which is manifestly incorrect, and sometimes even nonsensical, like a couple of million people changing their voting intentions within the space of seventy-two hours.]

After our knock-down in 1970 the Labour Party picked itself up, dusted itself off, and began preparing for the next round. The National

Executive Committee realised that we had to write a fresh political prospectus getting us back to the Party's principles which the recent Government had partially abandoned, a prospectus widely distanced from the restrictive, deflationary, sometimes even defeatist measures which had marred the last couple of years of that Government. So we set in hand a wide-ranging process of problem-analysis and policy-formation: at one time we had nearly fifty study-groups and working-parties producing papers for the Home Policy and International Committee of the National Executive. (The equally wide-ranging policy review which the Party launched after the 1987 general election differed from the post-1970 review in two very important respects: (i) in our earlier effort we trawled for expertise and talent over a wide stretch of water: the work was shared between members of the NEC, members of the Shadow Cabinet, other MPs, trade union leaders, academics and other experts, local councillors and rank-and-file members, whilst the post-1987 review groups were cautiously fly-fished from a much smaller and narrower catchment area; and (ii) the earlier review was planned and controlled by the NEC, and the later one by the Parliamentary leadership. That latter change is a part of the general and continuing process, which was started by Hugh Gaitskell and pushed on by Harold Wilson and Jim Callaghan, of gradually, almost furtively, shifting decision-making from Annual Conference and the NEC to the Shadow Cabinet, or even the Leader's office – a switch from democracy to centralism very similar to the one which Margaret Thatcher made, after 1979, in the *modus operandi* of her Parliamentary Party and even of her Cabinet.)

The post-1970 policy review laid down a programme for simultaneously increasing the size of the national cake and sharing it more fairly. It is a standard Conservative-plus-City contention that these two objectives conflict with one another, that the socialist concern for fair shares gets in the way of growth, that the nation should first go all out for a bigger cake and only when they've got it should think about how it's shared out. In fact the two objectives go hand in hand: sharing the cake out more fairly actually contributes to increasing its size, because, as our wartime experience showed, people work hard and produce more when they're satisfied that the product of their hard work will be fairly shared rather than benefiting only the already-well-off minority.

A number of members of the Tribune Group contributed to this work of policy formation, either as members of the NEC or as co-optees to some of the study-groups and working-parties. Our Group had lost some of its members in the election defeat, but after the election it was still stronger than ever before because a number of the newly-elected MPs joined: in fact, after every one of the eight general elections beginning with 1964 the Group increased in size and strength. The minutes of the first post-election meeting of the Group record the welcome extended to three new members attending for the first time – Neil Kinnock, Caerwyn Roderick and Dennis Skinner.

The Group threw itself with élan into the fight against the new Tory Government, both in the House and out in the country. In recent years the Ministers sacked by Thatcher because they weren't ideologically pure, and the 'wet' Conservative MPs who support them, have popularised the theory that, by contrast with the disastrously divisive Thatcher administrations, Harold Macmillan and Edward Heath presided over warmhearted one-nation governments in the Disraeli mould: nobody articulated this theory more than the two ex-premiers themselves, Macmillan from the benches of the House of Lords in the last years of his life, and Edward Heath *passim*. But the truth is other: it was Heath's administration which began the process of making the rich richer and the poor poorer which Margaret Thatcher was later to elevate into the first article of the creed. It was this element of government policy which the Tribune Group selected as its main target: we felt that most members of the Opposition Front Bench were compromised because they had been the Ministers responsible for the Wilson Government's public-expenditure cuts and therefore lacked the credibility to oppose the (much larger and more serious) Heath Government's public-expenditure cuts, whereas we could claim that our opposition to the Wilson cuts gave us the authority to go on saying what we had been saying all along. Totally uninhibited by any false modesty, we spelled out this claim in one of our public statements:

'We members of the "Tribune Group" and those other Labour MPs who voted, in line with Party Conference decisions, against some similar, though less serious, proposals by the late Labour Government are the best qualified to mount the attack on these Tory cuts.

'Take, for example, the issue of prescription charges, which is a matter close to the hearts of Labour men and women. We warned that, having removed the charges, for the Labour Government to reimpose them was to open the door to the Conservatives, should they regain power, to go further along the same road.'

Rereading that statement at this distance I find it, like every other I-told-you-so, just a bit self-satisfied and sententious, but at the time it struck home as a very real truth, though for our Leader an uncomfortable one.

Edward Heath would be equally uncomfortable if ever he now reread a statement which we issued following one of his Government's budgets: it reads like a prelude to what most people, including Heath, said of the (much worse) Lawson budget of 1988:

'The Conservative leaders do not talk about the class struggle: they practise it. Their Government has made the meanest and most savage attacks on working men and women, and still more on their children and pensioner parents, since 1931.

'Their object is to take hundreds of millions out of the pockets of the poor and the sick and give it to the rich. The average wage-earner with a wife and two children will gain the magnificent sum of 1s a week in income-tax relief. But he could lose up to 25s a week in the additional charges now imposed. As against that, the £20,000 a year man with a wife and two children will benefit by £195 a year.'

So much for the contention of Edward Heath and his undehydrated friends that Tory governments before Margaret Thatcher's consisted of civilised beneficent pursuers of social justice.

The regular exchanges which we had established before 1970 with some left-wing trade-union leaders became even closer now that we were in opposition. As the months passed both we and they became increasingly impatient of what we saw as the halfhearted, limited and ineffective opposition to the Government's policies, and not least to its anti-trade-union legislation, which our leaders were putting up, and that same disillusion spread through the rank-and-file of the Party and of the trade unions. We began to discuss seriously how our work in parliament could be reinforced by extraparliamentary activity.

Our first serious exploration of this possibility took place only a few months after the general election, over dinner in a Westminster restaurant attended by sixteen members of the Group and nine trade-union leaders (Cyril Cooper, Laurence Daly, George Doughty, George Elvin, Clive Jenkins, Jack Jones, Alex Kitson, Alan Sapper and Bob

Wright). We examined a number of possibilities: the most radical one proposed was calling on the TUC General Council to organise a one-day general strike – a proposal which drew support from only two members of the Group, Syd Bidwell and Neil Kinnock. (Neil seems to have developed since then some rather different views on extraparliamentary activity.)

We found some consolation from present frustrations in hopes for the future. The Party's policy review seemed to be going well and to promise that the next Labour government would break out of the conventional thinking that had limited the ambition and straitjacketed the movements of the 1966–70 Government.

I was a member of several of the policy review groups, but the research in which I was most involved and on which I had most to contribute was a programme for the regeneration of British industry. (It's a sad reflection that, because the 1974 Government shied away from fully implementing the recommendations we made, the post-1987 review had to go over all the same ground again.) In that research we came to the conclusion, central to all our thinking, that Britain's economic problems stemmed largely from the noncompetitiveness of its manufacturing industry, and that its noncompetitiveness stemmed largely from the failure of our entrepreneurs to invest as high a proportion of their surplus in modernisation as their overseas competitors did. The excuse which they gave for this failure – a plaintive dirge keened repetitively by the CBI and the Institute of Directors – was that they didn't make enough profit to provide enough money for new buildings and equipment and tooling, but that was an empty excuse: the fact was that they always gave priority to high dividends over re-investment. During Edward Heath's premiership he discovered this hard fact for himself: the discovery shocked him, and it also gave dramatic support to our own analysis. Invited to speak at one of the businessmen's conclaves (I think it was the Institute of Directors) he thundered at them, more in anger than in sorrow, a notable philippic: I have given you, he said, all you asked for – I've removed price controls and reduced corporate taxation – so that your profits have shot up, and still the level of industrial investment is falling.

Ted Heath was sadly rediscovering what his predecessors had long since discovered, which is that the generality of British entrepreneurs can't be bribed (which means that they certainly can't be cajoled) into spending enough money to keep their technology up to date.

Past governments had offered and provided generous – sometimes over-generous – grants and loans for investment, especially in the development areas and special development areas, with results that were only marginal. Our research groups, unlike Ted, were proposing not to weep over this diagnosis of the British disease but to prescribe some effective remedies for it. Since industrialists couldn't be induced by honey or money to invest adequately, the Government would have to do it for them.

Out of this analysis was born the twin-track policy of the National Enterprise Board plus planning agreements. The Board was to be a public holding company which would, through whole- or part-ownership, acquire control of underinvesting large companies and put them on the path of righteousness and expansion; and planning agreements between companies and the Government – a management-system which was being operated with great success in France – would introduce some public-interest and worker input into the investment (and other) policies of another group of large enterprises.

As the reports of this and the other new policy initiatives began to be made public, they inspired a fresh wave of hope and optimism throughout the Party. But after a while this satisfaction began to be clouded by doubt: the Leader of the Party seemed to be less than wildly enthusiastic about the new policy potentials which the Party was exploring, and we started to wonder whether many, or even any, of them would survive to be incorporated in the Party programme. Even before 1970 Harold Wilson had started changing the operations of both the Government and the Party from democratic management to presidential rule, and in opposition he seemed to be succumbing further to the temptations – and they are real temptations – of authoritarianism.

Our fears were sharpened by a pronouncement he made soon after the publication of *Labour's Programme for Britain* in 1973. At the very outset of the discussion of that programme Wilson announced that he and the Shadow Cabinet 'would not hesitate to use its veto at the appropriate time' to keep a specific item in the programme and out of the manifesto. The Tribune Group immediately issued a statement sharply challenging this tsarist ukase of Wilson's: 'We vigorously rebut,' we wrote, 'the Leader's claim that he and the Shadow Cabinet have any rights of veto over the policy to be included in the manifesto. There are no existing rights of veto for the Shadow Cabinet; there never have been such rights; and we are determined that no such rights, which would make a mockery of democracy within the Party, are ever conceded to any individual or section of the Party.'

Wilson never actually sought to carry out his threat to veto manifesto items, so all the kerfuffle he aroused by it was totally gratuitous – and there's no error, in politics or in anything else, as stupid as a gratuitous error. But at the time the threat gave us good reason to believe that he had specifically in mind a couple of the new policy proposals which he intended to get deleted from the manifesto. My guess was that one of them was our twin-track policy for industry, and another was a commitment to a large-scale, highly progressive redistribution of wealth which would have the consequential effect of creating a similar redistribution of power.

I was a member, in that year of two elections, of the drafting committee for both the 1974 manifestoes, as I had been for the previous four, and I played some part in ensuring that, at least on those two key items of policy, we didn't seriously depart from the programme we had worked out. In those manifestoes we wrote:

'. . . we shall create a powerful National Enterprise Board with the structure and functions set out in *Labour's Programme 1973*,'

and:

'A new and urgent Industry Act will provide for a system of Planning Agreements between the Government and key companies to ensure that the plans of those companies are in harmony with national needs and objectives and that Government financial assistance is deployed where it will be most effectively used. Wherever we give direct aid to a company out of public funds we shall reserve the right to take a proportionate share of the ownership of the company; and wherever possible this public support will be channelled through the Planning Agreements System,'

and

'It is . . . our intention to bring about a fundamental and irreversible shift in the balance of power and wealth in favour of working people and their families . . .'

So no veto. (Not this time, but it is widely believed that Jim Callaghan did exercise a veto, and successfully, on the committee drafting the 1979 manifesto. I can't write about that at first hand because by 1979 I was no longer on the National Executive Committee and therefore, for the first time since 1951, had no hand in drafting the manifesto; but it was a pretty open secret that at one stage in the drafting Jim threatened to resign if he didn't get his way on deleting one proposed commitment.)

This claim of Harold Wilson's of a right of veto was not the only method by which he sought to rule over the Party like a Roman emperor of old. Another was the edict he imposed on those of his Ministers who were members of the National Executive Committee requiring them to promote on that Committee the policies of the Government even when those policies were in conflict with the Party policy on which members of the NEC had been elected to the Committee and which they had a duty to sustain. Judged by any sort of standards this directive of Wilson's was a gross violation of basic democratic principles, since it required people to abandon any consideration for the constituency which elected them, and instead to hold themselves rigidly accountable to a quite different constituency, with the result that they were deceiving the Constituency Parties and holding their NEC seats by false pretences.

Not surprisingly many of the members in the constituencies deeply resented being treated as contemptuously as that, and some of them demanded that Ministers should be debarred from membership of the NEC. I supported that proposition, because in terms of simple logic it couldn't be faulted. But only one of the Ministers concerned shared my view. He was Dick Crossman, whose logical mind accepted that the double loyalty which the Leader was demanding could not be sustained with a clear conscience, and he carried this belief to its honest conclusion and dropped off the NEC of his own volition. Barbara Castle took the opposite view: she defended her foot-in-both-camps with one of her clanging barrages of amazonian bellicosity which were meat and drink to her.

She and her fellow-Ministers and the Leader got away with that one, but rank-and-file dissatisfaction with Wilson's leadership style grew apace. It took the form of a growing pressure for changes in the Party's constitution designed to make it more democratic. One of those proposed changes was that the Leader should be elected, and therefore influenced, not by only the Parliamentary Labour Party but by the Party as a whole. That demand was first spelled out in the Allaun-Sillars-Mikardo pamphlet, *Labour: Party or Puppet?*, which I mentioned earlier. It was a proposal that went hand-in-hand with the proposal that Labour MPs should be required to submit themselves for reselection in each Parliament: these two changes were eventually adopted after some years of struggle to overcome the resistance of the PLP and the Party establishment, and taken together they gave the rank-and-file members some say in the Party's policy-formation and implementation – not all that much say, but at least more than before, and at least enough to lift them a bit above their roles hitherto as mere spear-carriers during election campaigns and hod-carriers at all other times.

Without immodesty I can fairly claim to have opened the door to the reselection process. In 1973 I persuaded the NEC to adopt a self-denying ordinance by which it virtually surrendered its power to over-turn, on appeal, a Constituency Party's selection of a candidate or deselection of its Member of Parliament. I got away with this, and fairly easily, by arguing that if the Executive made no concession at all to the growing demand for greater autonomy for CLPs we would stir up a large pot of damaging divisions and confrontations. But I don't think I'd have got away with opening that particular door if my colleagues on the NEC had realised what was going to come in, six years later, through the open door.

Before this change an unsuccessful candidate or MP could appeal to the Executive, on grounds that were always subjective and generally insubstantial, against the heinous conduct of his Constituency Party in choosing, instead of him, somebody else who, in his modest and objective judgement, was less worthy than he. Most often the Executive, on grounds that were always arbitrary and generally biased, would uphold the appeal, particularly if the National Agent could produce, out of those McCarthyite dossiers pioneered by Sara Barker, some smear against the selected candidate. But at the 1974 Annual Conference I spelled out from the platform, on behalf of the NEC, the self-denying ordinance we had adopted of refusing to hear any appeal from the decision of a selection conference except on the grounds that there had been some breach of the constitution in carrying out the selection procedure.

Later in that speech I deployed the case for the introduction of a reselection process in terms that were designed to anticipate and discount the opposition which the Parliamentary Labour Party could be expected to mount against any change in the comfortable and comforting station in life to which they were accustomed. I strongly defended 'the right of the CLP, without any qualification at all, to be the only authority that decides who shall be the candidate that bears its name. They have got to carry the can; they have got to find the lolly; they have got to find the door-knockers; they have got to find the deliverers, so they should have the right, and nobody else should have the right, to decide for whom they should work. But of course if they have the right to select they must also have the right to deselect. That goes without saying, doesn't it?

'I don't believe, and have never believed, that the selection of a man as Labour candidate by a Constituency Labour Party is a ticket for life. It isn't, and it ought not to be, and I would never want it to be. If a situation develops in which there is an incompatibility between a Constituency Labour Party and its Member in the House, it is in its interest and in his interest as well that he should seek another constituency and it should seek another candidate. Divorce is always a difficult business, and it is always a painful business, but it is as true of the relations between a CLP and its Member as it is of the relations between husband and wife that, in the final issue, if the marriage has broken down through incompatibility then a divorce is better than carrying on with a pretence of living together.'

It was obvious that that speech had a decisive effect on the delegates. It also established that within a few years the Party would surely adopt some system for the reselection of MPs. In the meantime the NEC was adhering faithfully, as it has done ever since, to its self-denying ordinance, even when Shirley Williams tried repeatedly to get us to overturn the constitutionally correct deselection of Reg Prentice because he was an outstandingly good and loyal Labour man and therefore deserved exceptional support. (Not long after that the good and loyal Prentice joined the Conservative Party, and later became a Conservative MP.)

But the battle for reselection still had to be fought, and I will go through it in some detail because the full story of it has never been told. At the monthly meeting of the NEC's Organisation Committee in November 1977 I proposed, in implementation of a Conference resolution which had been remitted to the NEC, that we should set up a working party to examine how the principle of reselection could best be put into practice and into the Party's constitution, and this proposal of mine just scraped through on the chairman's casting vote. So the working party was set up: it consisted of four members of the NEC's Organisation Committee, three MPs chosen by the Parliamentary Party, two representatives of those trade unions who would be concerned because of their sponsorship of parliamentary candidates, and one representative of each of four other interested parties. We got to work, but quite soon after we started I began to be seriously worried about the possibility that our recommendations might produce a bitter and damaging division between the Constituency Parties and the trade unions (supported by the Parliamentary Party) which would re-create all the tortured conflicts of the 1950s.

On our working party only two of the NEC representatives, Eric Heffer and I, were fully in favour of reselection; two of the three PLP representatives, Sydney Irving and George Park, in accordance with the views of the majority of their colleagues, strongly opposed any form of reselection; so did one of the two trade-union representatives, Terry Duffy of the Engineers; the other, Moss Evans of the Transport and General, wasn't sure how his Executive would react; and the representative of the agents and the Co-operative Party were opposed to change of any sort. Although I wanted mandatory reselection I had a vision, and I was really scared by it, of our presenting that recommendation to the next Annual Conference and its being enthusiastically supported by the Constituency Parties and being crushingly voted down by the steamroller vote of the trade unions, and that would take us all the way back to a repeat of the horrendous Morecambe Conference of 1952 and its equally horrendous aftermath.

I put these fears to my three NEC colleagues on the working party – they were Bryan Stanley, Eric Heffer and John Cartwright (the only one of the subsequent SDP defectors whose departure I regretted) – and they accepted that the unhappy-ending scenario I was envisaging was a real possibility, and one that we should seek to avoid. So the four of us, together with Ron Hayward, had a meeting to see if we could work out a reselection formula which we could put to the other members of the working party and which had a reasonable chance of being accepted by both halves of the next Annual Conference.

The solution we came up with was to provide a reselection procedure and leave it to the management committee of each Constituency Party to decide, at the appropriate time during each Parliament, whether to activate it or not. This formula later became known, in the Party jargon, as 'The Mikardo Compromise', though in fact it wasn't a compromise: it was a recommendation with a strong independent justification of its own because it enhanced the autonomy of the CLP in that it provided that any CLP which wanted reselection could have it, while no CLP which didn't want reselection was compelled to have it.

In the end ten of the thirteen members of the working party subscribed to this recommendation, and the other three, led by Jo Richardson, produced a well-argued minority report in favour of the reselection process being mandatory at all times on every CLP.

The 1978 Annual Conference voted to accept the majority recommendation; but some delegates argued vigorously for the minority report, and some of the political adolescents who were members or supporters of the Campaign for Labour Party Democracy accused me of reneging on them – indeed the Campaign then ran a slate against me which got me knocked off the National Executive Committee. (A couple of years later, having learned better, they made some overtures to me which indicated that they had come to regret what they had done.)

Because there was some confusion in the voting at the 1978 Conference the matter was reopened the following year. By this time there had been, throughout the Party, including the trade unions, a considerable movement of opinion in favour of mandatory reselection. I went along with that, partly because I had always recognised the strength of the case for the mandatory option, but also because I was sure that in practice the choice between the two options would remain open because any CLP which clearly wanted to retain its MP would sidestep the commitment to reselection by selecting its candidate from 'a shortlist of one', i.e. its sitting Member. That is exactly what has happened: in both the 1979 and 1983 Parliaments a large proportion of the sitting MPs were reselected in this way.

That's how that conflict was resolved, and its resolution was hastened by the fact that, as the 1979 Parliament drew to its close, the whole Party switched its attention from internal organisation to the overriding task of winning the approaching general election. We had succeeded in getting some good manifesto commitments, and we therefore had the happy expectation of persuading the country to elect a Labour government that would have a radical outlook and the courage to introduce radical measures. Alas, regardless of their doom, the little victims played.

# Chapter 14

THE FIRST of the 1974 general elections, in February, produced a hung Parliament; the second, eight months later, gave Labour a small but working majority (which, however, became steadily eroded by by-election losses during the following four years).

The Queen's speech for the 1974–75 session included a lot of the forward thinking and measures set out in the election manifesto. The Tribune Group lined up enthusiastically in the vanguard of the troops who were embattled behind the Government to put those radical measures into legislation and fulfilment.

We were particularly enthused by the publication of the Industry Bill. Thought it didn't match up to all the hopes I'd had of it, there was enough in it to launch a new industrial revolution based on a large increase in manufacturing investment.

It was obviously going to be strenuously opposed, by both the Conservatives and the Liberals, throughout the whole of its passage, and especially in the committee stage. Several members of the Tribune Group, I among them, volunteered to serve on the Standing Committee, and were selected, and we played a major part, during a hundred hours of debate, in defending the Bill against all comers. (Michael Heseltine, in his speeches on the Committee, repeatedly tried to draw some abstruse sinister conclusions from our strong representation on the Committee: he was then serving his pristine apprenticeship in the technique of headline-grabbing which in later years became the principal weapon, the H-bomb, in his political-ambition armoury.)

Without much difficulty we frustrated the Opposition's attempts to murder the Bill, but we then saw it destroyed in an act of infanticide committed by its progenitors. Towards the end of the committee stage the Prime Minister entertained the leaders of the CBI who were, of course, bitterly opposed to the Bill. They asked him for five concessions which between them would have the effect of so emasculating the Bill as to make it incapable of fulfilling its stated purposes, and Wilson conceded all of them not merely tamely, but even happily. Those five demands of the CBI were that the capital available to the National Enterprise Board should be cut by eighty per cent (which meant that it couldn't tackle the big companies); that it should lose its power to acquire assets compulsorily (which meant that it couldn't acquire assets at all at a reasonable price); that planning agreements should be only voluntary (which meant that there wouldn't be any); that the trade unions should be excluded from them (which removed any inhibition on sweetheart agreements between Ministers and the bosses); and that Tony Benn should be taken out of the Department of Industry (which meant that even the emasculated Bill wouldn't be implemented vigorously). That wasn't just selling the pass – it was presenting it giftwrapped to Labour's most implacable opponents. Those CBI delegates must have Rollsed and Porsched away from their meeting with Harold scarcely believing how easily and totally and unconditionally they'd got away with every single thing they were asking for: the champagne must have flowed like Niagara.

Just as the CBI must have been startled by their unexpected blood-less victory, most of the Labour Party were shattered by Wilson's unexpected betrayal – that's not at all too strong a word for it – of the Party's commitments. Their frustration spilled over in indignation at the CBI's gratuitous success, and especially at their sidelining of Tony Benn for his sin of defending the Party's commitments, and many of us got on our chargers and rode into the lists in Tony's defence. It is ironic, in view of the bitchy relationship that later developed between Neil Kinnock and Tony Benn, that it was Neil who, in 1975, wielded the sharpest, the most determined and the most indignant lance on Tony's behalf. In a sizzling article in *Tribune* he wrote that

'the only reason for changing Benn's job ... was that it was demanded by interests who are the traditional and implacable enemies of the Labour movement.

'The appeasement, like most appeasements, won't work. Those who demanded the change will simply ask for more. But we are now in the extraordinary and dangerously undemocratic situation where our foes have a direct influence on the selection of Labour Ministers.'

But that was a defeat we need not have suffered if the left-wing members of the Cabinet had put themselves in the leadership of the Party's resistance to the Prime Minister's sell-out. He accompanied his sidelining of Benn with two other acts of reshuffle, which were to remove Judith Hart and Reg Prentice from the Cabinet. Prentice's position was saved, and easily, because his friend and supporter, Roy Jenkins, delivered an ultimatum to Wilson threatening to resign if Prentice were pushed out, and Wilson caved in immediately. If the Left members of the Cabinet – notably Foot, Castle, Silkin and Shore (a rightwinger who had acquired a false reputation as a leftist merely because he was anti-EEC) – had shown the same spunk as Jenkins they could easily have won the same victory, but they shied away from bearding the lion in his den.

On 9 June 1975 there was a continuous meeting of the Left ministers in Tony Benn's room stretching over several hours, with some changes of dramatis personae as various characters dropped in for a while, and then dropped out, and then came back again. For some reason which I can't recall, I was, though only a backbencher, invited to that meeting, and Tony and I were the only two participants who stayed right through it. I could scarcely contain my disappointment and anger: I thought the behaviour of those Ministers was both incomprehensible and gutless, and I said so more than once and in short sharp words of four letters. But they wouldn't move – except that Judith Hart shamed the rest of them by resigning and thus showing that she, even if she were alone in it, wasn't ready to abandon her convictions in order to hold on to office. Eric Heffer, Tony's number two, had similarly resigned some time before.

What I didn't know at the time – I learned it only many years later – was that those Left ministers were partly inhibited from effective protest by having compromised themselves on the issue of industrial policy nearly a year earlier. At a Cabinet meeting in August 1974 Harold Lever delivered a blistering attack on the Party's industrial policy not because he claimed there was anything wrong with it but because businessmen wouldn't like it – an argument which one wouldn't normally expect to hear from any member of a socialist Cabinet.

Harold Lever is very much a one-off in the Labour Party. He is

196

a successful and wealthy operator in the worlds of finance and business, a kind man with an attractive persona, a great charm of manner and a twinkling wit, an accomplished raconteur and mimic and a top-level bridge player. He gave good service to the Government by inventing effective pragmatic solutions to some short-term micro-problems, but he fitted into a would-be reforming Labour Cabinet like Falstaff in a monastery. Basically he was the City operators' honorary advocate in the Cabinet, and he did them proud.

His attack on the then projected Industry Bill wasn't by any means the only occasion and the only issue on which he succeeded in blocking progressive measures in Cabinet. For all the services, some of them very valuable services, which he gave to his colleagues, his overall contribution to the Party was on balance negative, and sometimes even damaging. I remember a question I got at a public meeting I addressed in 1975, 'Isn't Bennery a great threat to the success of the Labour Party?' to which I replied, 'No: our real problem today is not Bennery but Leverage.' Barbara Castle, a past-mistress of penetrating one-line judgements on her colleagues, wrote that 'the trouble with Harold Lever is that he plays too much bridge with too many representatives of the Establishment,' and she added that 'he is terrified of every socialist bit of our policy'.

At that August 1974 Cabinet meeting Tony Benn was the only Minister who opposed Harold Lever's chopping-down of the Party's industrial policy; none of his left-wing colleagues gave him any support. I wonder why. Perhaps it was because industrial policy was out of their depth, or perhaps they were overawed by Harold Lever's silver-tongued expert-sounding business jargon, or perhaps they didn't want to get into a row with the Prime Minister. Whatever the reason, it may well be that their surrender-by-silence on that occasion made them impotent to protest when the crunch came ten months later. But that was no excuse, and I just couldn't understand, and certainly couldn't condone, their unwillingness to use their bargaining-power with Wilson, as Roy Jenkins had done, to defend a principle and save a friend.

The Government's watering-down of the Industry Bill swept away the programme of regenerating British industry which was one of the two central pillars of the 1974 manifestoes. Because of the cuts in the size and powers of the National Enterprise Board it was never able to do more than tinker with a few marginal bits of industrial rationalisation. As for the planning agreements, whereas it had been envisaged that under the original Industry Bill we should within three years set up such agreements with the hundred companies which accounted for half the nation's manufacturing output, in practice under the emasculated Bill we set up in three years only one agreement, not with a company but with the National Coal Board, and that agreement was cosmetic and meaningless and valueless because it merely duplicated the powers already exercised over the Board by the Secretary of State for Fuel and Power.

The sweeping away of the second central pillar of the 1974 manifestoes, the 'fundamental and irreversible shift in the balance of power and wealth in favour of working people and their families', came a couple of years later, after Jim Callaghan had succeeded Harold Wilson as prime minister. In the two years of his premiership, from 1977 to 1979, there was actually a significant shift of wealth the other way round, from the poor to the rich – a process which was continued and rapidly escalated by the next prime minister, Margaret Thatcher.

Harold Wilson's Industry Bill victory over the Left (of which he had once proudly claimed to be a part) encouraged him further in his delusion that he was a president rather than a prime minister (a delusion which was also to afflict his two successors). He rapidly distanced himself from the Labour Party: he treated it as one would treat an elderly, boring maiden aunt, sending her a birthday card (in October) every year but never inviting her to visit and never listening to what she said. So while my 9 June anger was still incandescent I dashed off a letter to the Party's general secretary signed by enough NEC members to requisition a special meeting of the Executive to discuss the crisis which the Prime Minister had precipitated. It took place a month later, on 9 July, which was my birthday (and Mary cooked me a special high-protein birthday breakfast to keep my dander up). For what happened at that meeting I can't do better than quote Barbara Castle's diary entry for that day:

'Ministers were there in force. . . . Mik was soon in full spate with a bitter attack. After the last election, he said, the PM had promised closer contact between the Government and the party. Instead, contact had "never been worse". There had been no meeting between the NEC and the Cabinet since the election and the precious Liaison Committee between NEC and Government hadn't met once. Okay, so the Government was constantly talking to the TUC, but what about the party? "The Government is expressing contempt for the party even worse than the 1966–70 Government." It thought that party members were merely "dogsbodies to go and knock on doors". Time and again meetings arranged with Ministers are cancelled "and Peter Shore is the worst". He ended in a crescendo of viciousness: "We are in for a direct confrontation between the party and the Government." '

This tirade of mine (it was tough, but I don't accept that it was vicious) did have one effect in that it led to a renewal of the periodic meetings of the tripartite Liaison Committee of Cabinet plus NEC plus General Council of the TUC which had been set up in 1972 and which for a while had proved to be valuable as a forum for discussion and a mechanism for co-ordination. But the revived meetings didn't have that sort of value because Ministers considered them a nuisance and didn't treat them at all seriously. If one of them was asked for information he just brought along and read mechanically a brief written in civil-service Mandarin pictograms by one of his deputy assistants. The worst of the Ministers was the Secretary for Trade, Edmund Dell (yes, the same one who later walked out on us to become a merchant banker and a pillar of the SDP): when both the NEC and the trade-union delegates pressed him and the Chancellor on exchange controls he produced a departmental paper which argued that our exchange situation was improving: that argument rested on calculating percentages from base years and datum lines which were misleadingly selected to give the answer he wanted, and he glibly and arrogantly assumed (wrongly) that we would be too dim to see through it.

As that 1974 Government moved on towards its disastrous conclusion the dissatisfactions in the Party grew apace, and the Tribune Group forcefully articulated them. In a statement headed 'Appeal for the defence of the Labour Manifesto', we wrote that 'having worked for years to secure a Labour majority, we are desperately anxious to avoid mistakes like those of the 1966–70 period which inevitably led to our defeat at the polls,' and in a later statement we demanded a radical change of government action in five directions: a reversal of the policy of cutting the social wage, which mostly benefits the poor, in order to provide tax reductions, which mostly benefit the rich (where have I heard that before, and since?); a vigorous wide-ranging campaign to reduce unemployment; a Freedom of Information Act; democracy in the workplace; and a charter for council house tenants. All in vain: the Government staggered from error to error, including Jim Callaghan's final error in choosing the date of his general election not in the autumn of 1978 but in the spring of 1979. Although Jim had no great love for me, he had some respect for my experience in electioneering, and he chose me as one of the half-dozen people whose advice he asked, in the summer of 1978, on whether to have an election a couple of months after that or to wait till the following year. I strongly advocated October 1978.

'But,' he said, 'if we do it then there's a strong chance we may be defeated.'

'That's right,' I replied, 'but I can't see anything getting better for us during the winter, and I can see a lot getting worse.'

I suppose that amongst those he consulted there must have been a majority who took the opposite view to mine, with the result that he made the howling error of landing us in a general election at the end of a winter of discontent – an error from which his successor learned a lesson and which she never repeated.

In the period of which I am now writing I was involved in another and very different area of activity. When I was elected chairman of the Party's International Committee I automatically became the leader of our delegation to the Socialist International, with Ron Hayward, the general secretary, as my number two. Ron had been a delegate for some years before, and when he first got into the International he discovered that its management, and especially its financial management, was in a state of chaos. He immediately undertook to straighten out the finances, and with no little effort he rescued the organisation from imminent bankruptcy. But that merely got over the immediate crisis, and the endemic problem remained that the political prima donnas on the International's bureau were so absorbed in swanning all over the world to their conferences and delegations as if they were the United Nations, and in cobbling together political pronunciamentos in high-sounding internationalist phraseology which nevertheless preserved their own national interests, that they couldn't demean themselves to look at the low-level mundane question of how all this activity was going to be paid for. At meeting after meeting Ron and I tried to get at least a little time devoted to the practicalities of the International's operations, and all we got for our pains was to be treated with the impatient, condescending contempt which the old-school-tie amateur nabobs of the Rugby Union exhibit towards the despised professional proletarians of the Rugby League. At one stage some of the nabobs complained to Harold Wilson as our prime minister and Jim Callaghan as our foreign secretary that the British delegation were being disruptive, and we explained to Jim that of course we were being disruptive because we were trying to disrupt the International's thoughtless decline into an irreversible organisational and financial shambles. Jim took the point and said that if we'd give him chapter and verse for our complaints he'd look into them, and in reply we reminded him that he'd had all the chapters and verses in a report written for him two years earlier by his own personal assistant, Tom McNally, and had taken no notice of it. Collapse of stout party. But it didn't do much good: the problem persisted.

In the meanwhile the Callaghan Government dragged to its miserable close, and after its suicide in 1979 it was clear that Jim would resign from his office as Leader within the next year or eighteen months. When the time actually came, in October 1980, the question of who was to succeed him was complicated by the fact that, while the constitution provided that the Leader and his Deputy were elected by the Parliamentary Party alone, there was a proposal before the Party to amend the constitution so as to widen the franchise by setting up an electoral college of the PLP plus the Constituency Parties plus the trade unions, and that amendment was due to be put to a special Party Conference to be held a few months later.

The Left in the PLP were keen to postpone the election of a new Leader till then by appointing the current Deputy Leader, Michael Foot, as a caretaker for the short period up to the constitutional conference. The Right, by contrast, wanted the election held at once by the PLP alone, because they could be expected to elect the Right's favoured candidate, Denis Healey. Some of Callaghan's ex-Ministers issued statements in support of this proposal: they included three or more of those who later became the Gang of Four and a number of their friends who also defected to the SDP. They got their way, and the election went ahead with the PLP as the electoral constituency.

To go back to the beginning, Jim announced his resignation to the Shadow Cabinet at their regular Wednesday afternoon meeting on 15 October 1980. As soon as he'd finished his resignation statement Michael Foot paid a long and warm tribute to him. (Michael had characteristically given continuously faithful and selfless loyalty to Jim throughout the two turbulent years of Jim's premiership, and Jim returned evil for good by undermining Michael's leadership during the 1983 election campaign.) After the Shadow Cabinet meeting three of the leftwing members of the Shadow Cabinet and one semi-leftwinger – Albert Booth, Stan Orme, John Silkin and Peter Shore – went off to Silkin's room to discuss what to do next. The remaining two of their little group, Michael himself and Tony Benn, were tied up and weren't able to attend. The four who were there agreed that their objective must be to try to prevent the election of Denis Healey: Peter Shore said that he thought he had a good chance of beating Denis; John Silkin went much further and claimed confidently that he would certainly beat Healey and anyone else who might stand ('O wad some Pow'r the giftie gie us . . .').

The stop-Healey urge was one which I shared in full measure, but more than once I asked myself sharply why I was so keen to keep out of the Party's top position a man for whom I had, as I still have, great admiration and a very high regard. Denis is an outstanding talent, equalled by very few people I've met in the whole of my long innings. When he speaks on international affairs, he speaks with the authority that derives from an unmatched knowledge of what's going on in almost every country in the world, and his analysis of all those movements of events is almost always penetrating and enlightening. He is a cultured man of parts, of many interests outside politics (those politicians whose lives contain nothing but politics are always second-class politicians). He's a bubbly, witty man who can be a charming and entertaining companion.

Now that he has mellowed, as we all do (not least I) after we get our senior-citizens' bus-passes, he exudes the milk of human kindness; but in the 1960s and 1970s he was a political bully wielding the language of sarcasm and contempt like a caveman's cudgel. He didn't argue with those members of the Party who didn't agree with him, he just wrote them off. He once described a Cabinet colleague who dared to differ from him as having a 'tiny Chinese mind'. More than once, in my own arguments with him, he didn't reply to what I'd said but instead quoted me as saying something nonsensical which I had never said. He knew all the tricks, and used them ruthlessly.

When the leadership election loomed in 1980 my friends in the Tribune Group and many other people in the Party and the trade unions wanted to stop Healey because he was way out to the Right and was likely to go even further than Wilson and Callaghan in leading the Party away from its socialist principles. But even though I shared that view I had an even stronger motivation for frustrating his

202

leadership bid. I had seen at first hand his emery-paper abrasive manner, his crude strong-arm all-in-wrestling ways of dealing with dissent, his undisguised contempt for many of his colleagues, his actual enjoyment of confrontation, his penchant for pouring petrol on the flames of controversy, and I was thoroughly convinced that if he became Leader of the Party it wouldn't be long before these aggressive characteristics of his would split the Party from top to bottom; and that was a prospect which scared me.

It happened that I was away from London on Wednesday and Thursday, 15 and 16 October, and so I missed all the buzz of speculation and calculation that vibrated round the corridors and tea-rooms and bars of the Palace of Westminster right through those two days. I heard about it only when I got back to London on the Thursday evening. My immediate reaction was to wonder how anyone could possibly imagine that either Peter Shore or John Silkin had any chance whatever of defeating Healey. It was clear to me that if anyone could stop Healey it could only be Michael Foot, and I was amazed when I was told that he had decided not to stand but to put his backing behind Peter Shore.

The minute I opened my eyes the next morning, even before I'd filled my pre-breakfast pipe (disgusting!), I phoned Michael. It was the only time in all my long friendship with him that I've ever spoken roughly with him: on this occasion my vocabulary was more Wapping than Westminster. I told him he was adjectivally potty if he thought Peter Shore, or anyone else but himself, could beat Denis Healey, and that he would be adverbially letting us all down if he didn't run. He listened patiently, and said he'd think about it, and I knew he meant it.

What I didn't know at the time was that he was receiving many representations to the same effect. Some of them came from trade-union leaders: Clive Jenkins, who wanted Michael as Leader not just to stop Healey but on his own merits and for his close understanding with the unions, had talked about the election to some of his colleagues. They all agreed that Michael ought to stand, and they sent him letters or telegrams to say so. Clive wanted to organise a get-together over the weekend to talk the problem through: the difficulty was that Michael was going off to Dublin to speak in St Patrick's Cathedral at a commemoration of the death of his first literary hero, Jonathan Swift. (When a brash but foolhardy Dublin reporter asked Michael about the leadership election, the only thing that he would say was that everyone standing for political office should have a compulsory examination in *Gulliver's Travels*.)

However, Michael was returning from Dublin early on the Sunday evening, and a small dinner party was set up in his house to welcome him back. The trade unionists who were there were Moss Evans of the TGWU, Alan Fisher of NUPE, Clive Jenkins of ASTMS, Bill Keys of SOGAT, Alec Smith of the Tailors and Garment Workers, and Arthur Scargill of the NUM; the other participants were Jill Foot, Jo Richardson, Mary and I. We had our lively and satisfying discussion over a good dinner: Mary brought along the fish course (one of her specials, sweet-and-sour mackerel in an egg-and-cream sauce), Jill produced an equally *haute-cuisine* meat course, and Clive contributed a case of a friendly claret. At the beginning of the evening we were pretty sure that Michael would run, and at the end of it we were quite sure.

A small group of Michael's friends constituted themselves a campaign committee for the election: the outstanding contribution was made by Neil Kinnock. Right through the campaign everybody outside our own group, including the media, made Denis a hot favourite; but we did our canvassing round the PLP, Jo recorded the results, and as the days went by we became more confident. I combined my role as a canvasser with my other role as the parliamentary bookmaker: both Ladbroke's and Coral's had Healey at 5–2 on and Michael at 9–4 against (for once I also became a punter and won a holiday backing Michael at that price). But when I looked at our final canvass returns I laid Healey at evens, and took a lot of money, the last of it two minutes before the result was declared: as I walked into committee room 14 to hear the declaration, a senior ex-Minister who happened to walk in with me handed me a five-pound note as a bet on Denis, and ten minutes later it paid for the first round of the victory-celebration drinks.

# Chapter 15

AFTER the 1983 general election I knew that the new Parliament was going to be my last. I passed on that information to my Constituency Party as early as November 1984 in order to give them plenty of time to choose my successor. The following day I was asked by a politically illiterate television interviewer (how do these people get their jobs?) whether I was standing down because I was afraid that if I didn't I would be deselected. I told her that at the end of the Parliament I would be only a little short of eighty years old, and asked her if she thought I needed any other reason for not going on. Needless to say, that part of the interview didn't appear on the screen.

Going into that last Parliament I resolved to make three changes in the life-style of my declining years. First, I would cease to be Mik the battler and become old Uncle Mik, the guide, philosopher, friend and adviser to the younger and better troops who were lining up in the forefront of the battle; second, I would find some things to do in which my work would produce some concrete results while I was still around to see them; and third, I would prepare plenty of activity for my after-Parliament life so that I'd be too busy to suffer withdrawal symptoms.

My first opportunity to act as avuncular philosopher and counsellor came quite soon, at the Party Conference of 1983. At the beginning of that Conference Neil Kinnock was elected Leader of the Party, and three days later we were both amongst the speakers at the Wednesday evening *Tribune* rally. We agreed that I should speak before him, and I told him that I was planning to forecast some of the things which were going to happen in the world, and for which he should prepare himself, in the first few years of his leadership.

Some fairy godmother must have waved her magic wand over me that evening and endowed me with the gift of prophecy. One of the things I said was that within the next five years at least one major debtor country would default on its repayments and thereby cause some turmoil in the banking world; and the next was 'in the next five years we shall see, somewhere in the world, a horrendous nuclear accident – a monster Three Mile Island disaster – which could change the whole world's thinking not only about nuclear arms but about nuclear energy as well.' Latin America for one, as it turned out, and Chernobyl for the other: I reckon those two prophecies put me in the same league as Isaiah, one above Nostradamus and a long way above Ronald Reagan's astrologer.

The first job I tackled in the House in the hope of getting some concrete result reasonably quickly was to investigate in depth the Government's policies and actions in relation to the Falkland Islands and the Falklands war. From the beginning of that affair I had suspected, as many other people did, that the Government had deceived the House and the country, that they hadn't fully exhausted all the possibilities of a solution without bloodshed, and that therefore the deaths of 250 Britons and many more Argentines might possibly have been avoided. In the 1979 Parliament I had served on the Select Committee on Trade and Industry, but in 1983 I transferred to the Foreign Affairs Committee specifically in order to try to persuade that Committee to carry out an in-depth investigation into the Falklands affair.

The Committee consisted of a Conservative chairman, six other Conservative MPs and four Labour MPs: the other three were Dennis Canavan, Nigel Spearing and Mick Welsh. Not without some difficulty we persuaded the Committee to enquire into the events surrounding the weekend of 1–2 May 1982, the weekend in which the cruiser *General Belgrano* was sunk with the loss of 368 lives – the act which determined that the ensuring war would be bitter and bloody.

That enquiry was hampered by the fact that the Government were engaged in a cover-up of the false information and the no-information which they had given to the House in the weeks before the fateful weekend, and during and after it. We dug out some of the facts of that cover-up by patient research, and some of them were brought to light by Clive Ponting's leak for which the Government tried, and failed, to get him imprisoned.

The Labour members of the Committee soon came to suspect that when we asked the Foreign Office and the Ministry of Defence for information their first consideration in deciding whether to give it to us was not whether it was in the public interest to do so but only whether it was in the political interests of Ministers to do so. Our suspicions were soon confirmed: two leaked civil-service minutes, one of them written by a department head at the Defence Ministry, disclosed that the Government machine wasn't going to give us any information which conflicted with any previous statement made by a Minister, even when that statement was totally inaccurate and misleading.

We tried to dig more deeply into this cover-up, and produced a long list of further questions we wanted to put to Ministers, but this effort was frustrated by the Conservative majority on the Committee who, in a series of votes, deleted many key questions from our list.

We were repeatedly denied relevant information because of what were described as considerations of secrecy, which in some cases were genuine and in others pure fiction. One such denial was achieved through an act of pantomime – or Whitehall farce. When Michael Heseltine became Secretary of State for Defence he asked the Department to produce for him a dossier covering the whole Falklands story: it was compiled by Clive Ponting and became known as the Crown Jewels. After some resistance it was agreed that we should be allowed to go along to the Ministry, and sit round a table under the invigilation of one of the Department's civil servants like schoolboys taking the GCSE, and each be given a copy of the Crown Jewels, but strictly on condition that we didn't copy anything or even make any notes. I found the dossier fascinating. It contained some naval operational information on which blanket secrecy was fully justified, but it also included one short document devoid of any naval or other service details: it was a purely political despatch which revealed that the Government had summarily rejected a last attempt by US Secretary of State Al Haig to get a diplomatic settlement of the Falklands controversy and thus avoid the loss of life and limb and ships. That document contained no secrets whatever; but because its publication would have seriously embarrassed the Prime Minister it was put into the same file as the Crown Jewels, to which it didn't belong. This was just a dishonest device whose purpose was to give that despatch a top-secret classification which its contents did not at all justify and which it would not otherwise have had.

At the end of that invigilated examination of the Crown Jewels, I walked out of the back door of the Department of Defence and plonked my notebook on the bonnet of the nearest parked car and wrote down what I wanted to remember of what I'd been reading, none of which had the least connection with naval operations or signals or anything else that was genuinely secret.

As the Select Committee's enquiry drew to a close, we four Labour members of it could forecast that the Committee was likely to produce a report owing something to the spotlight of investigation and a lot to the manipulation of a whitewash-brush. We decided that the gap between our views and those of our Conservative colleagues was so wide that the normal process of our moving amendments to the Chairman's draft report would not be practicable, and that therefore the only way in which we could project our analysis of events would be to write a complete report, a minority report, of our own. We realised that it was going to be a huge task, and I had serious doubts about whether it could be accomplished by backbenchers out of their own resources and without any equivalent of the research and drafting skills which would be provided to the Committee's majority by our highly competent team of Committee clerks and the backup they could call on. In the end it was almost as an act of faith that we decided to tackle the task of writing a comprehensive and detailed minority report.

It turned out to be an even bigger task, much bigger, than we had anticipated. The minority report is considerably longer than the official majority report, more deeply researched, and more closely argued. Its compilation was made possible by the fact that one of its four authors, Nigel Spearing, is the best and most productive researcher I've ever met.

We did most of the work that went into the report during a series of all-day Friday meetings in my flat. We put in a long day on every one of those Fridays, with Mary continuously feeding us coffees like a conveyor-belt, and with a midday break consisting of a walk round to the local watering-hole for a pint and pub-grub. We had some help from a small number of our friends who had followed the Falklands events closely, though our contacts with them were inhibited by the fact that we couldn't discuss in their presence any of the knowledge we had gained from the confidential papers and proceedings of the Select Committee.

At the end of our report we called for a further enquiry, at a high level and perhaps on Privy Council terms, to discover what we ourselves had been unable to discover partly because, as I've said, we hadn't been able to ask all the questions that ought to be asked, and partly because in some cases the Government refused to answer some of the questions that we did manage to ask and in other cases answered them at best misleadingly and at worst untruthfully.

In Chapter 7 of our report we listed eight statements which had been made by the Prime Minister and other Ministers, on each of which we set out detailed evidence (which nobody has even attempted to refute) to show that they were totally untrue. Perhaps the most glaring of them was John Nott's assertion, later reinforced by the Prime Minister herself, that at the time the ancient and obsolescent *General Belgrano* was torpedoed she and her escorts were 'closing on elements of our Task Force' and therefore represented a threat to that Force: the truth, subsequently admitted by the Minister of State for Defence, was that at the time the cruiser was torpedoed she was steaming directly away from the Falklands and towards the security of her home port as fast as her ageing boilers would push her without bursting at the seams.

But the basic deception, from which all else flowed, and which we did manage to uncover in spite of deliberate ministerial obstruction, is that a week before the critical *Belgrano* weekend the Government decided to make a radical change in its announced Falklands policy, and decided at the same time to deceive the House and the country by not announcing the change and pretending that the original stated policy was being continued. That original stated policy was to use the minimum warlike force necessary to secure a diplomatic solution to the conflict.

During the weekend of 23–24 April the War Cabinet decided to abandon that policy and instead to carry out an act of aggression sufficiently large and dramatic to precipitate and escalate military action in order to impose a solution by force.

The large and dramatic act they chose was to sink the aircraft-carrier *Veinticinco de Mayo*, a modern ship carrying modern aircraft which was therefore a potential source of danger to our forces. So they searched the seas for the aircraft-carrier, but even with all the information which the Americans were feeding into GCHQ Cheltenham from their spy-satellites they failed to find it. So in order to pursue the new strong-arm policy they had to find something else to sink, and they sank the *General Belgrano*, which they knew perfectly well

209

was not in any way a danger to our forces. Over the next few months the Prime Minister and other Ministers were asked many times why they had sunk the cruiser, and they gave a series of answers to that question, but never once did they give the honest answer, which would have been, 'The only reason we sank the *Belgrano* was that we couldn't find the *Veinticinco de Mayo*.'

During that same weekend of 1–2 May the Foreign Secretary, Francis Pym, flew off on a visit to Washington and New York: that visit was part of the pretence that our Government were still seeking a diplomatic solution. Pym himself was not a party to the deception – indeed, he was one of the victims of it. He was sent off, an innocent abroad, to talk peace with Al Haig and the UN's Pérez de Cuéllar without being told that while he was engaged in those talks they were going to be scuppered by the sinking of one of the Argentine ships.

Both Haig and Pérez de Cuéllar were in contact with the President of Peru, who was equally in contact with the Argentine Junta in an effort to negotiate a peaceful agreement between Great Britain and Argentina. After Pym had left Washington to fly to New York for his talk with Pérez de Cuéllar, the British ambassador deputised for him in a final meeting with Secretary Haig. At that meeting Al Haig sounded out the ambassador on the possibility of our government agreeing to a further cease-fire of a few days to provide the opportunity for a last attempt, through the intermediacy of the Peruvians, to avoid a bloody and destructive war, but the ambassador made it clear that the War Cabinet had cast the die in favour of exercising the military option. The torpedo which sank the *Belgrano* also shot down the dove of peace.

The key question which still remains to be answered is whether the Government knew of the Peruvian peace plan before the *Belgrano* was sunk. If they did, the sinking constituted not merely the gratuitous shooting of a sitting duck but also deliberate sabotage of the peace negotiations.

Our Government's case is that the first they heard of the peace plan was at a meeting, a short time after the fatal torpedo was fired, between the British ambassador in Lima and the Peruvian Foreign Minister. Pressed on the point, they declared that this meeting was the only official contact between the two governments during that period. But the purport of the word 'official' is to suggest that there was also some unofficial contact. What was it? In a debate in the House of Lords there was a suggestion that such a contact might have involved Lord Thomas, a confidant of the Prime Minister, who was believed to have been in Lima during the critical period. The record of the meeting of the Foreign Affairs Committee on 23 January 1985 includes the following minute: '*Ordered*, that Lord Thomas of Swynnerton be asked to provide information about any contacts he had with British and Peruvian Government representatives in Peru in early May 1982'; but we never got that information from him, and the refusal or failure to provide it clearly suggests that here, too, there was something fishy that the Government were covering up. The conclusion we drew in our minority report was the inescapable one: 'The possibility of a link,' we wrote, 'between the Peruvian peace initiative and the sinking of the *Belgrano* is still an open question. The Government's suppression of evidence and giving of false evidence throughout the whole of this affair make it risky to base a firm conclusion on what they have said, and that is why we recommend a further enquiry.'

It is still a source of puzzlement to me (and, of course, of disappointment as well) that our thoroughly documented exposé of the Government's duplicity, and indeed of its unwillingness to explore every avenue of avoiding death and destruction, aroused so much less interest throughout the country than one might reasonably have expected. I am quite sure that if it had been a Labour government which had been shown up in this way the tabloids would have had a field-day with it; and I'm quite sure that if our minority report had been produced not by Labour MPs but by a team of investigative journalists in a Sunday newspaper or on *Panorama* or *World in Action* it would have reverberated for months on end. As it was, the Government got away with its evocation of jingoism, and of course it had the support of the newspapers, even down to their use of the term 'Argies' as a synonym for 'wops' and to the obscenity of the *Sun*'s picture of the sinking *Belgrano* with its headline 'Gotcha!' which must have warmed the hearts of the 368 mothers whose sons were gotched in those few minutes. But I have the consolation of a firm conviction that some day, though probably not in my lifetime, the full truth will emerge like a laser beam piercing right through the clouds of deceit.

There were two other items in my programme of doing something in my last few public years which could produce some concrete results while I was still around to enjoy them, and they both concerned the hard-hit and deprived borough of Tower Hamlets, half of which was my constituency.

That area, between Hackney and the river and between the City and Newham, had been for centuries an area of poverty, deprivation and overcrowding whose problems were intensified, at least for a while, by each of those successive waves of immigrants that I described earlier. By the 1920s the degradation had become so intolerable that it precipitated the Poplar revolt. In the 1940s large parts of the area were devastated by the Luftwaffe, and in the succeeding decades there was more devastation of a different kind as the up-river seaborne traffic declined and as companies were encouraged by the Government to move out of the inner city and into the development areas and the New Towns and take their younger employees with them.

The theory behind that policy was that, as the south-east region had the lowest unemployment rate, there was a case for moving work out of that region and into those regions where unemployment was higher. But what the Government failed to realise, until too late and until a great deal of damage had been done, was that within the overall low-unemployment south-east there are pockets, including Tower Hamlets and its neighbouring boroughs, in which the unemployment rate is at least as high as in nearly all the development areas, and the dispersal of firms from those pockets was creating disaster areas in parts of the inner cities. Later the economic troubles of Tower Hamlets, as of many other places, were further seriously aggravated by the Thatcherite policy of deflation, just as its social problems were further and just as seriously aggravated by the Thatcherite policy of making the rich richer and the poor poorer.

In 1978 the Borough Council of Tower Hamlets joined in a consortium with the Greater London Council, the City of London Polytechnic (which is the polytechnic of the East End as much as of the City) and the London Chamber of Commerce and Industry to set up one of the first enterprise agencies in the country, the Tower Hamlets Centre for Small Business: its function was to preserve and create jobs by preventing existing small businesses from collapsing or moving out of the borough, and encouraging and helping new small businesses to start up in the borough. It was a management consultancy unit which didn't charge fees, and because of my long experience in that field I was invited to become its chairman.

When I took up that post the Centre had one officer, who didn't have an office or a secretary or even a telephone of his own: when I resigned ten years later it was a large and busy organisation which

212

provided for its clients not only management and financial counselling but also grants and soft loans out of substantial funds provided by two City institutions.

Of course the beneficial effects of a modest effort of this sort don't weigh heavily against the damaging effects of a government pursuing defective economic/industrial policies: you can't cure macro-ills with micro-remedies. I saw my work at the Centre as running madly up an escalator going down in order to stay in the same place – but that's better than standing still on the escalator and finishing right down in the bargain basement. In spite of all the work we did at the Centre, and in spite of all the overstated and overtrumpeted achievements of the London Docklands Development Corporation, the overall unemployment rate in Tower Hamlets didn't go down; but in the period of my chairmanship of the Centre I had the great satisfaction of seeing many hundreds of men and women who were at work because they had been kept out of the dole queue by the advice and help we had given them or their employers.

My other piece of practical communal activity in Tower Hamlets involved quite as much effort but didn't achieve as much success. It concerned relations between the ethnic communities and the police.

All over the country, but to a greater extent in the Metropolitan Police area than anywhere else, the blacks and Asians and other ethnic groups are deeply distrustful of the police, and many of them (and some whites as well) believe that a lot of police officers, of all ranks, are racists.

Over the years I had many exchanges on this subject, based on my first-hand experience in the East End, with successive Home Secretaries and successive Commissioners of Police for the Metropolis. At the time when Willie Whitelaw was Home Secretary, I put it both to him and to his Commissioner, and neither of them was able to deny it, that the basic problem of police-community relations was not that there is a minority of racist officers but that almost all the officers felt less commitment to protecting the interests of black citizens than of white: one evidence of that phenomenon was that in cases of assault the police were more likely when the victim was black than when he was white to recommend him to take out a private prosecution instead of initiating a prosecution themselves. Another evidence was that often a racist attack was not so classified because the officer involved preferred to ascribe to the attacker some motive other than racism.

213

Only a small proportion of racist incidents are reported to the police. One reason why many victims don't report them is the fear, all too often justified, of retaliation through further harassment or violence; but the main reason why most victims don't report an incident is that they think it's a waste of time because the police won't do anything about it anyway. There seemed to me to be only one way through this barrier, and that was to set up a body, sufficiently wide-based and authoritative to command public confidence, which would closely monitor what action the police had taken on every racist incident reported to them, and make it widely known that they were doing so. Since that monitoring could provide a reasonable guarantee that the police would give serious and proper attention to every racist incident reported to them, it could be hoped that more victims of racist incidents would be encouraged to report them.

It was obvious to me that an idea as fresh and unconventional and radical as that was never going to be generally accepted unless it had been tested in practice. So I set out to create a pilot plant in the form of a Tower Hamlets Panel on Racist Incidents. I realised the task wasn't likely to be easy, and it wasn't. I got some encouragement from New Scotland Yard, but the reaction of the higher-level officers in Tower Hamlets was mixed: some were co-operative, none with any great enthusiasm and some even grudgingly, and others were actually obstructive.

There were similarly mixed reactions from the community organisations of the ethnic groups I was seeking to serve. They all suspected, quite wrongly but nevertheless quite understandably, that the effect of the Panel would be not to improve the performance of the police, as I claimed it would, but merely to whitewash it. Some of them sent representatives to the Panel, at first tentatively and later with more conviction; some others pointedly distanced themselves from it; one or two openly condemned it. Nevertheless I got it going. The Panel was greatly helped in its work by a change of definition introduced by Sir Kenneth Newman to the effect that an incident must be classed as racist not just if the investigating officer thought it was but also if the victim or any witness thought it was.

We met every month and closely examined a list setting out all the details of every racist incident reported in the previous month and of what the police had done about it. An officer was present at every meeting to deal with the questions and criticisms we put to him, and the members of the Panel often pressed him quite hard on particular cases. This activity did actually produce, over a period, a discernible improvement in police performance: there was a notable reduction in the elapsed time between the reporting of an incident and the arrival of one or more officers, and there was also more effort in following incidents through to identifying the perpetrators and acting against them by prosecution or other means.

But I always felt that this enterprise was sitting on shaky foundations. To many of the local higher-level police officers it was something to be tolerated rather than welcomed. To some of them the monitoring of their performance by a publicly-selected group of laymen smacked of the concept of the accountability of the police to the public who pay their wages, and that concept is the ultimate anathema to most police officers (and to most Tory Home Secretaries and MPs). In the end, just before I ended my connection with Tower Hamlets, and at a moment when it was planned to extend and improve the Panel's work by merging it with another community group, the police stepped in and sabotaged the whole operation. Ah well, some you win and some you lose.

And that brings me to the end of my time as a Member of Parliament. My last act in that capacity was to write a threnody to be published on the day of my parliamentary demise, and it appeared that morning in the ill-fated *London Daily News*. I wrote:

'For more than a year I've been preparing myself carefully for the day when I would suffer the sea-change from being a busy, active Member of Parliament, much in demand in his constituency and all round the country, to becoming an obscure retired nobody.

'I planned a graceful but stiff-upper-lip rundown towards the end, and – more importantly – I planned in detail what work I was going to do to keep myself occupied in retirement. Having done all that, I thought I had succeeded in ensuring that when the time came to go I would be cushioned against any traumatic shock.

'I was wrong. The shock is there; the wrench is an anguish. It's like being divorced, after forty years of happy marriage, by a woman one's still in love with.'

But what a lucky, favoured man I've been to have had that experience. If I had a second innings I'd do the same thing all over again.

# *Epilogue*

WHEN I entered the House of Commons in 1945 I did so as one
of the representatives of a people whose most common characteristics
were caring, compassion and commitment. When I left it in 1987
that people had become one whose most common characteristics
seemed to be acquisitiveness, selfishness and indifference. How firmly
based is that change, and what has brought it about?

The outlook and attitudes of the British people in 1945 had been
forged in the searing heat of the War. From Dunkirk onwards we
ceased to be mere individuals: our common objective – to end the
destruction and bring the troops home and get back to our normal
lives – welded us into a team in which every one of us accepted a
responsibility not only to do his share but also to lend a hand to his
team-mates. The all-absorbing nature of this communal effort was
illustrated by the obloquy which was heaped on the handful of spivs
and blackmarketeers who opted out of it: the clearest indication of
how public attitudes have changed since then is that the present-day
equivalents of those spivs and blackmarketeers, who are the insider
dealers and the tax-haven dropouts, don't attract that much condemnation, and are even admired in some quarters: very few of them
get punished, and some of them get knighted.

I am proud to have been a member of that postwar generation and
to have taken part in the radical changes it wrought, and wrought
in the face of the most adverse circumstances and the most crippling
handicaps. The 1945–48 period was a time when anyone who looked
for excuses to put off tackling a fresh task had no difficulty in finding

216

them. We had sold a lot of our overseas assets to pay for the war effort, and had left ourselves poor and shabby; many of our cities were blighted by large areas of rubble and many of our homes needed urgent repairs; much of our industry was disorganised by dispersal, and it faced a hideously difficult conversion from making armaments to making civilian products; millions of men and women had to be demobbed and got back to work (and we did it without creating large-scale unemployment); the tasks of recovery, and even of day-to-day existence, were hampered by shortages of even basic necessities.

But we were a tough lot in that generation: we didn't look for excuses and we weren't put off by difficulties. We measured the tasks ahead, and got on with them.

For over four hundred years the casualties of our society had suffered the humiliations, the degradation, of a Poor Law based on the hard-faced concept that poverty was not just a misfortune which had to be suffered but rather a crime which had to be expiated. We had long since become ashamed of it, but had never summoned up the will to get rid of it. Beveridge lit up the path, and we set our feet upon it. No matter that the times were out of joint: the time to do a good deed was now.

As far back as 1918 we had passed an Act giving every child the right to secondary education. That Act had never been implemented: in twenty-seven years there had been no moment which was the right moment to put it into operation: if there were enough buildings there weren't enough teachers, and if there were enough teachers there weren't enough desks or books or blackboards or what-have-you. The 1945 Government broke that log-jam in the only possible way: it fixed a date a couple of years ahead and said that from that date every child will get secondary education, and we'll do our best to get into place by that date everything that is needed, and if in spite of that there are some gaps we'll get by: we'll just do it. That decision was an act of faith – an act of faith which moved a mountain.

For very many years the conscience of the British people had been ravaged by the unequal and unfair treatment of disease. It was obscene that the chance of a sick man or woman or child getting proper treatment and cure depended not on the nature and gravity of the sickness but on ability to pay for treatment, on whether there was a balance in the bank or some coins in the Umbrella Cup. We had always known that that was wrong, but we had never bestirred ourselves to put it right. The determination of the 1945 Government and the organising and negotiating skills of Aneurin Bevan created a health service of a new kind, one in which help was given according to need and not according to payment.

The Britons of that generation were prepared, as no nation before had ever been, to bear one another's burdens. We accepted the responsibility of seeking to ensure that from then onwards the dependence of childhood, the vulnerability of sickness, the misfortune of accident, the deprivation of unemployment, the bereavement of widowhood, the weakness of old age would be borne not by the individual but by the community. In those difficult years we sought to answer, for the first time in the recorded history of man, the first question a man ever asked, Am I my brother's keeper?, and we said Yes, brother, you *are* your brother's keeper.

There was an MP in that 1945 Parliament who encapsulated what we were doing in a simple, beautiful parable. He was a Welshman named Rhys Davies, white-haired but vigorous, a Lloyd George look-alike and soundalike. In a speech he delivered in his Lancashire constituency he put his finger directly on the nature of the change the country was undergoing. In the old days, he said, we were in a stage coach, and it got to the bottom of a steep hill, and the coach stopped, and the driver got down and put his head inside the coach and roared in a loud voice, 'First-class passengers stay where you are, second-class passengers get out and walk, third-class passengers get out and push'; but today, he added, when the coach gets to the bottom of a steep hill the driver gets down and says, 'The old and the sick, the blind and the lame, the pregnant women and the small children stay where you are, all the rest get out and push.'

It's not easy to recapture, forty years later, the heady atmosphere of that sense of being members one of another. One man who has recaptured it is Mervyn Jones. In his mémoir entitled *Chances* there is a passage which not only evokes the mood of those days but also illustrates painfully how far we have slipped back since then:

'What was most significant about the England of 1948: a sense of equality that was also a sense of community. The Health Service was *ours*, the new social services built on the wreckage of charity and the Poor Law were *ours*, the well-planned Council estates and the New Towns were *ours*. Up to a point – a point unique in British history – the government was *ours*, because its policies and most of its spending were aimed to benefit the majority and were meanly resented by the minority. People who cherished private schools, private life insurance and pensions, private medicine were felt to be rejecting a generally accepted way of life, and it was assumed that their numbers would dwindle.'

But those numbers didn't dwindle, they grew. They grew in response to the continuous Tory appeal, loud in itself and hugely amplified by the popular press, to individual self-interest. In saying that, I'm not libelling the Conservatives. They never seek to disown the central thesis of their political philosophy, which is that the best way to maximise the welfare of the community is for each individual to do all he can to maximise his own personal welfare, and to do that single-mindedly and without being distracted by any other considerations, including consideration for others.

Even if you don't agree with that thesis, as I don't, you have to admit that it's a tenable one, and that it has certain attractions. The quickest way to fill a football stadium is to open all the gates wide and tell the waiting crowd that the first hundred to get into the stadium will receive a handsome bonus: that will get the stadium filled in a shorter time, and with much more fun, than the slow, boring procedure of crocodiling through turnstiles.

There's only one snag about it, which is that the race is to the strong: those who get through the gates at the head of the crowd will be the men with broad shoulders and iron muscles and sharp elbows: the women will be pushed behind, and the old and the frail and the kids will be pushed aside, and some of them will be knocked down and trampled on. In 1988 Margaret Harkness wrote (under the *nom-de-plume* John Law) of the great army of unemployed and deprived in East London 'whose commander-in-chief is *Laisser-faire*, upon whose banners "Grab who can" and "Let the devil take the hindmost" are written in large letters ... drink and crime follow close on the steps of *Laisser-faire*'s army.' Isn't that as precisely true today as it was a century ago?

Starting with Macmillan's you-never-had-it-so-good we've elevated self-interest into virtue, and that carries with it the corollary that we've reduced caring and commitment and community consciousness to objects at best of condescension and at worst of derision.

That change has even had an effect on our use of language. Until the last decade or two it was a compliment to call somebody a do-gooder: today that's a pejorative term – to those who are concentratedly making their way in the world a do-gooder is a nuisance interrupting the even tenor of conscienceless living. (If 'do-gooder' is a pejorative term, is 'do-badder' a term of commendation?)

Or look at what's happened to the word 'activist'. Not so long ago an activist was a man or woman to look up to: the Five Members who opposed Charles I, and William Wilberforce, and the Tolpuddle Martyrs, and Florence Nightingale, and the Chartists, and the social reformers, and the suffragettes were activists who were honoured, if not in their day at least posthumously, for what they did to improve the lot of their fellow-citizens. Today the tabloids call a man an activist to suggest that at best there's something fishy about him, and at worst that he might be a conspirator, or a revolutionary, a saboteur, a KGB agent or some other secret enemy of all good men and true.

Or, to take a third and last example, let's look at what is now the widely admired, the most highly esteemed, the almost revered sector of the nation, the Silent Majority.

What is this Silent Majority? It's all the people who stay silent, who don't utter a word of protest, against the fruits of social injustice and deprivation; or against the system which hoards mountains of food in cold stores in rich countries whilst millions starve in the wastelands; or against the erosion for company profit of the world's natural resources, and the pollution of its air and its rivers and its oceans; or against the slide towards nuclear war and nuclear winter and nuclear holocaust. It's all the people who stay silent either because they don't care or because, if they care a bit, they're content to let others raise their voices and bestir themselves to do something. The Good Samaritan was an activist: those who passed by on the other side were members of the Silent Majority.

What is true of dealings between individuals is often equally true of dealings between nations. In the decades since the War in which, within each of the world's capitalist countries, market forces have ensured that the gap between the rich and the poor has steadily widened, so in the global context market forces have ensured that the gap between the rich nations and the poor nations has steadily widened. It is no accident that in the last ten years the Britain which has most rapidly enriched its rich and impoverished its poor is also the Britain which has continuously and sharply cut the meagre aid it gives to the poorest peoples of the world.

Most of the world's economic problems derive from the single cause that throughout two centuries we have rapidly improved and refined our instruments of production without any corresponding updating of our instruments of distribution, exchange and finance, which are not much different from those that were in use at the beginning of the Industrial Revolution. When a rich country suppplies goods in trade to a poor country it charges for them at the highest price it can get; and if it gives credit it charges interest on that credit at the highest rate it can get; and if the interest isn't paid on the due date it charges interest on the unpaid interest.

In a market-oriented world there is only one exception to that game of trading snakes-and-ladders, and that exception arises only in the course of a war. War, which is a disaster in every other respect, does have one economic advantage: in a system in which the extraction of profit makes it impossible for the totality of people to consume all that they produce, war narrows this production/consumption gap by getting rid of some products without requiring payment for them and therefore without encroaching on purchasing-power. When the Nazis sent a fleet of bombers to knock down Coventry Cathedral they didn't post us an invoice next day demanding payment for the cost of the bombs they had supplied and the cost of the fuel required to deliver them, and nor did the Allies demand payment for the similar goods they had made available to Dresden to ensure the destruction of its historic art-galleries.

Why should this economic benefit of supplying goods without encroaching on purchasing-power be confined to the supply of war-heads and shells and bullets? In what way is the equation altered if the uninvoiced goods are instruments of life and not instruments of death? In economic terms what is the difference between supplying butter without charge to people who want it and supplying bombs without charge to people who don't want them? Is it too much to hope that some time before it's too late the world which could make the leap in imagination needed to escape from earth's gravity will make the leap in imagination needed to escape from the traditions of Victorian trading values?

Looking back over the years I ask myself whether our present I'm-all-right-Jack attitude; our present addiction to the drug of acquisitiveness; our present failure, all too often, to be ever mindful of the wants of others are a half-century cyclical phase or a permanent mutation.

There is evidence of some stirrings of conscience, of some revulsion against the uglier features of the society which we've created, of a desire amongst many people to rediscover the joy of altruistic service.

There are all those large sums that people have given, and go on giving, to relieve suffering at home and abroad: it's true that some of those subscriptions may be no more than conscience-money, and it's true that even those large sums are tiny in relation to both what is needed and what has been salted away – but nevertheless they're a straw which shows a new breeze springing up. There are the things that people say in opinion polls: for example 62 per cent (that's four times as many as five years earlier) would be willing to pay higher taxes to provide more aid to the Third World; and 61 per cent think we've become more selfish in the last ten years (only 19 per cent think we've become more generous); and 48 per cent think that though we've become richer in the last ten years we've also become more unhappy (only 21 per cent think we're happier): it's true that there may be a difference between what a man may say to a pollster and what he is prepared to do in practice – but nevertheless these things are a straw which shows that a new breeze is springing up.

Men sometimes behave like lemmings, but we're not lemmings: when we get to the cliff we take a peek over the edge before we decide whether to jump. And there are rapidly increasing numbers of us who don't like, and are drawing back from, what we've seen in that peek over the edge – from nuclear destruction in war and nuclear radiation in peace; from our arrogance in using up more than our fair share of Nature's resources, and thus robbing our children and grandchildren of *their* fair shares; from polluting and poisoning the air we breathe and the water we drink; from knocking a hole in the ozone layer that keeps us alive; and – perhaps above all – from some painful pangs of guilt and remorse. We surely can't let Man perish from the earth leaving only a silicon chip as a memento of his existence.

# *Index*